WeightWatchers®

In One Pot

200 Favorite One-Dish Meals
the Family Will Love

WEIGHT WATCHERS PUBLISHING GROUP

Creative and Editorial Director
Nancy Gagliardi

Art Director
Ed Melnitsky

Production Manager
Alan Biederman

Associate Art Director
Jennifer Bowles

Office Manager and
Publishing Assistant
Jenny Laboy-Brace

Food Editor
Eileen Runyan, M.S.

Recipe Developers
David Bonom

Maureen Luchejko

Deborah Mintcheff

Photographer
Ann Stratton

Food Styling
Michael Pederson

Prop Styling
Cathy Cook

Designer/Illustrator
Julia Michry

On the Cover: Country-Style
Beef Short Ribs with Horseradish
Cream, page 246

Roast Chicken Provençal,
page 84

ICON KEY

HOT / SPICY

NO COOK

30 MINUTES OR LESS

VEGETARIAN

Introduction

In my line of work, I get to cross paths with a lot of "foodies," the affectionate nickname for bigwigs (chefs, editors, authors, recipe developers, etc.) in the food industry. They're a fabulous source of cooking information, helping me keep on top of the latest trends, ideas, and tips. During lunch with one sophisticated editor, she regaled me with stories of a book she was working on by a big name chef (think lots of truffle oil, quail eggs, and foie gras). This woman is a fabulous cook, as well, who seeks out only the finest ingredients. She's the one I call when I want to find the best bacon or the finest coffee. She can tell me where to eat when I'm in San Francisco or where to buy spices when I'm in Minneapolis. So you can imagine my surprise when she recounted the dinner her family loves when she's short on time: "You take a pound box of uncooked pasta, put into a baking dish, then pour in a 32-ounce jar of a good bottled sauce. Mix them together, then sprinkle with grated Parmesan and shredded mozzarella. Cover with foil and pop in a moderate oven for about 45 minutes. The kids love it and it tastes pretty good."

Whether you consider yourself a gourmet or a classic home cook, streamlined dishes—those recipes we know that can be tossed in a pot and forgotten about—are the new "gold standard" for busy cooks. It's multitask cooking at its best: You whip it together and do other chores—or rest—while the meal cooks.

Our *Weight Watchers In One Pot: 200 Favorite One-Dish Meals the Family Will Love* takes this type of cooking to a new level. Sure, we've tried to keep the cooking simple, but we've also paid attention to the other part of this cooking equation: The food has to taste great. These recipes are hearty and they fill you up—not out. And don't let the ingredient lists scare you off—if you have a well-stocked pantry, freezer, and spice rack, plenty of these delicious dishes can be put together at the drop of a hat. We promise, these recipes are just like Mom used to make with one big difference: No one has to fight over who cleans the one pot!

NANCY GAGLIARDI
CREATIVE AND EDITORIAL DIRECTOR

Lemon-Blueberry Bundt Cake,
page 267

Contents

Hearty Soups and Chowders

Big enough for a meal

Pork Ball, Noodle, and Watercress Soup

This favorite Chinese soup can be served in smaller portions as an appetizer, or as one hearty main-dish bowlful to satisfy the hungriest. To save time, buy watercress in a 4-ounce bag, already trimmed and cleaned, from the produce section of your supermarket.

1 pound lean ground pork (10% or less fat)

1 large egg, lightly beaten

1 tablespoon minced peeled fresh ginger

2 teaspoons cornstarch

2 garlic cloves, minced

½ teaspoon salt

¼ teaspoon freshly ground pepper

6 cups low-sodium chicken broth

1 tablespoon reduced-sodium soy sauce

4 ounces thin, dried Chinese noodles or thin spaghetti, broken in half

¼ pound fresh shiitake mushrooms, stems discarded, caps thinly sliced

1 bunch watercress, trimmed

4 scallions, thinly sliced (white and light green portions only)

1 teaspoon Asian (dark) sesame oil

MAKES 6 SERVINGS

1. Combine the pork, egg, ginger, cornstarch, garlic, salt, and pepper in a medium bowl. Shape mixture into 24 balls; set aside.
2. Bring the broth and soy sauce to a boil in a Dutch oven. Add the noodles and mushrooms; return to a boil, stirring occasionally. Gently add the pork balls; return to a boil. Reduce the heat and simmer, partially covered, until the pork balls and noodles are cooked through, about 15 minutes. Gently stir in the watercress and simmer until just wilted, about 1 minute.
3. Remove the soup from the heat, then stir in the scallions and oil.

PER SERVING (1¼ cups): 233 Cal, 9 g Fat, 3 g Sat Fat, 84 mg Chol, 409 mg Sod, 16 g Carb, 2 g Fib, 23 g Prot, 78 mg Calc. *POINTS: 5.*

tip Since it's often cheaper to buy dried shiitake mushrooms in bulk than it is to buy them fresh—and dried mushrooms keep well for months—substitute 5 to 6 dried whole shiitake mushrooms for the fresh, if you like. Before using dried mushrooms, simply soak them in ½ cup boiling water for about 15 minutes; drain, then discard the tough stems.

Pork Ball, Noodle,
and Watercress Soup

Vietnamese Pork and Snow Pea Bowl

This colorful and flavorful soup cooks in minutes. Simply prep the vegetables and pork while you bring the broth to a boil. If you own a mandoline (a slicing machine), use it to get nice thin slices of carrots. Otherwise use a sharp knife—the carrot slices won't be as thin, so cook them a minute or two longer. For a spicy touch, add a pinch of crushed red pepper to this soup.

  6 cups low-sodium
     chicken broth
3½ carrots, thinly sliced
     on the diagonal
  ½ pound lean pork
     tenderloin, cut into
     2 x ¼-inch strips
  4 ounces vermicelli or
     very thin spaghetti,
     broken in half
  1 (8-ounce) can sliced
     water chestnuts,
     rinsed and drained
  4 ounces fresh snow
     peas, trimmed and
     sliced diagonally
     in half
2½ tablespoons rice-wine
     vinegar
  1 tablespoon pickled
     ginger, chopped
  1 tablespoon tamari or
     soy sauce
  2 teaspoons Asian (dark)
     sesame oil
  3 scallions, sliced (white
     and light green
     portions only)
  2 tablespoons toasted
     sesame seeds

MAKES 4 SERVINGS

1. Bring the broth to a boil in a Dutch oven. Add the carrots and cook until tender, about 5 minutes. Stir in the pork and vermicelli; return to a boil. Reduce the heat to medium and cook, stirring occasionally, until the pork and vermicelli are cooked through, about 3 minutes.

2. Add the water chestnuts, snow peas, vinegar, ginger, tamari sauce, and oil; return to a boil. Reduce the heat and simmer until the snow peas are crisp-tender, about 1 minute. Serve sprinkled with the scallions and sesame seeds.

PER SERVING (2 cups): 331 Cal, 9 g Fat, 2 g Sat Fat, 36 mg Chol, 402 mg Sod, 40 g Carb, 5 g Fib, 24 g Prot, 72 mg Calc. POINTS: 7.

tip For a change of pace try using black sesame seeds. Toast them as you would regular sesame seeds, but don't rely on any change of color to signal readiness—you can't see any difference in appearance to toasted black sesame seeds. You can taste the difference, however. All sesame seeds keep best stored in the freezer.

Beef Borscht

Borscht—the national soup of both Russia and Poland—is traditionally a peasant soup of beets, cabbage, and potatoes. We transform "peasant" into "fit for a king" with the addition of lean beef, a cheesecloth bundle of aromatic spices, and an elegant topping of sour cream and fresh dill. For an extra *2 POINTS* per serving, dish up this soup with a slice of fresh pumpernikel bread.

MAKES 6 SERVINGS

2 teaspoons canola oil

1 pound beef top round, trimmed of visible fat and cut into ½-inch chunks

1 large onion, chopped

2 teaspoons mixed pickling spice

1 teaspoon dill seeds

2 bay leaves, broken up

4 cups low-sodium beef broth

1 (14½-ounce) can diced tomatoes

½ small green cabbage, shredded (about 4 cups)

2 medium fresh beets, peeled and shredded (about 2 cups)

2 all-purpose potatoes, peeled and cut into ½-inch cubes

1 tablespoon red-wine vinegar

1 teaspoon sugar

½ teaspoon salt

6 tablespoons light sour cream

3 tablespoons minced dill

1. Heat the oil in a nonstick Dutch oven over medium-high heat. Add the beef and cook, turning occasionally, until browned on all sides, about 8 minutes. Add the onion and cook, stirring frequently, until softened, about 3 minutes. Tie the mixed pickling spice, dill seeds, and bay leaves in a cheesecloth bag.

2. Add the broth, tomatoes, cabbage, beets, potatoes, vinegar, sugar, salt and the cheesecloth bag of spices to the Dutch oven; bring to a boil. Reduce the heat and simmer, covered, until the beef and vegetables are tender, about 1 hour.

3. Remove the bag of spices. Serve the soup with the sour cream and dill.

PER SERVING (scant 1½ cups soup with 1 tablespoon sour cream): 223 Cal, 7 g Fat, 2 g Sat Fat, 46 mg Chol, 412 mg Sod, 21 g Carb, 4 g Fib, 20 g Prot, 84 mg Calc. POINTS: 4.

tip To save time, buy a 1-pound bag of already shredded cabbage from the produce section of your supermarket and substitute a 15-ounce can of sliced beets for the fresh beets.

Sopa de Albóndigas

Tender, savory meatballs in a well-seasoned broth of rice, corn, and tomatoes make this Mexican meatball soup true comfort food. A side salad of arugula with a light balsamic dressing would complete the meal, but if it's easier, simply stir 2 cups chopped fresh arugula or spinach into the soup with the cilantro.

MAKES 6 SERVINGS

2   teaspoons canola oil

1   large onion, chopped

3   garlic cloves, minced

5   cups low-sodium
    chicken broth

1   (14½-ounce) can
    stewed tomatoes

½   cup long-grain
    white rice

¾   pound lean ground
    beef (10% or less fat)

¼   cup seasoned dry
    bread crumbs

¼   cup shredded
    reduced-fat cheddar
    cheese

1   egg, lightly beaten

1   jalapeño pepper,
    seeded and finely
    chopped (wear gloves
    to prevent irritation)

½   teaspoon ground
    cumin

1   cup fresh or frozen
    corn kernels

½   cup chipotle salsa

⅓   cup chopped fresh
    cilantro

6   lime wedges

1. Heat the oil in a nonstick Dutch oven over medium-high heat. Add the onion and garlic and cook, stirring frequently, until softened, about 3 minutes. Transfer half of the onion mixture to a medium bowl; set aside.
2. Add the broth, tomatoes, and rice to the remaining onion mixture in the Dutch oven; bring to a boil. Reduce the heat and simmer, covered, until the rice is tender, about 20 minutes.
3. Meanwhile, add the beef, bread crumbs, cheese, egg, jalapeño pepper, and cumin to the onion mixture in the bowl; mix well. Shape into 24 meatballs.
4. Stir the corn and salsa into the simmering mixture in the Dutch oven; return to a simmer. Carefully drop the meatballs into the mixture. Cover and simmer, stirring gently once or twice, until the meatballs are cooked through, about 20 minutes. Stir in the cilantro and serve with the lime wedges.

PER SERVING (1½ cups): 284 Cal, 9 g Fat, 3 g Sat Fat, 70 mg Chol, 330 mg Sod, 31 g Carb, 3 g Fib, 21 g Prot, 107 mg Calc. *POINTS: 6.*

Scotch Broth

Barley, lamb, and mushrooms are the typical identifying ingredients in this soothing winter soup. We add green beans for color, crunch, and fiber.

MAKES 4 SERVINGS

1   teaspoon canola oil
½   pound lean boneless
    shoulder of lamb,
    trimmed of all visible
    fat and cut into
    ¾-inch chunks
2   onions, chopped
6   cups low-sodium
    chicken broth
¾   cup pearl barley
3   carrots, diced
1   cup diced turnip or
    rutabaga
2   bay leaves
2½ teaspoon salt
¼   teaspoon freshly
    ground pepper
½   pound fresh green
    beans, trimmed and
    cut into ½-inch pieces
½   pound fresh white
    mushrooms, sliced

1. Heat the oil in a nonstick Dutch oven over medium-high heat. Add the lamb and cook, turning occasionally, until browned on all sides, 7–8 minutes. Transfer the lamb to a plate and set aside.

2. Add the onions to the same Dutch oven and cook, stirring occasionally, until golden, 7–10 minutes. Add the broth, barley, carrots, turnip, bay leaves, salt, pepper, and the browned lamb; bring to a boil. Reduce the heat and simmer, covered, until the lamb and barley are tender, about 45 minutes. Discard the bay leaves.

3. Add the green beans and mushrooms to the pot; return to a boil. Reduce the heat and simmer, covered, until the vegetables are tender, 5–6 minutes.

PER SERVING (2¼ cups): 348 Cal, 8 g Fat, 2 g Sat Fat, 41 mg Chol, 453 mg Sod, 49 g Carb, 12 g Fib, 24 g Prot, 91 mg Calc. *POINTS: 7.*

tip Most grain-based soups thicken on standing, so you may need to add a little water if reheating.

Moroccan Lamb and Lentil Soup

In Morocco, a long-simmering, sweet-spiced soup such as this is made with lamb shanks and served to break the fast of Ramadan. We've adjusted the recipe to use quick-cooking lean lamb cubes, so the whole thing is ready in just about one hour. Serve with pita bread to mop up the juices, if you like.

2 teaspoons olive oil

¾ pound lean boneless shoulder of lamb, trimmed of all visible fat and cut into ¾-inch chunks

1 large onion, chopped

5 garlic cloves, minced

3½ cups low-sodium chicken broth

1 (14½-ounce) can diced tomatoes

¾ cup dried lentils, rinsed and picked over

1 cinnamon stick

1 teaspoon turmeric

1 teaspoon ground cumin

¾ teaspoon ground ginger

¾ teaspoon salt

½ teaspoon coarsely ground black pepper

2 medium zucchini, diced

1 teaspoon grated lemon zest

1 tablespoon fresh lemon juice

MAKES 4 SERVINGS

1. Heat the oil in a nonstick Dutch oven over medium-high heat. Add the lamb and cook, turning occasionally, until browned on all sides, 5–6 minutes. Transfer the lamb to a plate and set aside.

2. Add the onion and garlic to the same Dutch oven and cook, stirring occasionally, until golden, 7–8 minutes. Add the broth, tomatoes, lentils, cinnamon, turmeric, cumin, ginger, salt, pepper, and the browned lamb; bring to a boil. Reduce the heat and simmer, covered, until the lamb and lentils are tender, about 35 minutes.

3. Add the zucchini; return to a boil. Reduce the heat and simmer, covered, stirring occasionally, until the zucchini is softened, about 8 minutes. Remove the cinnamon stick, then stir in the lemon zest and juice just before serving.

PER SERVING (1¾ cups): 358 Cal, 10 g Fat, 3 g Sat Fat, 61 mg Chol, 709 mg Sod, 35 g Carb, 12 g Fib, 34 g Prot, 99 mg Calc. *POINTS: 7.*

Chicken and Escarole Soup

Pancetta (pan-CHEH-tuh), a flavorful Italian bacon found in large supermarkets and in specialty-food stores, adds authentic Italian flavor here. If you prefer, omit the cannellini beans and round out the meal with crusty Italian bread instead.

MAKES 4 SERVINGS

1 ounce thinly sliced pancetta, or 1 slice thick-cut bacon, chopped

1 large onion, chopped

4 garlic cloves, minced

3 cups low-sodium chicken broth

1 (14½-ounce) can Italian stewed tomatoes

1 pound skinless chicken thighs, trimmed of all visible fat

1 bunch escarole, cleaned and chopped

1 (15-ounce) can cannellini (white kidney) beans, rinsed and drained

2 tablespoons chopped fresh basil, or 2 teaspoons dried

½ teaspoon salt

¼ teaspoon crushed red pepper

2 tablespoons shredded Parmesan cheese

1. Spray a nonstick Dutch oven with nonstick spray and set over medium heat. Add the pancetta and cook until crisp, 4–5 minutes; transfer to a plate.

2. Pour off all but a coating of the drippings (about ½ teaspoon) from the Dutch oven. Add the onion and garlic. Cook, stirring frequently, until golden, 7–10 minutes. Add the broth, tomatoes, and chicken; bring to a boil. Reduce the heat and simmer, covered, until the chicken is cooked through and tender, about 30 minutes. Remove the chicken and set aside until cool enough to handle. Remove the chicken from the bone and return to the soup.

3. Add the escarole, beans, basil, salt, and crushed red pepper; return to a boil, stirring occasionally to mix in the escarole. Reduce the heat and simmer until the escarole is wilted and softened, about 5 minutes. Sprinkle with the crisped pancetta and the cheese just before serving.

PER SERVING (1¾ cups): 280 Cal, 8 g Fat, 3 g Sat Fat, 55 mg Chol, 1023 mg Sod, 26 g Carb, 6 g Fib, 26 g Prot, 139 mg Calc. *POINTS: 5.*

tip Escarole can be sandy and may need several rinses in cold water to clean it thoroughly. Substitute a (10-ounce) package frozen leaf spinach, thawed and squeezed dry, in place of the fresh escarole if you want to save a little time.

Classic Chicken Soup with Noodles

Chicken soup has long been considered a cure for all that ails you, and this long, slow-cooking favorite is perfect to make on a chilly day you plan to spend indoors. You'll be returning only half of the cooked chicken to this soup and saving the remaining 2 cups to use another day for sandwiches or salads.

3 pounds skinless chicken legs (drumsticks and thighs), trimmed of all visible fat

6 cups water

5 carrots, cut into 2-inch pieces

3 celery stalks, cut into 1-inch pieces

2 onions, each cut into 8 wedges

2 garlic cloves, minced

3 sprigs flat-leaf parsley

2 sprigs fresh thyme

2 bay leaves

1½ teaspoons salt

¼ teaspoon freshly ground pepper

2 cups medium egg noodles

¼ cup chopped flat-leaf parsley

MAKES 6 SERVINGS

1. Bring the chicken, water, carrots, celery, onions, garlic, parsley, thyme, bay leaves, salt, and pepper to a boil in a Dutch oven. Reduce the heat and simmer, covered, until the chicken is no longer pink inside and the vegetables are tender, about 45 minutes. Discard the parsley, thyme, and bay leaves.

2. Remove the chicken from the soup. Skim any fat from the top of the soup with a large spoon. Add the noodles and return the soup to a boil. Reduce the heat and simmer, uncovered, until the noodles are tender, about 5 minutes.

3. When cool enough to handle, remove the chicken from the bones. Cut the chicken into chunks and return 2 cups to the soup. Reserve the remaining 2 cups chicken for another day. Sprinkle the soup with the chopped parsley just before serving.

PER SERVING (generous 1½ cups): 195 Cal, 5 g Fat, 1 g Sat Fat, 52 mg Chol, 693 mg Sod, 20 g Carb, 3 g Fib, 17 g Prot, 60 mg Calc. *POINTS:* 4.

tip When you make chicken soup with a whole chicken, the small bones from the breast and back of the chicken tend to get lost in the soup. Using only chicken drumsticks and thighs avoids this.

Mexican Tortilla Soup

Zesty chorizo sausage—flavored with garlic, chili powder, and paprika—is a staple in Spanish and Mexican cooking. If you can't find chorizo, use hot Italian turkey sausage, remove the casing, and break up the sausage with a wooden spoon while browning it.

MAKES 6 SERVING

6 ounces chorizo sausage, casings removed, sausage sliced into ¼-inch slices
1 large red onion, halved lengthwise, then sliced crosswise
1 green bell pepper, seeded and chopped
2 garlic cloves, minced
1 jalapeño pepper, seeded and chopped (wear gloves to prevent irritation)
5 cups low-sodium chicken broth
1 package (16 ounces) frozen baby white corn
2 tomatoes, chopped
3 (6-inch) corn tortillas
¼ cup chopped fresh cilantro or parsley
2 tablespoons fresh lime juice

1. Heat a nonstick Dutch oven over medium-high heat. Add the sausage and cook, stirring occasionally, until browned, 6–8 minutes. Add the onion, bell pepper, garlic, and jalapeño pepper. Cook, stirring frequently, until the vegetables are softened, about 7 minutes.

2. Stir in the broth, corn, and tomatoes; bring to a boil. Reduce the heat and simmer, uncovered, until the flavors blend, about 10 minutes.

3. Meanwhile, spray a small nonstick skillet with nonstick spray and set over medium-high heat. Add 1 tortilla and cook until golden and crisped, about 45 seconds on each side. Repeat with the 2 remaining tortillas. Cut each tortilla in half, then crosswise into strips; set aside.

4. Stir the cilantro and lime juice into the soup. Serve with the tortilla strips.

PER SERVING (1⅓ cups soup and ⅙ of tortilla strips): 262 Cal, 12 g Fat, 4 g Sat Fat, 25 mg Chol, 427 mg Sod, 28 g Carb, 4 g Fib, 13 g Prot, 48 mg Calc. *POINTS: 5.*

 To save time, use 1½ cups broken-up baked tortilla chips in place of the homemade tortilla strips.

Turkey Mulligatawny

Turkey Mulligatawny

A spicy curried rice soup from southern India, mulligatawny gets a hefty amount of turkey added here, making it a hearty one-dish meal. Madras curry powder is hotter than standard curry powder. If you use standard curry powder, you may need 3 to 4 teaspoons.

MAKES 4 SERVINGS

2 teaspoons butter
1 medium onion, chopped
3 garlic cloves, minced
⅔ cup long-grain white rice
2–3 teaspoons Madras curry powder
1 teaspoon turmeric
¼ teaspoon ground cloves
5 cups low-sodium chicken broth
1 green bell pepper, seeded and chopped
1 small red apple, unpeeled and diced
1 pound boneless, skinless turkey breasts, cut into ¾-inch chunks
½ teaspoon salt
Freshly ground pepper, to taste
1 small tomato, chopped
¼ cup chopped fresh cilantro

1. Melt the butter in a Dutch oven over medium heat. Add the onion and garlic. Cook, stirring, until golden, 7–10 minutes. Add the rice, curry powder, turmeric, and cloves. Cook, stirring occasionally, until fragrant, 2–3 minutes.

2. Stir in the broth, bell pepper, and apple; bring to a boil. Reduce the heat and simmer, covered, until the rice is tender, about 20 minutes.

3. Add the turkey and salt; return to a boil. Reduce the heat and simmer, covered, until the turkey is cooked through, about 5 minutes. Season with the pepper, then sprinkle with the tomato and cilantro just before serving.

PER SERVING (1¾ cups): 360 Cal, 7 g Fat, 3 g Sat Fat, 72 mg Chol, 441 mg Sod, 39 g Carb, 3 g Fib, 34 g Prot, 60 mg Calc. POINTS: 7.

tip In Indian dishes, to spice up the flavor, garam masala (an aromatic blend of dried chiles, black pepper, and sweet spices) is often added toward the end of cooking. If extra kick is what you're looking for, add about ½ teaspoon to this soup when you add the tomato and cilantro.

Turkey Tortellini Soup

Tortellini, a specialty of the Piedmont area of northwestern Italy, can be fussy to make from scratch. We use convenient frozen tortellini and quick-cooking boneless turkey chunks. You can substitute leftover turkey (about 2 cups) if you have it on hand. This soup is traditionally served with grissini—long, thin breadsticks—and a light sprinkling of Parmesan cheese.

2 teaspoons canola oil

2 carrots, cut into
   ¼-inch slices

2 celery stalks, cut into
   ¼-inch slices

1½ large onion, chopped

1 small parsnip, peeled
   and chopped

5 cups low-sodium
   chicken broth

½ pound skinless
   boneless turkey
   breasts, cut into
   ½-inch chunks

½ (1-pound) package
   frozen cheese-filled
   tortellini

⅓ cup chopped fresh
   parsley

Freshly ground pepper,
   to taste

MAKES 4 SERVINGS

1. Heat the oil in a nonstick Dutch oven over medium-high heat. Add the carrots, celery, onion, and parsnip and cook, stirring occasionally, until the vegetables are softened and lightly browned, about 10 minutes.
2. Add the broth; bring to a boil. Reduce the heat and simmer, covered, until the vegetables are tender, about 15 minutes.
3. Add the turkey and tortellini; return to a boil. Reduce the heat and simmer, covered, until cooked through, about 10 minutes. Stir in the parsley and season with the pepper.

PER SERVING (1½ cups): 259 Cal, 9 g Fat, 3 g Sat Fat, 81 mg Chol, 171 mg Sod, 21 g Carb, 3 g Fib, 22 g Prot, 97 mg Calc. *POINTS: 5.*

tip Instead of serving this soup with breadsticks and Parmesan cheese, make it a creamy soup—and enrich it in vitamins and fiber—by adding 1 cup of canned pumpkin puree to the mixture at the end and heating it through.

Canadian Bacon, Broccoli, and Corn Chowder

Corn has long been grown and revered by Native Americans. Today fresh corn on the cob is not only available locally in the summer months, but thanks to improved transportation, you can find fresh corn from May on, shipped from Florida and sold at a very reasonable price in supermarkets.

MAKES 4 SERVINGS

1   teaspoon canola oil
2   bunches scallions, sliced (white and light green portions only)
3   ounces Canadian bacon, diced
4   cups chopped fresh small broccoli florets
2   tablespoons all-purpose flour
3   cups low-fat (1%) milk
2   cups fresh or frozen corn kernels
½   teaspoon salt
½   cup shredded sharp cheddar cheese
Freshly ground pepper, to taste

1. Heat the oil in a nonstick Dutch oven over medium-high heat. Add the scallions and bacon. Cook, stirring occasionally, until the scallions are softened and the bacon is cooked, about 7 minutes. Add the broccoli. Cook, stirring occasionally, until the broccoli is slightly softened, 3–5 minutes.

2. Sprinkle in the flour and cook, stirring constantly, until the flour is lightly browned, 1–2 minutes. Gradually stir in the milk. Cook over medium heat, stirring constantly, until the mixture bubbles and thickens slightly, about 5 minutes. Stir in the corn and salt. Cook, stirring occasionally, until heated through, about 3 minutes.

3. Remove the soup from the heat. Add the cheese and pepper and stir until the cheese melts.

PER SERVING (1⅓ cups): 302 Cal, 10 g Fat, 5 g Sat Fat, 32 mg Chol, 780 mg Sod, 38 g Carb, 7 g Fib, 20 g Prot, 402 mg Calc. **POINTS: 6.**

tip To remove the kernels from the cobs, stand the cobs upright on a cutting board and with a sharp knife, working from top to bottom, scrape away the kernels. One ear of fresh corn yields about ½ cup kernels. For this recipe you will need about four ears. When fresh corn is not available, use frozen.

Red Snapper Soup Veracruz

Native olives and fiery peppers—introduced to Mexico by early Spanish settlers—are central to the cooking of Veracruz, Mexico's principal seaport. A touch of cinnamon and cloves amplifies the flavors in this soup. For more fire, use canned diced tomatoes seasoned with jalapeño peppers instead of the stewed tomatoes.

MAKES 4 SERVINGS

2 teaspoons olive oil
1 onion, chopped
2 garlic cloves, minced
1 jalapeño pepper,
   seeded and finely
   chopped (wear gloves
   to prevent irritation)
1 green bell pepper,
   seeded and chopped
1 tablespoon all-purpose
   flour
3 cups fish or vegetable
   broth, or bottled
   clam juice
1 (14½-ounce) can
   stewed tomatoes
⅛ teaspoon cinnamon
⅛ teaspoon ground
   cloves
2 cups fresh or frozen
   corn kernels
1 pound red snapper,
   tilapia, cod, haddock,
   or halibut fillets, cut
   into 1-inch pieces
¼ cup chopped cilantro
2 tablespoons sliced
   pimiento-stuffed olives
1 tablespoon fresh
   lime juice

1. Heat the oil in a nonstick Dutch oven over medium-high heat. Add the onion, garlic, and jalapeño pepper. Cook, stirring frequently, until softened, about 3 minutes. Add the bell pepper and cook, stirring frequently, until softened, about 5 minutes.
2. Sprinkle in the flour and cook, stirring constantly, until the flour is lightly browned, 1–2 minutes. Gradually stir in the broth, tomatoes, cinnamon, and cloves. Cook, stirring constantly, until the mixture bubbles and thickens slightly.
3. Add the corn and fish; return to a boil. Reduce the heat and simmer, uncovered, until the fish is just opaque in the center, about 5 minutes. Stir in the cilantro, olives, and lime juice.

PER SERVING (scant 2 cups): 256 Cal, 5 g Fat, 1 g Sat Fat, 60 mg Chol, 431 mg Sod, 28 g Carb, 4 g Fib, 28 g Prot, 71 mg Calc. *POINTS: 5.*

Red Snapper Soup Veracruz

Spanish Cod and Rice Chowder

Regular brown rice takes 40 minutes to cook, so we use convenient quick-cooking brown rice, which cooks in about 8 minutes. Quick-cooking brown rice comes in convenient boil-in-a-bag packets (four 1-cup packets to a box).

MAKES 4 SERVINGS

- 2 teaspoons olive oil
- 1 large onion, chopped
- 2 garlic cloves, minced
- 1 teaspoon paprika
- 1 green bell pepper, seeded and chopped
- 1 red bell pepper, seeded and chopped
- 3 cups fish or vegetable broth, or bottled clam juice
- 1 (14½-ounce) can diced tomatoes
- 1 cup quick-cooking brown rice
- 1 tablespoon chopped fresh thyme, or 1 teaspoon dried
- ½ teaspoon saffron threads, crushed (optional)
- 1 pound cod or haddock fillet, cut into 1-inch pieces
- 2 tablespoons chopped pitted manzanilla olives
- ¼ cup chopped fresh parsley
- Freshly ground pepper, to taste

1. Heat the oil in a nonstick Dutch oven over medium-high heat. Add the onion, garlic, and paprika. Cook, stirring frequently, until softened, about 3 minutes. Add the green and red bell peppers and cook, stirring frequently, until softened, about 6 minutes.

2. Add the broth, tomatoes, rice, thyme, and saffron; bring to a boil. Reduce the heat and simmer, covered, until the rice is tender, about 8 minutes.

3. Add the cod and olives; return to a boil. Reduce the heat and simmer, covered, until the cod is just opaque in the center, about 4 minutes. Stir in the parsley and ground pepper just before serving.

PER SERVING (scant 2 cups): 362 Cal, 6 g Fat, 1 g Sat Fat, 60 mg Chol, 416 mg Sod, 48 g Carb, 6 g Fib, 30 g Prot, 91 mg Calc. *POINTS: 7.*

CUT *POINTS* Omit the olive oil, spray the Dutch oven lightly with nonstick spray, and reduce the amount of fish to ¾ of a pound to save a *POINT* per serving.

Scandinavian Flounder and Spinach Bisque

Bisque is a thick pureed soup, usually made rich by adding cream. Ours is a traditional thick smooth bisque, made rich in flavor from seasonings and fresh dill. For contrasting texture and an extra *POINT* per serving, serve each portion with two crisp rye crackers.

2 teaspoons canola oil

1 large onion, chopped

2 garlic cloves, minced

2 cups fish or vegetable broth, or bottled clam juice

1 pound all-purpose potatoes, peeled and cut into 1-inch chunks

1 bay leaf

½ teaspoon salt

¼ teaspoon ground nutmeg

¼ teaspoon ground white pepper

¾ pound flounder fillet, cut into 1-inch pieces

1 (10-ounce) package frozen chopped spinach, thawed and squeezed dry

1½ cups low-fat (1%) milk

¼ cup chopped fresh dill

MAKES 4 SERVINGS

1. Heat the oil in a nonstick Dutch oven over medium-high heat. Add the onion and garlic. Cook, stirring occasionally, until golden, 7–10 minutes.

2. Add the broth, potatoes, bay leaf, salt, nutmeg, and pepper; bring to a boil. Reduce the heat and simmer, covered, until the potatoes are tender, about 20 minutes. Discard the bay leaf.

3. Stir the flounder and spinach into the broth mixture; return to a boil. Reduce the heat and simmer until the fish is just opaque in center and spinach is tender, about 3 minutes.

4. Transfer half of the mixture to a blender or food processor and puree; transfer the puree to a bowl. Repeat with the remaining soup mixture, then return all the puree to the Dutch oven. Add the milk; bring to a simmer, then stir in the dill.

PER SERVING (generous 1½ cups): 258 Cal, 4 g Fat, 1 g Sat Fat, 45 mg Chol, 477 mg Sod, 32 g Carb, 4 g Fib, 23 g Prot, 218 mg Calc. *POINTS: 5.*

tip This soup is delicious cold—the flavors, especially the dill, shine even stronger after sitting overnight in the refrigerator. If you like, stir in 1 to 2 tablespoons of milk to thin the cold soup a little. If you bought a whole bunch of dill for this recipe, chop the remaining dill and freeze it in small zip-close freezer bags to add to soups, casserole dishes, or dips another time.

Bourride

Once thought of as peasants' fare, this fish-and-bread soup appears in many fine restaurants today. It is usually thickened with egg yolks and seasoned with aïoli, but we simplify by using mayonnaise and garlic. Fresh spinach, stirred in towards the end of the cooking time, rounds out the soup, making it a complete meal.

2 tablespoons low-fat mayonnaise

2 garlic cloves, minced

5 ounces French baguette, cut into 16 rounds

1 teaspoon olive oil

1 medium onion, halved lengthwise, then thinly sliced crosswise

3 cups fish or vegetable broth, or bottled clam juice

¼ cup dry white wine

1 thick lemon slice

1 large parsley sprig

1 fresh thyme sprig

1 (6-ounce) bag triple-washed baby spinach leaves

1 pound halibut, cod, or flounder fillets, cut into 1-inch pieces

1 teaspoon chopped fresh thyme, or ¼ teaspoon dried

MAKES 4 SERVINGS

1. Combine the mayonnaise and half of the minced garlic in a small bowl; cover and refrigerate until the flavors blend, at least 15 minutes or up to 2 hours.

2. Preheat the broiler. Place the bread rounds on a baking sheet; spray lightly with olive-oil nonstick spray. Spread the remaining garlic on top of the rounds. Broil 5 inches away from the heat until golden and fragrant, 2–3 minutes.

3. Heat the oil in a large nonstick saucepan over medium-high heat. Add the onion and cook, stirring occasionally, until golden, 7–10 minutes. Add the broth, wine, lemon, parsley sprig, and thyme sprig; bring to a boil. Reduce the heat and simmer, covered, until the flavors blend, about 10 minutes. Discard the lemon, parsley, and thyme.

4. Stir the spinach into the broth mixture and simmer, covered, until the spinach just begins to wilt, about 1 minute. Stir about ½ cup of the hot broth into the mayonnaise mixture; whisk until smooth. Return the mayonnaise mixture to the saucepan, stirring constantly until blended. Add the fish and simmer, covered, until the fish is just opaque, about 5 minutes. Stir in the chopped thyme.

5. Place 4 garlic toasts in the bottom of each of 4 soup bowls. Pour about 1¼ cups of the soup over the toasts in each bowl.

PER SERVING (1 bowl): 259 Cal, 4 g Fat, 1 g Sat Fat, 60 mg Chol, 448 mg Sod, 25 g Carb, 3 g Fib, 28 g Prot, 104 mg Calc. *POINTS: 5.*

New England Fish Chowder

Creamy, comforting, and satisfying, this favorite chowder is great served with oyster crackers. We mash a few of the cooked Yukon Gold potatoes right in the soup—a simple thickening technique, which in this case also gives the soup a delightful golden hue.

MAKES 6 SERVINGS

3   slices thick-cut bacon
1   large onion, chopped
2   carrots, diced
1   cup fish or vegetable broth, or bottled clam juice
3   Yukon Gold potatoes, peeled and diced (about 3 cups)
2   bay leaves
4   cups low-fat (1%) milk
1   pint chopped fresh clams in juice, or 2 (6½-ounce) cans minced clams in juice
1   pound flounder fillets, cut into 1-inch pieces
1 ¼ teaspoons salt
¼   cup chopped fresh parsley
Freshly ground pepper, to taste

1. Heat a nonstick Dutch oven over medium heat. Add the bacon and cook until crisp, about 4 minutes; set aside. Drain off all but a coating of fat (about 1 teaspoon).
2. Add the onion to the same Dutch oven and cook, stirring occasionally, until golden, 7–10 minutes. Add the carrots and cook 2 minutes. Add the broth, potatoes, and bay leaves; bring to a boil. Reduce the heat and simmer, covered, until the potatoes are tender, 12–15 minutes. Discard the bay leaves. Slightly mash some of the potatoes with a potato masher against the bottom of the Dutch oven to thicken the soup.
3. Add the milk, clams and their juice, the flounder, and salt; bring to a boil. Reduce the heat and simmer, uncovered, until the fish is just opaque in the center, 2–3 minutes. Stir in the parsley and season with the pepper. Crumble the bacon and sprinkle over the soup just before serving.

PER SERVING (1⅔ cups): 267 Cal, 5 g Fat, 2 g Sat Fat, 62 mg Chol, 723 mg Sod, 26 g Carb, 2 g Fib, 27 g Prot, 254 mg Calc. *POINTS: 5.*

tip Stir in a bunch of chopped cleaned arugula (about 4 cups) instead of the parsley to make it more of a complete meal, and to give it a fresh peppery flavor.

Bouillabaisse

Every bustling Mediterranean seaport has a favorite seafood soup or stew, and bouillabaisse is the world-celebrated fish soup of Provence. Made with fish, shellfish, onions, garlic, tomatoes, wine, and herbs, it is traditionally served with French bread. A touch of orange zest and Pernod (anise-flavored liqueur) provide extra zing, and a few potatoes make it a complete meal.

MAKES 6 SERVINGS

1 tablespoon olive oil
1 large leek, cleaned and thinly sliced (4 cups)
4 garlic cloves, minced
½ fennel bulb (white part only), chopped
2 carrots, diced
4 (8-ounce) bottles clam juice
1 (14½-ounce) can diced tomatoes
⅓ cup dry white wine
1–2 tablespoons Pernod
1 tablespoon chopped fresh thyme
2 teaspoons grated orange zest
½ teaspoon saffron threads, crushed
⅛ teaspoon cayenne
6 small red potatoes, cut into ½-inch chunks
1 pound halibut fillets, cut into 1-inch pieces
½ pound large shrimp, peeled and deveined
½ pound mussels, scrubbed, debearded
¼ pound shucked oysters or bay scallops

1. Heat the oil in a large nonstick Dutch oven over medium-high heat. Add the leek and garlic. Cook, stirring occasionally, until golden, 7–10 minutes. Add the fennel and carrots. Cook, stirring occasionally, 2–3 minutes. Add the clam juice, tomatoes, wine, Pernod, thyme, orange zest, saffron, and cayenne; bring to a boil. Reduce the heat and simmer, uncovered, until the flavors blend, about 10 minutes.

2. Add the potatoes; return to a boil. Reduce the heat and simmer, partially covered, until the potatoes are tender, about 15 minutes.

3. Add the fish fillets, shrimp, mussels, and oysters; bring to a boil. Reduce the heat and simmer, covered, until the fish and shrimp are just opaque in the center and the mussels open, about 5 minutes. Discard any mussels that don't open.

PER SERVING (1⅔ cups): 281 Cal, 4 g Fat, 1 g Sat Fat, 94 mg Chol, 647 mg Sod, 35 g Carb, 6 g Fib, 26 g Prot, 144 mg Calc. *POINTS: 5.*

tip After buying mussels, discard those with broken shells or shells that do not close tightly when gently tapped. Since mussels can be sandy, soak them in a bowl of cold water for 2 to 3 minutes. Repeat, using fresh water, until there is no more sand in the bowl. Then scrub them with a stiff brush under cold running water. The hairy filaments that protrude from a mussel are known as a beard. To remove, pinch the filaments between thumb and forefinger and pull firmly.

Thai Shrimp Soup

The heady aromatic blend of lime juice, sesame oil, garlic, fresh ginger, and spices adds a wealth of interesting flavors to this dish. If you have time, you can let the lime-spice mixture sit in the refrigerator, well covered, for up to two days.

MAKES 4 SERVINGS

4 teaspoons fresh lime juice

1 tablespoon minced peeled fresh ginger

1 tablespoon reduced-sodium soy sauce

1 teaspoon packed light brown sugar

1 teaspoon Asian (dark) sesame oil

3 garlic cloves, minced

½ teaspoon ground coriander

¼ teaspoon cayenne

6 cups fish or vegetable broth, or bottled clam juice

6 ounces thin, dried Chinese noodles or capellini

1 pound medium shrimp, peeled and deveined

½ pound fresh white mushrooms, sliced

¼ pound fresh snow peas, trimmed and sliced diagonally in half

2 scallions, thinly sliced

2 tablespoons chopped fresh cilantro

1. Combine the lime juice, ginger, soy sauce, sugar, oil, garlic, coriander, and cayenne in a small bowl. Set the mixture aside, at room temperature, to allow the flavors to blend, at least 15 minutes or up to 2 days.

2. Meanwhile, bring the broth to a boil in a Dutch oven. Add the noodles and simmer, uncovered, until almost tender, about 5 minutes. Add the shrimp, mushrooms, and snow peas; return to a boil. Reduce the heat and simmer uncovered, until the shrimp are just opaque in the center and the vegetables are softened, about 2 minutes.

3. Stir the lime juice mixture into the broth; return to a simmer. Serve the soup sprinkled with the scallions and cilantro.

PER SERVING (generous 1½ cups): 231 Cal, 2 g Fat, 0 g Sat Fat, 107 mg Chol, 365 mg Sod, 33 g Carb, 3 g Fib, 19 g Prot, 74 mg Calc. *POINTS: 4.*

Lobster Miso Soup

There are many kinds of bagged cleaned greens available in the produce section of the supermarket. For a more flavorful, almost peppery taste, substitute a bag of cleaned arugula or watercress for the spinach in this delicious, hearty soup. Japanese soba are thin buckwheat noodles with a robust, earthy flavor. You'll find them in health-food stores, Asian markets, or the ethnic aisle of large supermarkets.

MAKES 4 SERVINGS

6 dried whole shiitake
   mushrooms
6 cups water
4 (4-ounce) frozen rock
   lobster tails
2 teaspoons Asian (dark)
   sesame oil
2 garlic cloves, minced
2 teaspoons minced
   peeled fresh ginger
¼ teaspoon crushed
   red pepper
5 cups fish or vegetable
   broth, or bottled
   clam juice
5 teaspoons miso paste
1 tablespoon reduced-
   sodium soy sauce
6 ounces soba noodles,
   or thin spaghetti
1 (6-ounce) bag
   radishes, sliced
1 (6-ounce) bag
   triple-washed baby
   spinach leaves
2 scallions, thinly sliced

1. Combine the shiitake mushrooms with enough boiling water to cover in a small bowl; let stand 15 minutes. Drain the mushrooms, reserving ½ cup of the liquid. Discard the stems from the mushrooms, then cut the mushroom caps into ¼-inch pieces.

2. Meanwhile, bring the 6 cups water to a boil in a Dutch oven. Add the lobster tails and cook until they are bright red, 6–8 minutes. Rinse under cold running water to cool; drain. When the lobsters are cool enough to handle, gently pull the meat from the shells, cut into ½-inch chunks, and set aside.

3. Heat the oil in the same Dutch oven over medium heat. Add the garlic, ginger, and crushed red pepper. Cook, stirring frequently, until fragrant, 2–3 minutes. Add the reserved ½ cup mushroom liquid, the mushrooms, broth, miso paste, and soy sauce; bring to a boil. Stir in the noodles; return to a boil. Cook over medium heat, stirring occasionally, until the noodles are partially tender, about 5 minutes.

4. Stir in the radishes and spinach; return to a boil. Stir in the lobster meat and simmer 1 minute. Serve the soup sprinkled with the scallions.

PER SERVING (2 cups): 254 Cal, 4 g Fat, 1 g Sat Fat, 19 mg Chol, 634 mg Sod, 40 g Carb, 8 g Fib, 18 g Prot, 119 mg Calc. POINTS: 5.

tip For extra-fiery flavor, mix ½ teaspoon wasabi powder (Japanese horseradish) with ½ teaspoon warm water; let stand for 5 minutes to allow the flavor to develop. Stir into the soup during the last minute, along with the lobster.

Cuban Black Bean Soup

Black beans are a staple food in Cuba and other islands of the Caribbean. This spicy soup is served with chopped fresh tomatoes, onion, cilantro, and a dollop of yogurt, adding a welcome touch of color, crunch, and coolness.

MAKES 4 SERVINGS

1 cup dried black beans, picked over, rinsed, and drained

4 cups boiling water

2 teaspoons olive oil

2 celery stalks, thinly sliced

1 large onion, chopped

3 garlic cloves, minced

2 teaspoons chili powder

½ teaspoon ground cumin

½ teaspoon ground coriander

6 cups low-sodium vegetable broth

½ teaspoon hot pepper sauce

1 tablespoon sweet sherry (optional)

½ cup chopped ripe tomatoes

½ cup chopped red onion

¼ cup plain low-fat yogurt

¼ cup chopped fresh cilantro

1. Combine the beans and boiling water in a large bowl. Cover with a plate and let stand 1 hour; drain.

2. Heat the oil in a nonstick Dutch oven over medium-high heat. Add the celery, onion, garlic, chili powder, cumin, and coriander. Cook, stirring occasionally, until the vegetables are lightly browned and fragrant, about 10 minutes.

3. Add the soaked beans, the broth, and the hot pepper sauce; bring to a boil. Reduce the heat and simmer, covered, until the beans are tender, about 1¼ hours. Transfer 2 cups of the bean soup to a food processor or blender and puree. Return to the Dutch oven. Stir in the sherry, if using.

4. Serve the soup with bowls of the tomato, red onion, yogurt, and cilantro as garnishes.

PER SERVING (1⅓ cups soup and ¼ of toppings): 252 Cal, 4 g Fat, 1 g Sat Fat, 1 mg Chol, 174 mg Sod, 45 g Carb, 11 g Fib, 13 g Prot, 154 mg Calc. *POINTS*. 5.

tip Bean soups keep well in the refrigerator for up to three days or in the freezer for up to three months. The flavors are even better after standing. When reheating, thin with a little extra water, if necessary. The technique of pureeing some of the soup, then returning it to the pot, is an easy way of thickening the soup.

Minestrone

Recipes for minestrone, one of the world's classic soups, are as varied as the many ingredients called for. Our minestrone uses plenty of vegetables to make it nourishing, and convenient canned beans to keep it easy. Have fun with a small pasta such as farfallini instead of the traditional elbow macaroni. A basket of Italian bread transforms this into a favorite winter supper.

MAKES 6 SERVINGS

2 teaspoons olive oil
1 medium leek, cleaned and thinly sliced (about 3 cups)
1 small onion, chopped
3 garlic cloves, minced
5 cups low-sodium vegetable broth
1 (14½-ounce) can diced tomatoes
½ cup elbow macaroni or other small pasta
3 carrots, diced
¼ small green cabbage, shredded
1 large all-purpose potato, diced
1 (19-ounce) can cannellini (white kidney) beans, rinsed and drained
1 cup frozen green peas
⅓ cup chopped flat-leaf parsley
2 tablespoons chopped fresh basil, or 2 teaspoons dried
½ teaspoon salt
6 tablespoons shredded Parmesan cheese

1. Heat the oil in a nonstick Dutch oven over medium-high heat. Add the leek, onion, and garlic. Cook, stirring occasionally, until golden, 10–12 minutes.
2. Add the broth, tomatoes, macaroni, carrots, cabbage, and potato; bring to a boil. Reduce the heat and simmer, covered, stirring occasionally, until the macaroni and vegetables are tender, about 20 minutes.
3. Stir in the beans, peas, parsley, basil, and salt; return to a boil. Reduce the heat and simmer 1–2 minutes. Serve with the cheese.

PER SERVING (generous 1½ cups soup with 1 tablespoon cheese): 245 Cal, 4 g Fat, 2 g Sat Fat, 5 mg Chol, 678 mg Sod, 42 g Carb, 8 g Fib, 12 g Prot, 178 mg Calc. *POINTS: 4.*

tip No need to thaw the frozen peas—once they hit the hot soup, they'll thaw in a minute or two. Or if you make this recipe in spring, try using fresh peas, available in plastic (10- to 11-ounce) containers in the produce section of the supermarket.

Scandinavian Yellow Split Pea Soup with Dilled Yogurt

Leeks are one of the milder members of the onion family. Their fibrous leaves and distinctive sweet, earthy flavor make them well suited for use in long-simmering soups, where they get a chance to soften and impart flavor. For a change from plain black peppercorns, use a pepper grinder with multicolored whole peppercorns to freshly grind over the soup. For an extra *2 POINTS*, serve each bowl of soup with a slice of fresh pumpernickel bread.

MAKES 6 SERVINGS

1 tablespoon butter
1 large leek, cleaned and sliced (about 4 cups)
2 garlic cloves, minced
8 cups low-sodium vegetable broth
1 (1-pound) package dried yellow split peas, picked over, rinsed, and drained
2 bay leaves
3 carrots, sliced
2 celery stalks, sliced
1 teaspoon dried marjoram
¼ teaspoon freshly ground pepper
½ cup plain fat-free yogurt
3 tablespoons chopped fresh dill or parsley
2 teaspoons grated lemon zest

1. Melt the butter in a nonstick Dutch oven over medium-high heat. Add the leek and garlic. Cook, stirring occasionally, until golden, 7–10 minutes. Add the broth, split peas, and bay leaves; bring to a boil. Reduce the heat and simmer, covered, until the split peas are almost tender, about 25 minutes.
2. Add the carrots, celery, marjoram, and pepper; bring to a boil. Reduce the heat and simmer, covered, stirring occasionally, until the vegetables and split peas are tender, about 25 minutes.
3. Meanwhile, combine the yogurt, dill, and lemon zest in a small bowl; cover and refrigerate for 20 minutes to allow the flavors to develop. Discard the bay leaves. Serve with the dilled yogurt.

PER SERVING (1½ cups soup with scant 2 tablespoons yogurt topping): 341 Cal, 3 g Fat, 1 g Sat Fat, 6 mg Chol, 73 mg Sod, 61 g Carb, 21 g Fib, 21 g Prot, 144 mg Calc. POINTS: 6.

tip Dried split pea and bean dishes need occasional stirring during the last few minutes of cooking to prevent them from sticking to the bottom of the pan. If the mixture *does* burn on the bottom of the pan, simply pour off the unburned soup into another pan, leaving the scorched parts behind.

Middle Eastern Vegetable and Lentil Soup

Lentils—one of the most ancient foods known to man—have long been a favorite staple for soups and stews throughout the Middle East. They are a good source of protein, vitamins A and B, and calcium—and unlike dried beans, they cook in about 30 minutes. This soup's flavor is brightened at the last minute with the addition of fresh lemon zest and juice.

MAKES 4 SERVINGS

1   tablespoon olive oil
1   large onion, chopped
2   celery stalks, chopped
3   garlic cloves, minced
2   teaspoons ground
    cumin
6   cups low-sodium
    vegetable broth
½   pound (1¼ cups) dried
    lentils, picked over,
    rinsed, and drained
1   small eggplant, diced
    (about 5 cups)
2   zucchini, diced
1   tomato, chopped
½   teaspoon salt
2   teaspoons grated
    lemon zest
1   tablespoon fresh
    lemon juice
Freshly ground pepper,
    to taste

1. Heat the oil in a nonstick Dutch oven over medium-high heat. Add the onion, celery, and garlic. Cook, stirring occasionally, until the vegetables are lightly browned, 7–10 minutes. Add the cumin and cook until fragrant, about 1 minute.

2. Add the broth and lentils; bring to a boil. Reduce the heat and simmer, covered, about 15 minutes. Add the eggplant and return to a boil. Reduce the heat and simmer, covered, until the lentils and eggplant are tender, about 15 minutes.

3. Stir in the zucchini, tomato, and salt; return to a boil. Reduce the heat and simmer, covered, until the zucchini is just softened but still colorful, 3–5 minutes. Stir in the lemon zest, juice, and pepper.

PER SERVING (generous 2 cups): 313 Cal, 5 g Fat, 1 g Sat Fat, 0 mg Chol, 330 mg Sod, 54 g Carb, 18 g Fib, 18 g Prot, 96 mg Calc. *POINTS*: 6.

African Squash and Lima Bean Soup

Every bride in Ghana is expected to be able to make a good squash-and-bean soup, often flavored with smoked fish or pig's feet. We keep our version of this flavorful soup strictly vegetarian and very simple, and hike up the spices.

MAKES 4 SERVINGS

1 tablespoon vegetable oil
3 garlic cloves, minced
1 tablespoon grated peeled fresh ginger
1 teaspoon paprika
¼ teaspoon crushed red pepper
3 cups low-sodium vegetable broth
1 (20 ounce) bag frozen butternut squash chunks
½ (1 pound) bag frozen whole small onions
1 (10-ounce) box frozen baby lima beans
½ teaspoon salt
1 tomato, chopped

1. Heat the oil in a nonstick Dutch oven over medium heat. Add the garlic, ginger, paprika, and crushed red pepper. Cook, stirring frequently, until fragrant, about 2 minutes.

2. Add the broth, squash, onions, lima beans, and salt; bring to a boil. Reduce the heat and simmer, covered, until the vegetables are tender, about 10 minutes. Stir in the tomato and heat through, about 2 minutes.

PER SERVING (1½ cups): 230 Cal, 4 g Fat, 1 g Sat Fat, 0 mg Chol, 346 mg Sod, 45 g Carb, 12 g Fib, 7 g Prot, 103 mg Calc. *POINTS: 4.*

tip If you have any leftover cooked brown rice on hand, you can stir 1 cup into this soup for a heartier meal and an additional **POINT** per serving.

Japanese Tofu Noodle Soup

Although not low in fat, tofu is cholesterol-free and very low in saturated fat. It is an excellent source of protein, and some tofus are even fortified with calcium. Miso is a rich, savory paste made from fermented soybeans. You can find miso paste and soba noodles in health-food stores, Asian markets, or many large supermarkets.

MAKES 6 SERVINGS

2 teaspoons Asian (dark) sesame oil

1 (15-ounce) container firm tofu, drained and cut into ½-inch cubes

2 garlic cloves, chopped

2 teaspoons minced peeled fresh ginger

¼ teaspoon Chinese five-spice powder

6 cups low-sodium vegetable broth

2 tablespoons miso paste

2 carrots, thinly sliced on the diagonal

4 ounces soba noodles, or thin spaghetti

3 cups finely shredded green cabbage

¼ pound fresh brown button mushrooms, sliced

2 tablespoons sake wine (optional)

1. Heat the oil in a nonstick Dutch oven over medium-high heat. Add the tofu and cook, tossing frequently, until lightly browned on all sides, about 7 minutes. With a draining spoon, transfer the tofu to a plate and set aside.

2. Lower the heat to medium under the same Dutch oven. Add the garlic, ginger, and five-spice powder. Cook, stirring frequently, until fragrant, 1–2 minutes. Add about ½ cup of the broth and the miso paste; bring to a boil, stirring constantly to blend in the miso paste. Add the remaining 5½ cups broth and the carrots; return to a boil.

3. Stir in the soba noodles; return to a boil and cook rapidly until the noodles and carrots are almost tender, about 5 minutes.

4. Add the cabbage, mushrooms, sake, and tofu; return to a boil. Reduce the heat and simmer until the vegetables are softened, about 4 minutes.

PER SERVING (1⅓ cups): 233 Cal, 9 g Fat, 1 g Sat Fat, 0 mg Chol, 239 mg Sod, 26 g Carb, 6 g Fib, 16 g Prot, 193 mg Calc. *POINTS: 5.*

French Onion Soup

This rich, much-loved soup is easy to serve in individual ovenproof soup bowls. Use small casserole dishes if you don't have ovenproof soup bowls. Vidalia onions are especially sweet and good for caramelizing here, but you can substitute 6 medium regular onions, if you like. For a special treat and an extra ½ *POINT* per serving, stir in 3 tablespoons of cognac during the last minute of simmering the soup.

MAKES 4 SERVINGS

1   tablespoon butter
3   large Vidalia onions, halved lengthwise, then thinly sliced crosswise
6   cups low-sodium vegetable broth
½   cup dry red wine
1   bay leaf
1   sprig fresh thyme, or ¼ teaspoon dried
¼   teaspoon freshly ground pepper
5   ounces French baguette, cut into 16 rounds
1   cup shredded part-skim Swiss or Jarlsberg cheese
2   tablespoons shredded Parmesan cheese

1. Melt the butter in a nonstick Dutch oven over medium-high heat. Add the onions and cook, stirring occasionally, until translucent, about 8 minutes. Reduce the heat to medium-low and cook, stirring occasionally, until golden brown and well softened, about 12 minutes.
2. Add the broth, wine, bay leaf, thyme, and pepper; bring to a boil. Reduce the heat and simmer, uncovered, about 30 minutes. Discard the bay leaf and thyme.
3. Preheat the broiler. Place the bread rounds on a baking sheet and broil 5 inches away from the heat until toasted, about 2 minutes on each side.
4. Place 4 rounds of bread in each of 4 ovenproof soup bowls. Add the onion soup (about 1½ cups for each bowl). Sprinkle evenly with the Swiss cheese, then the Parmesan cheese.
5. Stand the bowls on the baking sheet and broil 5 inches from the heat until the cheese melts and is light golden brown, about 3 minutes.

PER SERVING (1 bowl): 269 Cal, 9 g Fat, 5 g Sat Fat, 19 mg Chol, 701 mg Sod, 34 g Carb, 3 g Fib, 15 g Prot, 441 mg Calc. *POINTS: 6.*

tip Getting the onions golden is essential for good flavor and color in onion soup. If necessary, raise the heat and cook the onions a little longer, until they become truly golden. Simmering the soup uncovered for 30 minutes reduces the broth and intensifies the flavors—you should be left with about 6 cups of soup.

Cheddar Cheese Soup

Cheddar cheese was first made in the village of Cheddar, in southwest England, in the sixteenth century. Early English settlers brought the formula for making cheddar cheese to the United States and Canada. It is now one of our most popular cheeses. Extra-sharp cheddar is especially full of flavor, making it possible to use only small amounts. If you like, omit the beer and substitute an extra cup of milk.

MAKES 4 SERVINGS

- 2 teaspoons canola oil
- 1 large onion, chopped
- 2 celery stalks, chopped
- 2 carrots, chopped
- ½ teaspoon dry mustard
- 2 cups low-sodium vegetable broth
- 1 pound baking potatoes, peeled and cubed
- ¼ teaspoon freshly ground pepper
- 1 cup beer
- 1 cup low-fat (1%) milk
- 3 ounces extra-sharp cheddar cheese, shredded (¾ cup)

1. Heat the oil in a nonstick Dutch oven over medium-high heat. Add the onion, celery, and carrots. Cook, stirring occasionally, until the vegetables are lightly browned, about 8 minutes. Stir in the mustard and cook 1 minute.

2. Add the broth, potatoes, and pepper; bring to a boil. Reduce the heat and simmer, covered, until the vegetables are tender, about 20 minutes.

3. With a potato masher or fork, gently mash some of the vegetables against the bottom of the pan to slightly thicken the soup. Add the beer and milk; bring to a simmer. Remove the soup from the heat. Add the cheese, then stir until the cheese melts.

PER SERVING (scant 1½ cups): 276 Cal, 10 g Fat, 5 g Sat Fat, 25 mg Chol, 103 mg Sod, 35 g Carb, 4 g Fib, 10 g Prot, 227 mg Calc. *POINTS: 6.*

tip Soups are often pureed to thicken them. If you want to save time and cleanup, try our back-to-basics method of mashing some of the vegetables against the bottom of the pan to help thicken the soup.

Chilled Salmon and Cucumber Soup

Cool cucumber soup is the perfect refresher for any steamy summer day. We add salmon to make it main-dish. For a change of pace, substitute an equal amount of cooked small shrimp for the salmon. You can prepare the soup (without the dill) and the salmon up to 24 hours ahead. Keep them refrigerated in separate containers, then stir together, with the dill, just before serving.

MAKES 4 SERVINGS

1 cup fish or vegetable broth, or bottled clam juice
¼ cup dry white wine
¾ pound salmon fillet
2 large seedless cucumbers, peeled and coarsely chopped
2 tablespoons white balsamic vinegar
2 garlic cloves, halved
¾ teaspoon salt
¼ teaspoon freshly ground pepper
2 cups low-fat buttermilk
¼ cup finely chopped fresh dill

1. Bring the broth and wine to a boil in a large skillet. Add the salmon. Reduce the heat and simmer, covered, until the salmon is just opaque in the center, about 10 minutes. With 2 wide spatulas, transfer the salmon to a plate until cool enough to handle. Discard the skin from the salmon, then cut or flake the salmon into ½-inch pieces. Cover and refrigerate until well chilled, at least 1 hour or up to 24 hours. Transfer the cooking broth from the skillet to a small bowl and refrigerate, covered, until chilled, at least 1 hour or up to 24 hours.

2. Puree the cucumbers, the chilled cooking broth, vinegar, garlic, salt, and pepper in a blender or food processor until smooth. Transfer to a large bowl; stir in the buttermilk. Cover and refrigerate until well chilled, at least 2 hours, or up to 24 hours. Stir in the salmon and dill just before serving.

PER SERVING (scant 2 cups): 180 Cal, 5 g Fat, 2 g Sat Fat, 54 mg Chol, 741 mg Sod, 11 g Carb, 1 g Fib, 21 g Prot, 186 mg Calc. POINTS: 4.

tip A blender is our first choice over a food processor for getting smooth soups, and the cleanup is a little easier. Scandinavians add chopped fresh dill to this soup, but for a different and equally refreshing experience, try substituting an equal amount of chopped fresh mint for the dill.

Chicken Gazpacho

If you can't stand the heat, get into the kitchen and whip up this classic chilled soup, full of crunchy, nourishing vegetables and spicy flavors. We add chicken and a few croutons and it becomes a meal in itself. If just a few more crunchy, savory croutons would make you happier—and for an extra *POINT*—serve your portion of the soup with an extra ¼ cup fat-free croutons. And for an extra ½ *POINT*, serve with a tablespoon of reduced-fat sour cream.

MAKES 6 SERVINGS

1 beefsteak tomato, chopped
1 yellow bell pepper, seeded and diced
1 small zucchini, diced
½ seedless cucumber, diced
1 small red onion, finely chopped
1 garlic clove, minced
3 cups tomato juice
2 cups low-sodium chicken or vegetable broth
2–3 tablespoons white balsamic vinegar
2 tablespoons chopped fresh parsley
¼ teaspoon salt
⅛ teaspoon hot pepper sauce
2 cups diced cooked chicken
1 cup fat-free croutons

1. Combine the tomato, bell pepper, zucchini, cucumber, red onion, and garlic in a large bowl.
2. Combine the tomato juice, broth, vinegar, parsley, salt, and hot pepper sauce in another large bowl; pour over the vegetables. Cover and refrigerate until well chilled, at least 3 hours or up to 2 days.
3. Just before serving, stir in the chicken. Serve with the croutons.

PER SERVING (1⅔ cups soup and scant ¼ cup croutons): 148 Cal, 4 g Fat, 1 g Sat Fat, 37 mg Chol, 627 mg Sod, 13 g Carb, 2 g Fib, 16 g Prot, 45 mg Calc. POINTS: 3.

tip You can make this soup, without the chicken, up to two days ahead of time and store it, covered, in the refrigerator. Stir in the chicken just before serving.

Chicken Gazpacho

The Meat Market

Beef, pork, and lamb dishes

Mushroom-Crusted Beef Tenderloin with Potatoes and Tomatoes

Imported dried mushrooms (whole, sliced, or in pieces)—readily available in supermarkets at a reasonable price—give a nice woodsy flavor to many dishes, such as bean or vegetable soups, tomato sauces, pasta dishes, and casseroles. Here we grind the dried mushrooms into a powder to coat the beef before browning it. You can use tiny red potatoes, cut in half, instead of baking potatoes, if you prefer.

MAKES 4 SERVINGS

1 (1-pound) beef tenderloin, trimmed of all visible fat

1 teaspoon salt

½ teaspoon freshly ground pepper

1 (½-ounce) container imported dried mushrooms

1 tablespoon all-purpose flour

¼ cup fat-free egg substitute

4 teaspoons extra-virgin olive oil

3 baking potatoes (about 5 ounces each), peeled and cut into ⅛-inch-thick slices

3 tomatoes, cut into ¼-inch-thick slices

1 teaspoon dried thyme

1. Preheat the oven to 400°F.

2. Sprinkle beef with ½ teaspoon of the salt and ¼ teaspoon of the pepper. Grind the mushrooms to a powder in a spice grinder or small food processor. Place the flour and mushroom powder on separate pieces of wax paper. Put the egg substitute in a pie plate. Roll the beef in the flour, coating it evenly and shaking off the excess. Coat the beef with the egg substitute, allowing the excess to drip off. Roll the beef thoroughly in the mushroom powder, using it all to coat the beef.

3. Heat the oil in a heavy roasting pan over medium-high heat. Add beef and cook until browned on all sides, about 8 minutes. Transfer to a plate. Remove the roasting pan from the heat.

4. Arrange the potatoes in the pan in slightly overlapping rows, covering the bottom of the pan. Sprinkle with the remaining ½ teaspoon salt and ¼ teaspoon pepper. Arrange the tomato slices in a single row around the inside edge of the pan, on top of the potatoes. Season tomatoes with the thyme, then lightly spray the tomatoes and potatoes with nonstick spray.

5. Roast the potatoes and tomatoes until partially cooked, about 20 minutes. Place the beef in the center of the pan on top of the potatoes. Roast until an instant-read thermometer, inserted in the center of the beef, registers 145°F for medium-rare and the potatoes are cooked through, about 20 minutes. Transfer the beef to a cutting board and let rest about 10 minutes. Cut the beef into 12 slices and serve with the vegetables.

PER SERVING (3 slices beef and ¼ of vegetables): 340 Cal, 14 g Fat, 4 g Sat Fat, 65 mg Chol, 673 mg Sod, 26 g Carb, 3 g Fib, 28 g Prot, 30 mg Calc. *POINTS: 7.*

Mushroom-Crusted Beef Tenderloin
with Potatoes and Tomatoes

Beef and Pepper Fajitas

Fajitas are casual, fun-to-eat fare. Increase the fun factor and let each person create his own personalized wrap by serving bowls of tomato salsa (homemade or store-bought), lime wedges, sliced fresh or pickled jalapeño peppers, and—for an extra *POINT* per 2 tablespoons—guacamole or fat-free sour cream.

MAKES 4 SERVINGS

¼ cup fresh lime juice

2 teaspoons olive oil

2 large garlic cloves, minced

1 teaspoon salt

1 (1-pound) flank steak, trimmed of all visible fat

2 large red bell peppers, seeded and cut into ½- inch-wide strips

1 large green bell pepper, seeded and cut into ½-inch-wide strips

1 large onion, sliced

1–2 jalapeño peppers, seeded and finely chopped (wear gloves to prevent irritation)

4 (8-inch) fat-free flour tortillas

1. Combine the lime juice, oil, garlic, and ½ teaspoon of the salt in a zip-close plastic bag; add the beef. Squeeze out the air and seal the bag; turn to coat the beef. Refrigerate, turning the bag occasionally, at least 2 hours or up to 4 hours.

2. Spray the grill rack with nonstick spray; prepare the grill.

3. Put the red and green bell peppers and onion in a bowl. Lightly spray the vegetables with nonstick spray and sprinkle with the remaining ½ teaspoon salt; toss to coat. Grill the vegetables over medium heat, turning frequently, until tender, about 8 minutes. Transfer to a bowl and toss with jalapeño pepper; keep warm.

4. Remove the flank steak from the plastic bag; discard marinade. Place the steak on the grill rack and grill, turning once, until an instant-read thermometer, inserted in the center of the steak, registers 145°F for medium-rare, about 12 minutes. Transfer the meat to a plate; keep warm. Grill the tortillas until browned in spots, about 1 minute on each side. Transfer to a basket.

5. Thinly slice the flank steak on the diagonal. Fill each tortilla with 3 to 4 slices of the flank steak and about 1 cup of the vegetables. Or serve the tortillas in a basket and arrange the meat and vegetables on a platter, then let each person assemble his own fajita.

PER SERVING (1 fajita): 337 Cal, 9 g Fat, 3 g Sat Fat, 65 mg Chol, 626 mg Sod, 33 g Carb, 4 g Fib, 29 g Prot, 78 mg Calc. *POINTS: 7.*

 **tip** This dish is cooked completely on the grill, but if you prefer you can cook it under the broiler, on a nonstick ridged grill pan, or in a large nonstick skillet.

Beef Stroganoff

This is an authentic version of beef stroganoff, which was named for a prominent member of the Stroganov family in Russia. As the story goes, old Count Grigory Alexandrovich Stroganov lost his teeth and was no longer able to chew. So his personal chef sliced beef paper-thin and served it coated with a delicate brown sauce in hopes of pleasing his employer. The dish was a great success—and the rest is history.

MAKES 6 SERVINGS

1   cup low-sodium beef broth
2   tablespoons all-purpose flour
1   teaspoon dry mustard
1   (1-pound) beef tenderloin, trimmed of all visible fat and cut into 2½-inch strips
½   teaspoon salt
¼   teaspoon freshly ground pepper
2   teaspoons olive oil
1   small onion, thinly sliced
1   (10-ounce) package cremini, white, or baby portobello mushrooms, halved or quartered
¼   cup water
2   tablespoons light sour cream
2   tablespoons chopped fresh parsley
4   cups hot cooked egg noodles

1. With a whisk, stir the broth, flour, and mustard in a large nonstick skillet until blended and smooth. Cook over medium-high heat, stirring constantly, until the mixture comes to a boil and thickens, about 2 minutes. Pour into a small bowl and cover to keep warm. Wipe the skillet clean.

2. Pat the beef dry with a paper towel; sprinkle with the salt and ⅛ teaspoon of the pepper. Heat 1 teaspoon of the oil in the same skillet over medium-high heat. Add half of the beef and cook, turning once, until browned but still pink on the inside, about 2 minutes. With a slotted spoon, transfer the beef to a plate; keep warm. Repeat with the remaining 1 teaspoon oil and the remaining half of the beef.

3. Add the onion to the skillet. Cook, stirring, until translucent, 3–5 minutes. Add the mushrooms, water, and the remaining ⅛ teaspoon pepper. Cook, stirring, until the mushrooms are tender, 3–4 minutes. Add any accumulated meat juices to the sauce mixture in the small bowl. Return the beef to the skillet with the onions and mushrooms. Cook, stirring occasionally, until just heated through, about 1 minute. Transfer the meat mixture to a platter; keep warm.

4. Rewhisk the sauce mixture and pour into the skillet. Cook over medium-low heat, stirring occasionally, until the sauce is heated through, about 2 minutes. Remove the skillet from the heat and stir in the sour cream. Pour the sauce over the meat, then sprinkle with the parsley. Serve with the egg noodles.

PER SERVING (⅔ cup stew and ⅔ cup noodles): 311 Cal, 9 g Fat, 3 g Sat Fat, 80 mg Chol, 255 mg Sod, 32 g Carb, 2 g Fib, 23 g Prot, 33 mg Calc. *POINTS:* 7.

Sesame Beef and Asparagus

Broccoli florets work as well as asparagus—and skinless, boneless chicken breasts work as well as beef—in this versatile stir-fry. For an extra *2 POINTS*, serve each portion with ½ cup cooked brown rice.

MAKES 4 SERVINGS

1 pound fresh asparagus, tough ends trimmed

¾ cup low-sodium chicken broth

3 tablespoons reduced-sodium soy sauce

1 tablespoon cornstarch

1 tablespoon vegetable oil

1 pound beef top round, trimmed of all visible fat and cut into 2 x ⅛-inch strips

1 tablespoon minced peeled fresh ginger

2 garlic cloves, minced

1 tablespoon sesame seeds, toasted

1. Cut off the asparagus tips and put in a medium bowl. Cut the asparagus spears on a long diagonal into ⅛-inch-thick slices; add to the asparagus tips.
2. Combine the broth, soy sauce, and cornstarch in a cup.
3. Heat a nonstick wok or large deep skillet over high heat until a drop of water sizzles. Swirl in the oil, then add the beef. Stir-fry until just cooked through, 3–4 minutes. Transfer to a plate.
4. Add the asparagus, ginger, and garlic to the wok; stir-fry until the asparagus is crisp-tender, about 2 minutes. Return the beef with any accumulated juices to the wok. Add the broth mixture and cook, stirring constantly, until the sauce bubbles and thickens, about 1 minute. Transfer the beef and asparagus to a platter, then sprinkle with the sesame seeds.

PER SERVING (1¼ cups): 211 Cal, 8 g Fat, 2 g Sat Fat, 60 mg Chol, 508 mg Sod, 7 g Carb, 2 g Fib, 26 g Prot, 28 mg Calc. *POINTS: 4.*

tip Toasting sesame seeds brings out their nuttiness and turns them a lovely deep golden brown. Cook them over medium heat in a small skillet, tossing them often, until they begin to look shiny and just turn color. Be sure to transfer them to a plate: they will continue to darken if left in the skillet.

Spicy Orange Beef

Beef (or pork or chicken) for stir-frying is best when very thinly sliced. This is most easily accomplished if the meat is partially frozen first. Place the still-wrapped meat in the freezer for at least one hour, or until very firm—then slicing will be a breeze.

MAKES 4 SERVINGS

2   navel oranges
²/₃ cup low-sodium chicken broth or water
2   tablespoons reduced-sodium soy sauce
1   tablespoon cornstarch
½   teaspoon crushed red pepper
1   tablespoon vegetable oil
1   pound beef top round, trimmed of all visible fat and cut into 2 x ⅛ inch strips
1   pound broccoli crowns, cut into small florets
1   red bell pepper, seeded and cut into ¾-inch pieces
3   scallions, cut into 1-inch pieces
2   tablespoons minced peeled fresh ginger
2   large garlic cloves, minced
2   cups hot cooked brown rice

1. With a vegetable peeler, remove enough zest from one of the oranges to make 2 tablespoons very thinly sliced strips; set aside. Remove the peel and pith from the oranges. Holding an orange over a bowl to catch the juice, cut along either side of each membrane to release the orange sections, allowing the juice to fall into the bowl. Repeat with the other orange; set sections aside.
2. Combine ⅓ cup of the broth, the orange juice, soy sauce, cornstarch, and crushed red pepper in a cup until smooth.
3. Heat a nonstick wok or large deep skillet over medium-high heat until a drop of water sizzles. Swirl in the oil, then add the beef. Stir-fry until lightly browned, about 4 minutes. Transfer the beef to a plate.
4. Add the broccoli, bell pepper, orange zest strips, and the remaining ⅓ cup broth to the wok. Cook, covered, until the vegetables are parcooked, about 2 minutes. Uncover, then add the scallions, ginger, and garlic. Stir-fry until fragrant, about 30 seconds. Return the beef to the wok; add the orange sections and cornstarch mixture. Cook, stirring constantly, until mixture bubbles and thickens, about 1 minute. Serve with the rice.

PER SERVING (1½ cups orange beef with ½ cup rice): 368 Cal, 9 g Fat, 2 g Sat Fat, 60 mg Chol, 393 mg Sod, 44 g Carb, 8 g Fib, 31 g Prot, 113 mg Calc. **POINTS: 7.**

tip Think like a Chinese chef—prep all the ingredients, including the sauce mixture, ahead, place in separate bowls, then cover (or place in zip-close plastic bags for less cleanup) and refrigerate for up to 24 hours.

Beef and Spinach Sukiyaki

Beef and Spinach Sukiyaki

Bring out the chopsticks when you sit down to enjoy this popular Japanese dish. Serve it in shallow soup bowls and drink the flavorful broth from the bowl. Japanese people consider sukiyaki the perfect food to have when friends or relatives get together, because of the easy one-pot cooking style.

MAKES 8 SERVINGS

8 ounces capellini or angel hair pasta

4 teaspoons vegetable oil

2 tablespoons sugar

1 (1-pound) beef tenderloin, trimmed of all visible fat, cut lengthwise in half, then cut crosswise into very thin slices

½ pound napa cabbage, cut into 1-inch pieces

1 bunch scallions, cut into 1-inch pieces

6 ounces fresh white mushrooms, halved or quartered, if large

1⅓ cups low-sodium chicken broth

⅓ cup sake, dry white wine, or dry vermouth

¼ cup reduced-sodium soy sauce

½ pound firm tofu, cut into ½-inch cubes

1 (6-ounce) package triple-washed fresh baby spinach

1. Cook the pasta according to package directions in a large heavy pot; drain. Rinse under cold running water; drain again. Wipe the pot dry.

2. Meanwhile, heat the oil in the same pot over medium heat. Sprinkle the sugar evenly in the pot and cook, stirring frequently, until the sugar turns caramel-colored, about 2 minutes. Add half of the beef and cook over medium-high heat until just cooked through, about 2 minutes. Transfer the beef to a plate. Repeat with the remaining beef. Reduce the heat to medium to prevent the sugar from burning, if necessary.

3. Return the beef to the pot along with the pasta, cabbage, scallions, mushrooms, broth, sake, and soy sauce. Bring to a boil. Reduce the heat and simmer, covered, stirring occasionally, until the vegetables are tender, about 5 minutes. Stir in the tofu and spinach; cook until the spinach wilts, about 1 minute.

PER SERVING (generous 1 cup): 312 Cal, 10 g Fat, 2 g Sat Fat, 32 mg Chol, 367 mg Sod, 33 g Carb, 3 g Fib, 23 g Prot, 130 mg Calc. *POINTS:* 6.

Vietnamese Beef and Noodle Salad

Rice noodles, available in Asian markets and some supermarkets, come very thin and round, resembling capellini, or flat and long, resembling fettuccine. For this recipe use thin noodles, called rice sticks or rice vermicelli (sold in packages weighing 7 or 8 ounces). A time-saving bonus to rice noodles is that it is not necessary to cook them. They are simply stirred into boiling water, where they soften after several minutes.

⅓ cup fresh lime juice

4 teaspoons vegetable oil

4 garlic cloves, crushed

⅛ teaspoon freshly ground pepper

1 pound beef top round, trimmed of all visible fat and cut into 2 x ⅛-inch strips

1 (7-ounce) package rice sticks (vermicelli)

1 small head Boston lettuce, torn into bite-size pieces

3 carrots, coarsely grated

1 large tomato, seeded and chopped

1 cup lightly packed fresh cilantro leaves

¼ cup sliced mint

3 tablespoons Asian fish sauce (nam pla)

1 tablespoon sugar

1 teaspoon hot pepper sauce

⅓ cup unsalted dry-roasted peanuts, chopped

MAKES 6 SERVINGS

1. Combine 1 tablespoon of the lime juice, the oil, three-fourths of the garlic, and the pepper in a zip-close plastic bag; add the beef. Squeeze out the air and seal the bag; turn to coat the beef. Refrigerate, turning the bag occasionally, at least 30 minutes or up to 4 hours.

2. Plunge the noodles into a large bowl of boiling water; let soak until soft, about 3 minutes. Drain well, rinse under cold running water, and put in a large bowl. Add the lettuce, carrots, tomato, cilantro, and mint to the noodles; toss until mixed. Cover and refrigerate.

3. Heat a large nonstick skillet over high heat. Add one-third of the beef and cook until browned along the edges, about 2 minutes. Transfer the meat to a plate. Repeat in two more batches with the remaining beef.

4. Meanwhile, combine the remaining lime juice (about ¼ cup), the fish sauce, sugar, the remaining garlic, and the pepper sauce in a small bowl. Pour over the noodle-salad mixture; toss until evenly coated. Mound the salad on a platter, then top with the beef. Sprinkle with the peanuts just before serving.

PER SERVING (2 cups salad with scant ½ cup beef and scant 1 tablespoon peanuts): 286 Cal, 10 g Fat, 2 g Sat Fat, 40 mg Chol, 402 mg Sod, 30 g Carb, 3 g Fib, 20 g Prot, 43 mg Calc. *POINTS: 6.*

tip Many of the ingredients for this salad can be prepared ahead. Cut up the vegetables and store in separate zip-close plastic bags in the refrigerator for up to one day. The meat can marinate and the dressing can sit in the refrigerator for up to four hours.

Chuck-Wagon Stew

The unusual addition of coffee, molasses, and chili sauce to the stew adds down-home richness to an otherwise basic recipe. For strong brewed coffee, use a scoop and a half of coffee to 6 ounces of water.

MAKES 4 SERVINGS

2 thin slices reduced-sodium bacon
1 pound beef top round, trimmed of all visible fat and cut into ¾-inch chunks
¾ teaspoon salt
¼ teaspoon freshly ground pepper
1 tablespoon all-purpose flour
½ pound frozen small white onions
4 carrots, cut into 2-inch pieces
1½ cups water
1 cup strong brewed coffee
2 tablespoons chili sauce or ketchup
1 tablespoon mild molasses
1 pound all-purpose potatoes, peeled and cut into ¾-inch chunks
½ pound green beans, trimmed and halved
½ teaspoon liquid smoke
½ teaspoon hot pepper sauce

1. Heat a nonstick Dutch oven over medium heat. Add the bacon and cook until crisp. With a slotted spoon, transfer the bacon to a paper towel to drain. Remove all but 2 teaspoons of the fat from the Dutch oven.
2. Meanwhile, pat the beef chunks dry with a paper towel; sprinkle with the salt and ⅛ teaspoon of the pepper. Put the beef and flour in a zip-close plastic bag. Shake the bag until the beef is evenly coated with the flour. Add half of the beef to the bacon fat in the pot and cook over medium-high heat until browned on all sides, about 5 minutes. Transfer the beef to a plate. Repeat with the remaining beef.
3. Add the onions and carrots to the pot. Cook, scraping up the browned bits with a wooden spoon, until the onions are golden, about 3 minutes. Return the beef to the pot. Crumble the bacon and add to pot. Stir in the water, coffee, chili sauce, molasses, and the remaining ⅛ teaspoon pepper.
4. Bring the stew to a boil. Reduce the heat and simmer, covered, about 1 hour. Add the potatoes, green beans, liquid smoke, and pepper sauce. Simmer, covered, until the beef is fork-tender, about 20 minutes longer.

Per serving (2½ cups): 351 Cal, 8 g Fat, 3 g Sat Fat, 65 mg Chol, 647 mg Sod, 43 g Carb, 7 g Fib, 28 g Prot, 84 mg Calc. *POINTS: 7*.

CUT*POINTS* Make this stew serve five instead of four and save a *POINT* per serving.

Provençal Beef Daube with Mushrooms

In France, a *daube* is a stew cooked in a round, deep earthenware casserole called a *daubière*. Its shape prevents the stew's liquid from evaporating too quickly while it simmers its way to perfection. The most traditional daubes are prepared in Provence, where they are slowly cooked over an open fire, on top of the stove, or in the oven.

1½ pounds beef top round, trimmed of all visible fat and cut into 1½-inch chunks
1 cup dry red wine
3 (4 x ½-inch) strips orange zest
1 teaspoon dried rosemary
1 teaspoon dried thyme
1 tablespoon olive oil
1 large onion, coarsely chopped
2 large garlic cloves, minced
¾ cup boiling water
1 (14½-ounce) can Italian plum tomatoes, cut up
1 teaspoon salt
¼ teaspoon freshly ground pepper
1 (½-ounce) container imported dried mushrooms
6 carrots, sliced
1 pound fresh white mushrooms, halved
4 cups hot cooked ziti

MAKES 6 SERVINGS

1. Combine the beef, wine, 2 of the orange strips, ½ teaspoon of the rosemary, and ½ teaspoon of the thyme in a bowl; toss well. Cover and marinate in the refrigerator for at least 4 hours or up to overnight, turning the meat occasionally.

2. Drain the beef, reserving the wine. Wipe the herbs off the beef and discard along with the orange zest. Pat the beef dry.

3. Heat the oil in a nonstick Dutch oven over medium-high heat. Add half of the beef. Cook until lightly browned on all sides, about 4 minutes. Transfer the beef to a plate. Repeat with the remaining beef.

4. Reduce the heat to medium. Add the onion, garlic, and ¼ cup of the water to the pot. Cook, stirring, until onion is translucent, 3–5 minutes. Return the beef with any accumulated juices to the pot. Add the tomatoes with their juice, salt, pepper, the reserved wine, the remaining orange strip, ½ teaspoon rosemary, and ½ teaspoon thyme; bring to a boil. Reduce the heat and simmer, covered, 1 hour.

5. Meanwhile, soak the dried mushrooms in the remaining ½ cup boiling water until soft, about 15 minutes. Lift out mushrooms and rinse to remove any grit. Pour the mushroom liquid through a small strainer lined with a paper towel.

6. Add the carrots, the fresh and dried mushrooms, and the mushroom liquid to the pot. Simmer, covered, until the meat and carrots are fork-tender, about 1 hour, partially covering the stew for the last 30 minutes. Serve with the pasta.

PER SERVING (1½ cups stew with ⅔ cup pasta): 368 Cal, 7 g Fat, 2 g Sat Fat, 60 mg Chol, 577 mg Sod, 45 g Carb, 6 g Fib, 31 g Prot, 68 mg Calc. *POINTS:* 7.

Braciole with Chunky Tomato-Mushroom Sauce

Braciole is a typical Italian-American dish, usually prepared as part of an expansive Sunday family dinner. We add a generous amount of mushrooms and zucchini to the pot while the braciole simmers in the bubbling tomato sauce, to add flavor to what Sicilian cooks refer to as "Sunday gravy."

2 slices white bread, made into coarse crumbs (1 cup)

¼ cup grated Parmesan cheese

¼ cup lightly packed thinly sliced fresh basil leaves

3 garlic cloves, minced

8 thin slices beef top round (about 1 pound), trimmed of all visible fat

½ teaspoon salt

¼ teaspoon freshly ground pepper

1 tablespoon extra-virgin olive oil

½ pound fresh white mushrooms, sliced

2 zucchini, halved lengthwise, then sliced crosswise

1 (14½-ounce) can Italian plum tomatoes, broken up

MAKES 4 SERVINGS

1. Combine the bread crumbs, cheese, basil, and one-third of the garlic in a small bowl.

2. Pound the beef slices between pieces of plastic wrap until ⅛-inch thick. Sprinkle the beef with ½ teaspoon of the salt and ⅛ teaspoon of the pepper. Sprinkle the bread-crumb mixture evenly over the beef slices, pressing it so it adheres. Roll up each beef slice beginning with a short side. Secure each beef roll with a wooden pick.

3. Heat the oil in a large nonstick skillet over medium-high heat. Add the beef rolls and cook, turning occasionally, until browned on all sides, about 4 minutes. Transfer the braciole to a plate.

4. Add the mushrooms, zucchini, and the remaining two-thirds garlic, ½ teaspoon salt, and ⅛ teaspoon pepper to the skillet. Cook, stirring frequently, until the mushrooms are golden, about 5 minutes. Return the beef with any accumulated juices to the skillet and stir in the tomatoes with their juice; bring to a simmer. Cook, covered, until the meat is very tender, about 30 minutes.

5. Transfer the braciole to a platter; remove the wooden picks. Spoon the vegetables and sauce around and over the braciole.

PER SERVING (2 braciole with 1½ cups vegetables and sauce): 273 Cal, 10 g Fat, 3 g Sat Fat, 65 mg Chol, 687 mg Sod, 17 g Carb, 3 g Fib, 30 g Prot, 157 mg Calc. *POINTS: 6.*

tip An old-fashioned egg slicer makes quick work of slicing mushrooms. Simply wipe the mushrooms with a damp paper towel to remove any grit and trim the stems before placing them in the slicer.

**Braciole with Chunky
Tomato-Mushroom Sauce,
page 57**

Light Veal Milanese

In most veal Milanese recipes, the meat is heavily coated with a flour-egg-crumb mixture and then pan-fried in a good amount of butter. Here the cutlets are seasoned and broiled, allowing the flavor of the meat to come through while keeping the dish low in fat. The blender cucumber dressing contains no fat but is still deliciously thick and flavorful. For variety, add a small clove of garlic along with the lemon juice. For an extra *POINT*, serve each portion with a long sesame breadstick.

1 cucumber, peeled, seeded, and coarsely chopped

Juice of 1 lemon (about 2 tablespoons)

1 teaspoon salt

4 cups lightly packed torn romaine lettuce leaves

1 bunch arugula (about 6 ounces), stems removed and leaves torn

½ small red onion, very thinly sliced

16 cherry tomatoes, halved

8 veal cutlets (about 1 pound)

4 teaspoons extra-virgin olive oil

⅛ teaspoon freshly ground pepper

MAKES 4 SERVINGS

1. Puree the cucumber with the lemon juice and ½ teaspoon of the salt in a blender. Toss the romaine, arugula, onion, and tomatoes in a large bowl.

2. Pound the veal cutlets between pieces of plastic wrap until ⅛-inch thick. Brush the veal with the oil, then sprinkle with the remaining ½ teaspoon salt and the pepper.

3. Spray the broiler rack with nonstick spray; preheat the broiler.

4. Broil the cutlets 5 inches from the heat until cooked through, about 5 minutes. Pour the cucumber dressing over the salad and toss to coat. Divide the salad among 4 plates. Top each with 2 veal cutlets.

PER SERVING (2 cups salad and 2 veal cutlets): 193 Cal, 9 g Fat, 2 g Sat Fat, 74 mg Chol, 666 mg Sod, 8 g Carb, 2 g Fib, 20 g Prot, 112 mg Calc. *POINTS: 4.*

 To save time, pick up one or two of your favorite packaged salads and use in place of the arugula and romaine.

Easy Osso Buco

Though osso buco is most definitely an Italian preparation, *herbes de Provence*, a heady mix of dried herbs commonly used in southern French cooking, contributes just the right flavor. *Herbes de Provence* is usually a blend of thyme, rosemary, sage, savory, marjoram, and lavender. It is found in specialty-food stores and in some large supermarkets. If your Dutch oven doesn't have ovenproof handles, cover them with heavy-duty foil.

MAKES 4 SERVINGS

4   (7-ounce) veal shanks, trimmed of all visible fat
½   teaspoon salt
¼   teaspoon freshly ground pepper
1   teaspoon extra-virgin olive oil
4   carrots, cut into ¼-inch dice
3   celery stalks, cut into ¼-inch dice
1   onion, coarsely chopped
3   garlic cloves, minced
1½ cups low-sodium chicken broth
1   (14½-ounce) can Italian plum tomatoes, broken up
⅓   cup dry white wine
1   teaspoon herbes de Provence, or dried thyme
2   cups hot cooked brown rice

1. Preheat the oven to 325°F.

2. Sprinkle the veal shanks with the salt and pepper. Heat the oil in a nonstick ovenproof Dutch oven over medium-high heat. Add the veal shanks and cook until browned on all sides, about 10 minutes. Transfer the veal to a plate.

3. Add the carrots, celery, onion, garlic, and ¼ cup of the broth to the pot. Reduce the heat to medium. Cook, stirring, until the onions are soft, about 4 minutes. Return the veal with any accumulated juices to the pot. Stir in the tomatoes with their juice, the remaining 1¼ cups broth, the wine, and herbes de Provence; bring to a boil. Cover the pot and put in the oven. Braise until the veal is very tender, about 1½ hours.

4. Transfer the veal shanks to a platter; keep warm. Cook the sauce and vegetables in the Dutch oven over medium-high heat until the liquid is slightly reduced, about 5 minutes. Pour the sauce and vegetables over the veal and serve with the rice.

PER SERVING (1 veal shank, ¾ cup vegetables and ½ cup rice): 490 Cal, 13 g Fat, 5 g Sat Fat, 191 mg Chol, 700 mg Sod, 39 g Carb, 6 g Fib, 52 g Prot, 135 mg Calc. *POINTS: 10.*

CUT*POINTS* After cooking, remove the veal from the bones. Discard the bones, cut the veal into bite-size chunks, and return to the Dutch oven with the vegetables. This will make it easy to share this dish among six people and save about *3 POINTS* per serving.

Braised Herb-Crusted Pork Tenderloin with Vegetables

Pork tenderloin—reasonably priced, very lean, and easy to prepare—is a great cut of meat. Here it is rolled in a flavorful blend of fresh parsley, rosemary, and thyme. But you can substitute savory, oregano, marjoram, or sage for the rosemary or thyme, if you like. Be sure to brown the herbed crust well and turn the tenderloin over gently with tongs or with two wooden spoons so as not to disturb the crust.

1 pork tenderloin (about 1 pound), trimmed of all visible fat
¾ teaspoon salt
¼ teaspoon freshly ground pepper
¼ cup finely chopped fresh parsley
2 tablespoons finely chopped fresh rosemary
2 tablespoons finely chopped fresh thyme
4 teaspoons extra-virgin olive oil
4 carrots, cut into matchstick-thin strips
4 celery stalks, cut into matchstick-thin strips
3 parsnips, peeled and cut into matchstick-thin strips
1 large garlic clove, smashed with the side of a chef's knife, then cut in half
¾ cup low-sodium chicken broth

MAKES 4 SERVINGS

1. Preheat the oven to 425°F.
2. Sprinkle the pork with ½ teaspoon of the salt and ⅛ teaspoon of the pepper. Fold the narrow end of the tenderloin under. Combine the parsley, rosemary, and thyme on wax paper. Roll the pork in the herbs, lightly pressing them so they adhere.
3. Heat the oil in an ovenproof nonstick Dutch oven over medium-high heat. Add the pork and cook until browned on all sides, about 8 minutes. Add the carrots, celery, parsnips, and garlic to the pot. Sprinkle the vegetables with the remaining ¼ teaspoon salt and ⅛ teaspoon pepper. Pour in the broth.
4. Roast, tossing the vegetables once or twice, until an instant-read thermometer inserted into the center of the pork registers 160°F for medium and the vegetables are tender, about 20 minutes. Let the pork rest for 5 minutes, then transfer to a cutting board and cut into ½-inch-thick slices. Serve the pork with the vegetables and any pan juices.

PER SERVING (3–4 slices pork with 1 cup vegetables): 305 Cal, 10 g Fat, 2 g Sat Fat, 72 mg Chol, 568 mg Sod, 27 g Carb, 7 g Fib, 29 g Prot, 91 mg Calc. *POINTS: 6.*

Rosemary-Grilled Pork Chops with Potatoes and Zucchini

This recipe gives new meaning to the term "one pot." Although a grill isn't a pot, it is the ideal way to cook an entire meal. If you've never tried grilled potatoes or grilled zucchini, let this recipe be a delicious introduction.

Finely grated zest and
    juice of 1 large lemon
2   tablespoons chopped
    fresh rosemary
3   garlic cloves, crushed
    with a garlic press
1   tablespoon extra-virgin
    olive oil
4   (4-ounce) boneless
    center-cut pork loin
    chops, trimmed of all
    visible fat
1   teaspoon salt
½   teaspoon freshly
    ground pepper
1   pound baby potatoes,
    such as Yukon Gold,
    scrubbed and halved
2   medium zucchini, cut
    lengthwise into
    ⅛-inch-thick slices

MAKES 4 SERVINGS

1. Combine the lemon zest, rosemary, garlic, and oil in a small bowl. Sprinkle the pork with ½ teaspoon of the salt and ¼ teaspoon of the pepper. Rub half of the rosemary mixture over the pork. Put the pork on a plate, then cover and refrigerate at least 1 hour or up to several hours.

2. Spray the grill rack with nonstick spray; prepare the grill.

3. Toss the potatoes with the remaining rosemary mixture, ¼ teaspoon of remaining salt, and ⅛ teaspoon of remaining pepper in a medium bowl. Lightly spray the potatoes with nonstick spray, then place on the grill, cut-side down. Grill the potatoes 5 inches from the heat, turning once, until tender, 45 minutes. Transfer the potatoes to a bowl; cover with foil to keep warm.

4. Sprinkle the zucchini with the remaining ¼ teaspoon salt and ⅛ teaspoon pepper; lightly spray the zucchini with nonstick spray. Put the pork and zucchini on the grill. Grill the pork until an instant-read thermometer inserted in the center of the pork chops registers 160°F for medium, about 4 minutes on each side. Grill the zucchini until tender, about 4 minutes on each side. Put the pork and zucchini on a platter. Drizzle the lemon juice over the zucchini. Serve with the potatoes.

PER SERVING (1 pork chop with ¼ of zucchini and potatoes): 339 Cal, 13 g Fat, 4 g Sat Fat, 72 mg Chol, 638 mg Sod, 28 g Carb, 4 g Fib, 28 g Prot, 41 mg Calc. *POINTS: 7.*

tip For rich caramelized citrus flavor, cut a lemon in half and grill it, cut-side down, until lightly browned and slightly softened, about 5 minutes. Squeeze the warm juice over the zucchini just before serving.

**Maple-Brined Pork Chops
with Crispy Potato Wedges**

Maple-Brined Pork Chops with Crispy Potato Wedges

Brining pork with salt and other flavors before it is cooked adds complexity and juiciness. For best taste, use natural—not imitation—maple extract.

MAKES 4 SERVINGS

2 cups boiling water
2 tablespoons kosher salt
1 cup unsweetened apple cider or juice
¼ cup maple syrup
1 teaspoon maple extract
¼ teaspoon ground allspice
4 (5-ounce) bone-in rib pork chops
1 pound baking potatoes
½ teaspoon table salt
⅛ teaspoon freshly ground pepper
1 tablespoon olive oil
2 Granny Smith apples, cored and cut into ½-inch-thick wedges

1. Stir the boiling water and kosher salt in a medium bowl until the salt dissolves; refrigerate until cold. Stir in the apple cider, maple syrup, maple extract, and allspice. Put the pork chops in a single layer in a large baking dish. Pour the cold brine mixture over the chops. Cover and refrigerate for at least 4 hours or up to overnight, turning the pork occasionally.

2. Peel and coarsely grate the potatoes. With your hands, squeeze all the water out of the potatoes. Spray a large nonstick skillet with nonstick spray and set over medium-high heat. Add the potatoes and sprinkle with the table salt and pepper. Cook, lightly pressing down on the potatoes with a spatula, until deep golden on the bottom, about 5 minutes. Slide the potato cake onto a large flat plate. Invert the potato cake back into the skillet. Reduce the heat to medium; cook until the potatoes are tender, about 5 minutes. Slide the potato cake onto a plate; cover with foil to keep warm.

3. Remove the pork chops from the brine and pat them dry with paper towels. Discard the brine. Swirl the oil in the skillet, then add the pork. Cook until deep golden on the outside and an instant-read thermometer inserted in the center of the pork chops registers 160°F for medium, about 4 minutes on each side. Transfer the chops to a plate; cover with foil to keep warm.

4. Add the apple wedges to the skillet. Cook, tossing occasionally, until the apples are deep golden and tender, about 6 minutes.

5. Cut the potato cake into four wedges. Place a wedge on each of 4 plates, top with a pork chop, and spoon a few of the apple wedges alongside.

PER SERVING (1 pork chop with 1 wedge potato cake and ¼ of apple): 319 Cal, 10 g Fat, 3 g Sat Fat, 54 mg Chol, 905 mg Sod, 36 g Carb, 4 g Fib, 21 g Prot, 23 mg Calc. *POINTS:* 6.

Szechuan Pork and Vegetables

Szechuan dishes are often very spicy, sometimes bordering on the incendiary. This version is only mildly spicy, so feel free to up the amount of chili garlic sauce (found in the Asian section of large supermarkets or Asian specialty stores), if you're so inclined.

½ cup low-sodium chicken broth or water

1 tablespoon cornstarch

1 tablespoon reduced-sodium soy sauce

1½ teaspoons chili garlic sauce

1 red bell pepper, seeded and cut into ¾-inch pieces

1 tablespoon vegetable oil

1 (1-pound) pork tenderloin, trimmed of all visible fat, cut lengthwise in half, then thinly sliced crosswise

2 cups small broccoli florets

4 scallions, cut into ½-inch pieces

2 garlic cloves, minced

2 tablespoons dry sherry

1 cup drained canned baby corn

1 cup drained canned straw mushrooms

2 cups hot cooked brown rice

MAKES 4 SERVINGS

1. Combine the broth, cornstarch, soy sauce, and chili garlic sauce in a cup; set aside.

2. Spray a nonstick wok or large deep skillet with nonstick spray; set over medium-high heat until a drop of water sizzles. Add the bell pepper and stir-fry until lightly charred, 3–5 minutes. Transfer to a large bowl. Swirl the oil into the wok, then add the pork. Stir-fry until lightly browned and cooked through, about 4 minutes. With a slotted spoon, transfer the pork to the bowl with the bell pepper. Add the broccoli, scallions, and garlic to the wok and stir-fry until crisp-tender, about 2 minutes. Add the sherry; cover and cook about 1 minute.

3. Return pork mixture to the wok. Add the corn, mushrooms, and cornstarch mixture; cook, stirring constantly, until mixture bubbles and thickens, about 1 minute. Serve with the rice.

PER SERVING (1¼ cups pork mixture with ½ cup rice): 372 Cal, 9 g Fat, 2 g Sat Fat, 72 mg Chol, 546 mg Sod, 40 g Carb, 5 g Fib, 32 g Prot, 57 mg Calc. *POINTS: 7.*

Pork and Sausage Gumbo

Gumbo, a Cajun soup-like dish, is often prepared with at least ¼ cup oil. This is a terrific low-fat version, with all of the richness of the classic. Instead of making a roux by cooking equal amounts of flour and oil to a rich caramel hue, we toast the flour and cook it "dry" to lend the gumbo depth of flavor.

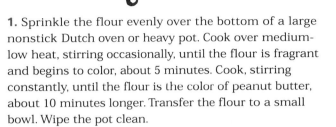

MAKES 4 SERVINGS

3 tablespoons all-purpose flour
1 tablespoon oil
¾ pound pork tenderloin, trimmed of all visible fat and cut into ½-inch chunks
¼ pound low-fat sweet Italian sausage links, casings removed
1 onion, chopped
1 green bell pepper, seeded and chopped
2 celery stalks, chopped
3 garlic cloves, minced
½ cup water
1 (14½-ounce) can diced tomatoes
1 (10-ounce) package frozen okra
2 cups low-sodium chicken broth
1 teaspoon dried thyme
½ teaspoon salt
¼ teaspoon freshly ground pepper
¼ teaspoon cayenne
1 bay leaf
2 cups hot cooked rice

1. Sprinkle the flour evenly over the bottom of a large nonstick Dutch oven or heavy pot. Cook over medium-low heat, stirring occasionally, until the flour is fragrant and begins to color, about 5 minutes. Cook, stirring constantly, until the flour is the color of peanut butter, about 10 minutes longer. Transfer the flour to a small bowl. Wipe the pot clean.

2. Heat the oil in the Dutch oven over medium-high heat. Add the pork and sausage and cook until very lightly browned, 6–8 minutes. Transfer to a plate. Add the onion, bell pepper, celery, garlic, and water to the Dutch oven. Cook, stirring occasionally and scraping up the browned bits with a wooden spoon, until the vegetables are softened, 3–5 minutes.

3. Return the browned flour to the pot and cook, stirring, about 1 minute. Add the tomatoes with their juice, the okra, broth, thyme, salt, pepper, cayenne, and bay leaf. Return the pork and sausage to the pot; bring to a boil. Reduce the heat and simmer, covered, until the pork is tender and the liquid thickens slightly, about 20 minutes. Discard the bay leaf.

4. Put a mound of the rice in the center of each soup bowl. Ladle the gumbo around the rice.

PER SERVING (1½ cups gumbo with ½ cup rice): 377 Cal, 9 g Fat, 2 g Sat Fat, 65 mg Chol, 781 mg Sod, 44 g Carb, 5 g Fib, 30 g Prot, 126 mg Calc. *POINTS: 7.*

tip You can cut up the onion, bell pepper, and celery a day ahead and store in zip-close plastic bags in the refrigerator. The garlic, however, is best if minced just before being used.

Pork Paprikash

Open the spice cupboard in just about any home and you are likely to come across a jar of paprika—a deep-reddish powder made from the capsicum pepper. It is most often sprinkled on food to lend a bit of color. In Hungary, however, it is an important element in many traditional dishes, where it is added with a generous hand. For the highest-quality paprika, look for the Hungarian variety in a decorative red and white metal container that says "Pride of Szeged." It is available both sweet and hot, but the sweet variety is most commonly used.

1 tablespoon all-purpose flour
½ teaspoon salt
¼ teaspoon freshly ground pepper
1 pound pork tenderloin, trimmed of all visible fat and cut into ¾-inch chunks
2 teaspoons olive oil
1 onion, chopped
1 large green bell pepper, seeded and coarsely chopped
1 tablespoon paprika, preferably Hungarian
¾ cup low-sodium chicken broth
3 tablespoons light sour cream
4 cups hot cooked egg noodles (about ½ pound dry)

MAKES 4 SERVINGS

1. Combine the flour, salt, and pepper in a zip-close plastic bag. Add the pork and shake to evenly coat.
2. Heat the oil in a large nonstick skillet over medium heat. Add half of pork and cook until lightly browned on all sides, about 4 minutes. Transfer to a plate. Repeat with the remaining pork.
3. Add the onion and bell pepper to the skillet. Cook, stirring frequently, until the onion is translucent, about 4 minutes. Stir in the paprika and cook, stirring constantly, until fragrant, about 20 seconds.
4. Return the pork with any accumulated juices to the skillet. Stir in the broth and bring to a boil. Reduce the heat and simmer, covered, until the pork is tender, 20–25 minutes. Remove from the heat, then stir in the sour cream. Serve over the egg noodles.

PER SERVING (¾ cup paprikash with 1 cup noodles): 430 Cal, 11 g Fat, 3 g Sat Fat, 129 mg Chol, 370 mg Sod, 47 g Carb, 3 g Fib, 35 g Prot, 50 mg Calc. *POINTS: 9.*

Greek-Style Meatballs in Cinnamon-Scented Tomato Sauce

Bulgur is wheat kernels that have been steamed, dried, and crushed. It is a staple in the Middle East and most often enjoyed in this country in tabbouleh salad. Bulgur is found in supermarkets and health-food stores in fine, medium, and coarse grinds. It is employed here as a tasty filler for the meatballs, where medium- or coarse-grained bulgur works best.

MAKES 6 SERVINGS

1 pound lean ground pork (10% or less fat)
½ cup bulgur
½ cup chopped flat-leaf parsley
1 large onion, chopped
3 garlic cloves, minced
¼ cup fat-free egg substitute
1 teaspoon ground cumin
1 teaspoon salt
¼ teaspoon freshly ground pepper
1 pound fresh green beans, trimmed and cut into 1-inch pieces
4 teaspoons extra-virgin olive oil
1 (14½-ounce) can Italian plum tomatoes, broken up
1 (8-ounce) can tomato sauce
1 cup water
1 (4-inch) cinnamon stick
2 cups hot cooked orzo

1. Combine the pork, bulgur, parsley, half of the onion, one-third of the garlic, the egg substitute, cumin, ½ teaspoon of the salt, and ⅛ teaspoon of the pepper in a bowl. Knead the mixture well, then cover and refrigerate for 30 minutes or up to 4 hours. Shape the meat mixture into 30 walnut-size meatballs.

2. Half-fill a large deep skillet with water; bring to a boil. Add the green beans and cook until crisp-tender, about 6 minutes. Drain the green beans, then plunge them into a bowl of ice water to stop the cooking; drain and set aside. Wipe the skillet dry.

3. Heat the oil in skillet over medium heat. Add the remaining onion and garlic. Cook, stirring frequently, until the onion is golden, 7–10 minutes. Add the tomatoes with their juice, the tomato sauce, water, cinnamon stick, the remaining ½ teaspoon salt and ⅛ teaspoon pepper, and the meatballs to the skillet; bring to a boil. Reduce the heat and simmer, covered, until the meatballs are cooked through and the sauce thickens slightly, about 20 minutes.

4. Add the green beans and simmer until heated through, about 5 minutes. Remove the cinnamon stick. Serve the meatballs and sauce over the orzo.

PER SERVING (5 meatballs with 1 cup sauce and ⅓ cup orzo): 314 Cal, 10 g Fat, 2 g Sat Fat, 46 mg Chol, 782 mg Sod, 53 g Carb, 7 g Fib, 35 g Prot, 87 mg Calc. *POINTS: 6.*

Thai One-Pot

There are several types of long-grain rice that work well in this easy-to-prepare, brightly colored one-pot meal. Regular long-grain white rice is a good foil for all the bold flavors in the dish. But you could use basmati, a long-grain white rice that is native to India and valued for its perfumed scent and delicate flavor, or jasmine rice, an aromatic variety that is slightly sticky when cooked and is frequently used in Southeast Asian cooking.

MAKES 4 SERVINGS

2 teaspoons vegetable oil

1 pound lean ground pork (10% or less fat)

2 red bell peppers, seeded and cut into strips

6 ounces fresh shiitake mushrooms, stems discarded, caps thickly sliced

2 cups low-sodium beef broth

1 cup long-grain white rice

1 tablespoon reduced-sodium soy sauce

¾ teaspoon chili-garlic sauce

4 ounces fresh snow peas, trimmed and halved

4 scallions, thinly sliced

½ cup coarsely chopped fresh cilantro

2 tablespoons fresh lime juice

1. Heat the oil in a large, deep nonstick skillet or a wok over medium-high heat. Add the pork and cook, breaking it up with a wooden spoon, until it almost loses its pink color, about 4 minutes. Add the bell peppers and mushrooms. Cook, stirring frequently, about 1 minute.

2. Stir in the broth, rice, soy sauce, and chili garlic sauce; bring to a boil. Reduce the heat and simmer, covered, until the rice is tender and the broth is absorbed, about 20 minutes.

3. Remove the pan from the heat, then stir in the snow peas, scallions, and cilantro. Let stand 5 minutes then drizzle with the lime juice.

PER SERVING (2¼ cups): 438 Cal, 12 g Fat, 4 g Sat Fat, 70 mg Chol, 241 mg Sod, 49 g Carb, 3 g Fib, 32 g Prot, 55 mg Calc. *POINTS: 9.*

 **tip** Chili-garlic sauce, also known as chili-garlic paste or chili-bean sauce, is a potent mix of chile peppers, salt, rice vinegar, and garlic. This reddish-brown sauce is very spicy and fragrant; its heat is intoxicating. It is packaged in 8-ounce bottles and will keep for many months in the refrigerator.

Butterflied Leg of Lamb with Charred Tomatoes and Potatoes

If you've never grilled a marinated butterflied leg of lamb before, you're in for a treat. Have the butcher butterfly and trim the lamb of fat for you, but you'll still need to trim more fat when you get it home. The lamb should be marinated for at least 2 hours to give the flavors a chance to develop. You can marinate it for up to 6 hours—making the flavor even better.

MAKES 6 SERVINGS

¼ cup fresh lemon juice

3 tablespoons chopped fresh rosemary

2 tablespoons Dijon mustard

4 large garlic cloves, minced

1 teaspoon salt

½ teaspoon freshly ground pepper

1½ pounds butterflied leg of lamb, trimmed of all visible fat

1¼ pounds baking potatoes, peeled and cut lengthwise into ¼-inch-thick slices

3 large tomatoes, cut crosswise in half and seeded

1. Combine the lemon juice, rosemary, mustard, garlic, ½ teaspoon of the salt, and ¼ teaspoon of the pepper in a small bowl. Spread half of the mixture over the lamb. Place the lamb in a zip-close plastic bag. Squeeze out the air and seal the bag. Refrigerate for at least 2 hours or up to 6 hours.

2. Spray the grill rack with nonstick spray; prepare the grill for a medium fire.

3. Grill the lamb over medium heat, turning occasionally, until an instant-read thermometer inserted into the thickest part of the lamb registers 145°F for medium-rare, 30-40 minutes. Transfer the lamb to a cutting board and let rest 10 minutes.

4. Meanwhile, brush the reserved mustard mixture over the potatoes, then sprinkle with ¼ teaspoon of the remaining salt and ⅛ teaspoon of the remaining pepper. Lightly spray the potatoes with nonstick spray. Grill, turning occasionally, until lightly charred and tender, about 30 minutes. Sprinkle the tomatoes with the remaining ¼ teaspoon salt and ⅛ teaspoon pepper, then lightly spray the cut sides with nonstick spray. Grill the tomatoes until lightly charred, about 5 minutes on each side.

5. Cut the lamb into slices and serve with the potatoes and tomatoes.

PER SERVING (3–4 slices of lamb, about 4 slices potato, and ½ tomato): 282 Cal, 9 g Fat, 3 g Sat Fat, 78 mg Chol, 528 mg Sod, 23 g Carb, 3 g Fib, 27 g Prot, 33 mg Calc. *POINTS: 6.*

Egyptian-Style Pot Roast

This is, without doubt, a great one-pot meal. Juices from the lamb drip into the vegetables and infuse them with tantalizing flavor, while the diced tomatoes keep them deliciously moist. The lamb is just as tasty whether cooked medium-rare or well-done. If members of your family like their lamb cooked to different degrees of doneness, simply slice off pieces of the lamb and continue to roast the remaining meat.

2 pounds boneless leg of lamb, trimmed of all visible fat, then rolled and tied

1 garlic clove, cut in half

1 teaspoon salt

½ teaspoon freshly ground pepper

2 (6-ounce) eggplants

2 pounds very small potatoes, scrubbed and halved

1 pound fresh green beans, trimmed

2 zucchini, thickly sliced

2 cups low-sodium beef broth

1 (14½-ounce) can diced tomatoes

MAKES 8 SERVINGS

1. Preheat the oven to 375°F.

2. Rub the lamb all over with the cut side of the garlic. Sprinkle the lamb with ½ teaspoon of the salt and ¼ teaspoon of the pepper. Put the lamb in the center of a large heavy roasting pan.

3. Peel the eggplant. Cut lengthwise in half then crosswise into ½-inch-thick slices. Place the eggplant, potatoes, green beans, and zucchini in separate piles around the lamb. Sprinkle the vegetables with the remaining ½ teaspoon salt and ¼ teaspoon pepper. Pour the broth into the pan. Spoon the tomatoes over the vegetables.

4. Braise lamb and vegetables, uncovered, basting occasionally with the pan juices, until an instant-read thermometer inserted in the center of the lamb registers 145°F for medium-rare and the vegetables are very tender, 45–55 minutes. Slice the lamb, arrange on a platter, then surround with the vegetables.

PER SERVING (⅛ of lamb and vegetables): 363 Cal, 13 g Fat, 5 g Sat Fat, 82 mg Chol, 478 mg Sod, 33 g Carb, 6 g Fib, 29 g Prot, 79 mg Calc. *POINTS:* **8.**

tip If you prefer your lamb even more well-done, continue to roast it until the instant-read thermometer registers 160°F for medium or 170°F for well-done, 15 to 25 minutes longer.

Lamb Biryani

In India, biryani is an important dish often served at weddings or other family gatherings. Part of the reason for this may be that it's easy to prepare in great quantities—and all in one pot. Be sure to include all the enticing spices; the combination lends this dish its flavor complexity. Unlike some biryanis, which take almost two hours to prepare, this one is made fairly quickly and also has a shorter ingredient list, but it is just as long on flavor.

2 tablespoons minced peeled fresh ginger
2 garlic cloves, crushed with a garlic press
1½ teaspoons ground cumin
¾ teaspoon salt
½ teaspoon turmeric
¼ teaspoon cinnamon
⅛ teaspoon cayenne
Pinch ground cloves
1 pound boneless leg of lamb, trimmed of all visible fat and cut into ½-inch chunks
⅓ cup plain fat-free yogurt
4 teaspoons vegetable oil
1 large onion, thinly sliced
1 cup basmati or long-grain white rice
¼ cup chopped raisins or currants
1½ cups water
2 tablespoons chopped unsalted dry-roasted pistachios or cashews

MAKES 6 SERVINGS

1. Combine the ginger, garlic, cumin, salt, turmeric, cinnamon, cayenne, and cloves in a cup. Put the lamb in a bowl. Add the yogurt and half of the spice mixture; toss to coat. Refrigerate, covered, about 4 hours. Reserve the remaining spice mixture.

2. Heat the oil in a large nonstick skillet over medium-high heat. Add the onion and cook, stirring frequently, until the onion is translucent, 3–5 minutes. Add the reserved spice mixture and cook, stirring constantly, until the spices are fragrant, about 2 minutes. Add the lamb mixture to the skillet and cook, stirring occasionally, about 3 minutes. Stir in rice and raisins; cook, stirring, about 2 minutes. Stir in the water and bring to a boil.

3. Reduce the heat and simmer, covered, until the lamb is fork-tender and the rice has absorbed the liquid, about 20 minutes. Remove from the heat and let rest about 5 minutes. Spoon the biryani into a large bowl, then sprinkle with the pistachios.

PER SERVING (scant 1 cup biryani with 1 teaspoon nuts): 301 Cal, 9 g Fat, 2 g Sat Fat, 52 mg Chol, 345 mg Sod, 35 g Carb, 1 g Fib, 20 g Prot, 55 mg Calc. *POINTS: 7.*

Lemon-and-Oregano Marinated Lamb Kebabs

You can substitute almost any favorite vegetable here for the cherry tomatoes and zucchini—mushrooms, lengths of jumbo asparagus, red onion wedges (skewered through the layers to hold the onion together), and chunks of eggplant are all good possibilities. Bay leaves are threaded onto the skewers to give flavor to the food and for an attractive appearance. Avoid eating them, as they can be sharp and cut the mouth.

Finely grated zest and
    juice of 1 lemon
1   tablespoon olive oil
1   teaspoon salt
½   teaspoon dried
    oregano
¼   teaspoon freshly
    ground pepper
1   pound boneless leg
    of lamb, trimmed of all
    visible fat and cut into
    1-inch chunks
12 cherry tomatoes
2   zucchini, cut into
    ½-inch-thick slices
8   bay leaves
2   cups hot cooked orzo

MAKES 4 SERVINGS

1. Combine the lemon zest and juice, oil, salt, oregano, and pepper in a zip-close plastic bag; add the lamb. Squeeze out the air and seal the bag; turn to coat the lamb. Refrigerate, turning the bag occasionally, at least 30 minutes or up to several hours.
2. Spray the grill rack with nonstick spray; prepare grill.
3. Remove the lamb from the marinade. Discard the marinade. Thread the lamb, cherry tomatoes, zucchini, and bay leaves alternately on 4 (12-inch) metal skewers.
4. Grill the kebabs 5 inches from the heat, turning occasionally, until the lamb is cooked through, 10–12 minutes for medium-rare. Spoon the orzo onto a platter and place the kebabs on top.

PER SERVING (1 kebab with ½ cup orzo): 305 Cal, 9 g Fat, 3 g Sat Fat, 78 mg Chol, 215 mg Sod, 25 g Carb, 3 g Fib, 29 g Prot, 30 mg Calc. *POINTS: 6.*

tip When grating lemon, it is important to remove only the flavorful colored part of the peel, called the zest. The thick white part just under the zest, known as the pith, is very bitter and should not be grated. A microplane grater, which resembles a rasp, removes citrus zest easily and is a worthwhile investment. It is available in kitchenware stores.

Lemon-and-Oregano
Marinated Lamb Kebabs

Picadillo

Picadillo is a delectable savory, sweet, and salty combination and is a favorite dish in many Spanish-speaking countries. In Cuba it is often served with rice and beans, while in Mexico it is used as a flavorful stuffing for chiles rellenos, enchiladas, tacos, tamales, and tostados.

1 tablespoon vegetable
  oil
1 large red bell pepper,
  seeded and chopped
1 onion, chopped
2 large garlic cloves,
  minced
1 pound lean ground
  beef (10% or less fat)
1½ cups canned
  crushed tomatoes
1 cup frozen peas
¼ cup dark raisins,
  chopped
2 tablespoons chopped
  pitted green olives
1 teaspoon ground
  cumin
1 teaspoon hot pepper
  sauce
½ teaspoon salt
¼ teaspoon freshly
  ground pepper
2 cups hot cooked long-
  grain white rice

MAKES 6 SERVINGS

1. Heat the oil in a large nonstick skillet over medium heat. Add the bell pepper, onion, and garlic. Cook, stirring, until the onion is golden, 7–10 minutes. Add the beef and cook, breaking it up with a spoon, until the meat browns, about 6 minutes.
2. Stir in the tomatoes, peas, raisins, olives, cumin, hot pepper sauce, salt, and pepper; bring to a boil. Reduce the heat and simmer, covered, until the flavors meld, about 10 minutes. Serve with the rice.

PER SERVING (scant 1 cup picadillo with ⅓ cup rice): 275 Cal, 8 g Fat, 3 g Sat Fat, 43 mg Chol, 424 mg Sod, 29 g Carb, 3 g Fib, 20 g Prot, 47 mg Calc. *POINTS: 6.*

Keema Matar

Here is a great example of simply prepared food that yields rich, intricate flavor. The rich flavor comes from sautéing the spices first until they toast slightly and release their exotic fragrance and flavor, rather than stirring them into the sauce at the end of the cooking time.

MAKES 4 SERVINGS

2 teaspoons vegetable oil
1 onion, thinly sliced
1 tablespoon minced peeled fresh ginger
1 teaspoon salt
1 teaspoon ground cumin
½ teaspoon ground coriander
¼ teaspoon ground cardamom
¼ teaspoon cayenne
1 (4-inch) cinnamon stick
1 pound lean ground beef (10% or less fat)
¾ pound all-purpose potatoes, peeled and cut into ½-inch cubes
1 (14½-ounce) can diced tomatoes
½ cup water
1 cup frozen peas
3 tablespoons plain fat-free yogurt
⅓ cup chopped cilantro
1 large (about 4-ounce) nan (Indian flatbread), lavash, or pita bread, cut into eighths

1. Heat the oil in a large nonstick skillet over medium-high heat. Add the onion and cook, stirring, until lightly browned, about 6 minutes. Stir in the ginger, ½ teaspoon of the salt, the cumin, coriander, cardamom, cayenne, and cinnamon stick. Reduce the heat to low and cook, stirring constantly, until the spices are very fragrant, about 4 minutes.

2. Add the beef to the skillet. Cook over medium heat, breaking up the meat with a spoon, until it browns, about 6 minutes. Add the potatoes, tomatoes, water, and the remaining ½ teaspoon salt; bring to a boil. Reduce the heat and simmer, covered, until the potatoes are tender, about 30 minutes.

3. Add the peas and yogurt to the skillet, stirring until the yogurt is blended. Cook, uncovered, over medium-high heat until the mixture thickens slightly, about 7 minutes. Remove the cinnamon stick.

4. Spoon the keema matar into a large bowl, then sprinkle with the cilantro. Serve with the nan.

PER SERVING (1¼ cups keema matar with 2 pieces nan): 410 Cal, 11 g Fat, 4 g Sat Fat, 65 mg Chol, 1002 mg Sod, 45 g Carb, 6 g Fib, 32 g Prot, 113 mg Calc. *POINTS: 8.*

tip When browning and breaking up the ground beef, keep the chunks between ½ to ¾ of an inch for the most appetizing texture in the finished dish.

Lone-Star Chili

What could be more associated with the Lone-Star State than chili? Even though true Texas chili generally is a long, complicated recipe made without beans, we make this favorite one-pot meal quickly with ground beef and canned beans. For extra zip, serve the chili with a tablespoon or two of the minced pickled jalapeño peppers.

1 tablespoon olive oil
1 pound lean ground beef (10% or less fat)
1 green bell pepper, seeded and chopped
1 onion, chopped
2 garlic cloves, minced
2 cups canned crushed tomatoes
½ cup water
2 tablespoons finely chopped pickled jalapeño peppers
1 tablespoon chili powder
1 teaspoon ground cumin
1 teaspoon salt
½ teaspoon dried oregano
1 (19-ounce) can pinto beans, rinsed and drained
1½ cups baked tortilla chips
6 tablespoons reduced-fat shredded cheddar cheese
6 tablespoons chopped red bell pepper

MAKES 6 SERVINGS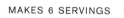

1. Heat the oil in a large nonstick skillet over medium heat. Add the beef and cook, breaking it up with a spoon, until the meat browns, about 6 minutes. Add the green bell pepper, onion, and garlic. Cook, stirring, until the onion is translucent, 3–5 minutes.

2. Stir in the tomatoes, water, jalapeño peppers, chili powder, cumin, salt, and oregano; bring to a boil. Reduce the heat and simmer, covered, stirring occasionally, about 30 minutes. Stir in the beans; cook until heated through, about 5 minutes.

3. Serve the chili in bowls with the tortilla chips, cheese, and red bell pepper on the side.

PER SERVING (1½ cups chili, ¼ cup chips, and 1 tablespoon each cheese and bell pepper): 297 Cal, 10 g Fat, 3 g Sat Fat, 47 mg Chol, 803 mg Sod, 28 g Carb, 8 g Fib, 25 g Prot, 123 mg Calc. *POINTS:* 6.

Ham-and-Egg Fried Rice

Fried rice is a wonderfully versatile dish that works well as a side or a main course. The key to great fried rice is to use fully cooked rice that is absolutely cold, which then easily separates into individual grains. This is authentic Chinese fried rice—it doesn't contain soy sauce.

MAKES 4 SERVINGS

- 4 teaspoons vegetable oil
- 2 garlic cloves, minced
- 6 ounces fresh shiitake mushrooms, stems discarded, caps sliced
- 1 red or yellow bell pepper, seeded and cut into ¼-inch dice
- 1 cup very small broccoli florets
- ½ cup fat-free egg substitute
- 2 cups cold cooked long-grain white rice
- 6 ounces ham steak, cut into ¼ inch dice
- 1 cup bean sprouts
- 2 scallions, thinly sliced
- ½ cup frozen baby peas
- ½ teaspoon salt

1. Heat a nonstick wok or large deep skillet over medium-high heat until a drop of water sizzles. Swirl in 2 teaspoons of the oil, then add the garlic. Stir-fry until fragrant, about 20 seconds. Add the mushrooms, bell pepper, and broccoli. Stir-fry until the vegetables are crisp-tender and the mushrooms begin to brown, about 5 minutes. Transfer to a bowl.

2. Add the remaining 2 teaspoons oil to the wok. Add the egg substitute and stir-fry until softly scrambled, about 2 minutes, breaking it up as it cooks. Transfer the egg substitute to the vegetables in the bowl.

3. Add the rice, ham, bean sprouts, scallions, peas, and salt to the wok. Stir-fry until heated through, about 3 minutes. Add the vegetables and egg substitute and stir-fry until heated through.

PER SERVING (2 cups): 278 Cal, 10 g Fat, 2 g Sat Fat, 21 mg Chol, 897 mg Sod, 32 g Carb, 4 g Fib, 18 g Prot, 57 mg Calc. *POINTS: 6.*

tip Plan ahead: Cook up a batch of rice the day before, let it cool, and store in a zip-close plastic bag in the refrigerator until ready to use.

Paella-Stuffed Peppers

Valencia is the birthplace of paella, where this famous saffron-infused rice dish may contain shrimp, rabbit, chicken, sausage, or squid, depending on who's doing the cooking. In Spain, paella is prepared in a round shallow metal pan with splayed sides and two brightly colored red or green handles. Short-grain Valencia rice is the rice of choice for paella, since its short grains absorb liquid and flavors well. Here all the enticing flavors and aromas of a good paella are captured and stuffed into colorful bell peppers.

MAKES 4 SERVINGS

4 large red, green, and/or yellow bell peppers, stems still attached
¼ teaspoon saffron threads
1 tablespoon olive oil
½ pound low-fat sweet Italian sausage links, casings removed
1 onion, chopped
2 large garlic cloves, minced
1½ cups low-sodium chicken broth
¾ cup short-grain white rice
1 tomato, seeded and chopped
1 (2-ounce) jar sliced pimientos, drained
½ teaspoon salt
¼ teaspoon freshly ground pepper
½ cup frozen baby peas

1. Half-fill a wok or large, deep skillet with water; bring to a boil.
2. Meanwhile, cut off the tops of the bell peppers and reserve. Cut out the ribs and remove the seeds from the peppers. Put the peppers and their tops in the boiling water. Cook, covered, just until tender, about 4 minutes, turning the peppers over after 2 minutes. Remove the peppers with tongs and drain on paper towels. Transfer 2 tablespoons of the hot water to a cup and stir in the saffron. Pour out the remaining water from the skillet; wipe the skillet dry.
3. Heat the oil in the skillet over medium heat. Add the sausage and cook, breaking it up with spoon, until very lightly browned, about 4 minutes. With a slotted spoon, transfer the sausage to a paper towel to drain.
4. Add the onion and garlic to the same skillet and cook, stirring frequently, until the onion is golden, 7–10 minutes. Add the broth, rice, tomato, pimientos, salt, pepper, and saffron water; bring to a boil. Reduce the heat and simmer, covered, until the rice is tender and has absorbed the liquid, about 20 minutes. Stir in the sausage and peas, then let stand, covered, for 5 minutes.
5. Meanwhile, preheat the oven to 350°F.
6. Fill the peppers with the rice mixture and replace the pepper tops. Stand the peppers in an 8-inch square baking dish. Cover with foil and bake until heated through, about 20 minutes.

PER SERVING (1 stuffed pepper): 309 Cal, 6 g Fat, 1 g Sat Fat, 22 mg Chol, 812 mg Sod, 49 g Carb, 5 g Fib, 15 g Prot, 45 mg Calc. *POINTS: 6.*

Country-Style Sausage and Peppers

This old-fashioned favorite—a staple of street fairs everywhere—becomes a satisfying one-pot meal with the addition of potatoes. Partially cooked cubed potatoes, a great time-saver found in the produce section of most supermarkets, are put to good use here.

MAKES 4 SERVINGS

½ pound (about 2) low-fat sweet or hot Italian sausage links, pricked with a fork

¼ cup water

1 tablespoon extra-virgin olive oil

1 (1-pound) package refrigerated partially cooked cubed potatoes

2 large red or green bell peppers, seeded and cut into ½-inch-thick strips

1 large onion, thickly sliced

1 large garlic clove, finely chopped

½ teaspoon salt

¼ teaspoon freshly ground pepper

1. Bring the sausage links and water to a boil in a large nonstick skillet. Reduce the heat and simmer, covered, about 5 minutes. Uncover and cook, turning the sausages occasionally, until well browned and cooked through, about 15 minutes. Transfer the sausages to a plate. When cool enough to handle, thinly slice.

2. Add the oil to the same skillet, then stir in the potatoes, bell peppers, onion, and garlic. Sprinkle with the salt and pepper. Cook, stirring frequently, until the vegetables are tender, about 12 minutes. Return the sausages to the skillet and cook until heated through, about 3 minutes.

PER SERVING (½ sausage link with 1¼ cups vegetables): 226 Cal, 5 g Fat, 1 g Sat Fat, 22 mg Chol, 773 mg Sod, 35 g Carb, 4 g Fib, 12 g Prot, 30 mg Calc. POINTS: 4.

Dinnertime Favorites

Chicken, turkey, and more

Roast Chicken Provençal

This is Sunday dinner at its best—and one pan cooks all. A fragrant herb paste is rubbed under the skin, leaving the chicken flavorful and moist even after the skin is removed. Since this is chock-full of vegetables, use your largest shallow roasting pan.

4   garlic cloves
1   tablespoon chopped
    fresh rosemary
1   tablespoon chopped
    fresh thyme
1   tablespoon chopped
    fresh tarragon
1   tablespoon extra-virgin
    olive oil
¾   teaspoon salt
1   (3½-pound) whole
    chicken
1   lemon, quartered
1   pound whole small
    red potatoes
2   red onions, each cut
    into 6 wedges
3   plum tomatoes, halved
1   teaspoon dried
    oregano
1   zucchini, cut into
    1½-inch chunks
1   yellow squash, cut
    into 1½-inch chunks
10 kalamata olives, pitted
    and chopped

1. Preheat the oven to 425°F. Spray an 11 x 16-inch shallow roasting pan with nonstick spray.
2. Chop 1 of the garlic cloves. Combine the chopped garlic, rosemary, thyme, tarragon, oil, and ¼ teaspoon of the salt in a small bowl to make a paste.
3. Gently loosen the skin from the breast and leg portions of the chicken; rub the paste evenly under the skin. Place the lemon in the cavity of the chicken, then tuck the wings behind the back and tie the legs with kitchen twine. Place the chicken, breast-side up, in the pan.
4. Combine the remaining 3 garlic cloves, potatoes, onions, tomatoes, oregano, and the remaining ½ teaspoon salt in a large bowl. Spray the vegetables lightly with olive-oil nonstick spray. Arrange the vegetables around the chicken. Roast, stirring the vegetables occasionally, about 45 minutes. Add the zucchini, squash, and olives to the vegetables in the pan and toss well. Continue roasting until an instant-read thermometer inserted in the inner thigh of the chicken registers 180°F and the vegetables are tender, 20–25 minutes longer.
5. Transfer chicken to a platter; let rest 10 minutes. Remove the skin, then carve. Serve the chicken with the vegetables.

PER SERVING (⅙ of chicken and vegetables): 299 Cal, 10 g Fat, 2 g Sat Fat, 77 mg Chol, 432 mg Sod, 23 g Carb, 4 g Fib, 30 g Prot, 61 mg Calc. *POINTS: 6.*

tip Harmful bacteria are destroyed when food is cooked to proper temperatures. Use a meat thermometer to determine that safe temperature. The U.S. Department of Agriculture recommends that whole chicken be cooked to at least 180°F.

Roast Chicken Provençal

Coq au Vin

Here is real comfort food, in traditional French style. This coq au vin can be cooked with an additional ½ cup chicken broth instead of the wine, if you prefer.

MAKES 6 SERVINGS

2 slices reduced-fat center-cut bacon, chopped
1 (3½-pound) chicken, cut into eighths, skin and all visible fat removed
½ pound fresh white mushrooms, sliced
1 onion, chopped
2 garlic cloves, chopped
1 tablespoon tomato paste
1 cup frozen whole small onions
2 carrots, chopped
1 (14-ounce) can low-sodium chicken broth
½ cup dry white wine
½ pound small Yukon Gold potatoes, unpeeled and cut in half
2 tablespoons all-purpose flour
2 tablespoons cold water
2 teaspoons browning and seasoning sauce
2 tablespoons chopped fresh parsley

1. Heat a nonstick Dutch oven over medium-high heat. Add the bacon and cook, stirring occasionally, until browned, about 5 minutes; transfer to paper towels to drain.
2. Add the chicken to the Dutch oven and cook over medium-high heat until lightly browned, about 3 minutes on each side. Transfer the chicken to a plate; set aside.
3. Add the mushrooms, chopped onion, and garlic to the Dutch oven. Cook over medium heat, stirring occasionally, until golden, about 8 minutes. Stir in the tomato paste until smooth. Add the whole onions and carrots; cook, stirring, 1 minute. Add the broth, wine, and potatoes; bring to a boil, stirring to scrape the browned bits from the bottom of the pan. Return the chicken and bacon to the Dutch oven. Reduce the heat and simmer, covered, until the vegetables are tender and the juices run clear when the chicken is pierced with a fork, about 25 minutes.
4. Combine the flour, water, and seasoning sauce in a small bowl until smooth; stir in about ¼ cup of the hot liquid from the Dutch oven until blended. Add the flour mixture and parsley to the pot and cook, stirring constantly, until the mixture bubbles and thickens, about 3 minutes.

PER SERVING (⅙ of chicken with 1 cup vegetables and sauce): 300 Cal, 9 g Fat, 3 g Sat Fat, 90 mg Chol, 220 mg Sod, 19 g Carb, 3 g Fib, 34 g Prot, 51 mg Calc. *POINTS: 6.*

Chicken Paprikash

This dish is usually heavily sauced with rich sour cream, but our trimmed-down version still has rich, hearty flavor—without the fat and calories of the Hungarian classic.

MAKES 4 SERVINGS

4 (5-ounce) skinless boneless chicken breasts
½ teaspoon salt
¼ teaspoon coarsely ground black pepper
2 teaspoons canola oil
1 large onion, chopped
1 green bell pepper, seeded and chopped
2 tablespoons paprika
1 tablespoon all-purpose flour
2 cups low-sodium chicken broth
½ pound fresh mushrooms, sliced
2 tablespoons light sour cream
1 tablespoon chopped fresh dill
4 cups hot cooked broad egg noodles

1. Sprinkle the chicken with the salt and pepper. Heat 1 teaspoon of the oil in a large nonstick skillet over medium-high heat. Add the chicken and cook until lightly browned, about 3 minutes on each side. Transfer the chicken to a plate; set aside.

2. Add the remaining 1 teaspoon oil to the same skillet, then add the onion and bell pepper. Cook over medium heat, stirring often, until very tender and lightly browned, about 8 minutes. Add the paprika and flour; cook, stirring constantly, about 1 minute. Gradually add the broth and cook, stirring constantly, until the mixture bubbles and thickens slightly. Add the mushrooms and simmer 3 minutes. Return the chicken to the skillet. Reduce the heat and simmer, covered, until the chicken is cooked through, about 5 minutes.

3. Stir the sour cream and dill into the skillet; bring to a gentle simmer, then remove from the heat. Serve with the noodles.

PER SERVING (1 chicken breast with ½ cup sauce and 1 cup noodles): 471 Cal, 11 g Fat, 3 g Sat Fat, 133 mg Chol, 409 mg Sod, 51 g Carb, 4 g Fib, 42 g Prot, 68 mg Calc. *POINTS: 10.*

Chicken Ratatouille with Penne

For a different twist—and a perfect contribution to a potluck dinner—spoon the vegetables and pasta into a lasagna pan, then sprinkle with ¾ cup shredded part-skim mozzarella cheese. Pop it in the oven to heat through and melt the cheese for the best "baked ziti" ever. The cheese will add an extra *POINT* per serving.

2	teaspoons olive oil
1	pound skinless boneless chicken breasts
1	onion, chopped
2	garlic cloves, chopped
½	pound eggplant, unpeeled and cut into 1-inch cubes
1	zucchini, cut into 1-inch cubes
1	yellow squash, cut into 1-inch cubes
1	green bell pepper, seeded and cut into 1-inch pieces
1	(28-ounce) can Italian peeled tomatoes, drained and chopped
½	cup dry white wine
2	teaspoons dried oregano
1	teaspoon sugar
¾	teaspoon salt
4	cups hot cooked penne
½	cup chopped basil
¼	cup grated Parmesan cheese

MAKES 6 SERVINGS

1. Heat 1 teaspoon of the oil in a nonstick Dutch oven over medium-high heat. Add the chicken and cook until golden on the outside and no longer pink inside, about 4 minutes on each side. Transfer the chicken to a plate and let rest 5 minutes for easier slicing. Cut diagonally into thin slices.

2. Add the remaining 1 teaspoon oil to the same Dutch oven. Add the onion and garlic. Cook over medium heat, stirring, until softened, about 5 minutes. Add the eggplant, zucchini, yellow squash, bell pepper, tomatoes, wine, oregano, sugar, and salt; bring to a boil. Reduce the heat and simmer, covered, until the vegetables are softened and the flavors are well developed, about 30 minutes.

3. Return the sliced chicken to the Dutch oven and briefly heat through. Stir in the cooked pasta, basil, and cheese.

PER SERVING (1½ cups): 318 Cal, 6 g Fat, 2 g Sat Fat, 45 mg Chol, 628 mg Sod, 41 g Carb, 5 g Fib, 25 g Prot, 137 mg Calc. *POINTS:* 6.

Italian Chicken Kebabs with Herbed Orzo

Just a few Italian-inspired ingredients turn ordinary kebabs into something special. A variety of vegetables would work here in place of the squash and mushrooms—try eggplant cubes, red onion wedges, even marinated whole, mild cherry peppers (canned or jarred variety), drained, rinsed, and dried.

MAKES 4 SERVINGS

1 pound skinless boneless chicken breasts, cut into 12 pieces

1 zucchini, cut into 12 pieces

1 yellow squash, cut into 12 pieces

8 whole cremini mushrooms

8 oil-packed sun-dried tomatoes, drained and patted dry with paper towels

2 teaspoons extra-virgin olive oil

1 teaspoon dried oregano

½ teaspoon salt

¼ teaspoon crushed red pepper

2 cups hot cooked orzo

¼ cup chopped fresh basil

2 tablespoons grated Parmesan cheese

1. Spray a broiler rack with nonstick spray. Preheat the broiler.
2. Combine the chicken, zucchini, yellow squash, mushrooms, sun-dried tomatoes, 1 teaspoon of the oil, the oregano, salt, and crushed red pepper in a large bowl. Thread 3 pieces each of chicken, zucchini, and yellow squash, 2 mushrooms, and 2 sun-dried tomatoes onto 4 (12-inch) metal skewers, alternating the ingredients. Place the skewers on the broiler pan.
3. Broil the skewers 4 inches from the heat, turning at least once, until the vegetables are tender and the chicken is cooked through, 8–10 minutes.
4. Combine the orzo with the remaining 1 teaspoon olive oil in a large bowl. Stir in 2 tablespoons of the basil and 1 tablespoon of the Parmesan cheese.
5. Spoon the orzo onto a platter, then top with the kebabs. Sprinkle the cooked kebabs with the remaining 2 tablespoons basil and the remaining 1 tablespoon Parmesan cheese.

PER SERVING (1 kebab with ½ cup orzo): 316 Cal, 9 g Fat, 2 g Sat Fat, 64 mg Chol, 443 mg Sod, 28 g Carb, 3 g Fib, 32 g Prot, 91 mg Calc. *POINTS: 6.*

Chicken and Dumplings with Sage

Nothing says "one-pot" more than chicken and dumplings—and since the chicken we use is boneless and cubed, the cooking time is much less than it is for traditional chicken and dumplings. Sage gives the dumplings a flavor reminiscent of stuffing and goes well with this comforting stew.

MAKES 6 SERVINGS

2   teaspoons canola oil
1   pound skinless
    boneless chicken
    breasts, cut into
    1-inch pieces
½   teaspoon salt
1   onion, chopped
2   carrots, chopped
2   celery stalks, chopped
3½ cups low-sodium
    chicken broth
1   russet potato
    (8 ounces), cubed
¼   cup fresh green beans,
    trimmed and cut into
    1-inch pieces
1   cup frozen peas
1⅔ cups reduced-fat
    all-purpose baking mix
⅔   cup fat-free milk
1   teaspoon chopped
    fresh sage, or
    ½ teaspoon dried
½   teaspoon coarsely
    ground black pepper

1. Heat 1 teaspoon of the oil in a nonstick Dutch oven over medium-high heat. Add the chicken; sprinkle with the salt and cook, turning occasionally, until browned, about 6 minutes. Transfer the chicken to a bowl; set aside.
2. Add remaining 1 teaspoon oil to the same Dutch oven, then add the onion, carrots, and celery. Cook, stirring occasionally, until the vegetables begin to soften and brown slightly, about 6 minutes. Add the broth and potato; bring to a boil. Reduce the heat and simmer, covered, until the potato is almost tender, about 10 minutes. Add green beans and cook until crisp-tender, about 6 minutes. Stir in the browned chicken and the peas; heat through, about 2 minutes.
3. Meanwhile, to prepare the dumplings, combine the baking mix, milk, sage, and pepper in a bowl until a soft dough forms.
4. Drop the dough, by rounded tablespoons, onto the simmering stew, making a total of 6 dumplings. Simmer, uncovered, 10 minutes. Then cover and simmer until the dumplings have doubled in size and are cooked through, about 10 minutes longer.

PER SERVING (1 cup stew with 1 dumpling): 337 Cal, 9 g Fat, 2 g Sat Fat, 40 mg Chol, 682 mg Sod, 39 g Carb, 4 g Fib, 22 g Prot, 104 mg Calc. *POINTS: 7.*

Chicken and Dumplings
with Sage

Mediterranean Chicken and Seafood Stew

Aromatic fennel, leek, and garlic combine well here with another Mediterranean specialty—seafood. We add lean chicken to stretch the seafood as well as to add texture and interest. For additional flavor, save a few of the fern-like fennel leaves, chop them, and sprinkle into the stew at the last minute.

MAKES 4 SERVINGS

2	teaspoons olive oil
¾	pound skinless boneless chicken breasts, cut into 1-inch chunks
½	fennel bulb, thinly sliced
2	carrots, cut into matchstick-thin strips
1	medium leek, cleaned and thinly sliced
1	plum tomato, chopped
2	garlic cloves, finely chopped
2	cups low-sodium chicken broth
¼	cup dry white wine
¾	pound Yukon Gold potatoes, unpeeled and quartered
1	bay leaf
12	littleneck clams, cleaned
12	mussels, scrubbed and debearded
½	pound small shrimp, peeled and deveined
1	tablespoon chopped fresh thyme leaves

1. Heat 1 teaspoon of the oil in a Dutch oven over medium-high heat. Add the chicken and cook, turning occasionally, until browned, about 4 minutes. Transfer to a bowl; set aside.

2. Add the remaining 1 teaspoon oil to the Dutch oven, then add the fennel, carrots, leek, tomato, and garlic. Cook over medium-low heat, stirring occasionally, until the vegetables are tender but not browned, about 8 minutes. Stir in the broth, wine, potatoes, and bay leaf; bring to a boil. Reduce heat and simmer, covered, until the potatoes are almost tender, about 10 minutes.

3. Add the clams and cook, covered, 3 minutes. Add the mussels, shrimp, thyme, and the browned chicken. Simmer, covered, until the shrimp are just opaque in the center, the clams and mussels open, and chicken is cooked through, about 3 minutes longer. Discard any clams or mussels that do not open. Remove the bay leaf before serving.

PER SERVING (2 cups): 336 Cal, 6 g Fat, 1 g Sat Fat, 129 mg Chol, 329 mg Sod, 29 g Carb, 4 g Fib, 39 g Prot, 119 mg Calc. *POINTS:* 6.

tip When purchasing mussels, look for unbroken, tightly closed shells or shells that close when lightly tapped. Scrub them with a stiff brush under cold running water to remove any sand. Discard any shells that remain open. The hairy filaments that protrude from a mussel are known as a "beard." To remove, pinch the filaments between thumb and forefinger and pull firmly.

Gingered Chicken and Vegetables

To have this stir-fry on the table in under 30 minutes, serve it with white rice, instead of brown rice (white rice cooks in 20 minutes, whereas brown rice takes 40 minutes), and use pre-cut vegetables from your supermarket's salad bar, or packaged cut vegetables from the produce section. If you like, substitute crunchy sugar snap peas for the snow peas.

MAKES 4 SERVINGS

¼ cup low-sodium
  chicken broth
2 tablespoons rice wine
  or dry white wine
1 tablespoon reduced-
  sodium soy sauce
2 teaspoons cornstarch
1 teaspoon Asian (dark)
  sesame oil
1 teaspoon sugar
2 teaspoons canola oil
1 pound skinless
  boneless chicken
  breast, cut into strips
4 scallions, cut into
  3-inch pieces
1 tablespoon minced
  peeled fresh ginger
2 garlic cloves, chopped
1 red bell pepper, cut
  into strips
2 carrots cut into
  matchstick-thin strips
¼ pound fresh shiitake
  mushrooms, sliced
¼ pound snow
  peas, halved
2 cups hot cooked
  brown rice

1. Combine the broth, rice wine, soy sauce, cornstarch, sesame oil, and sugar in a small bowl; stir until the cornstarch dissolves.

2. Heat a nonstick wok or large, deep skillet over medium-high heat until a drop of water sizzles. Swirl in 1 teaspoon of the oil, then add the chicken. Stir-fry until just cooked through, 5–6 minutes; transfer to a plate.

3. Swirl the remaining 1 teaspoon oil into the wok, then add the scallions, ginger, and garlic. Stir-fry until fragrant, about 1 minute. Add the bell pepper, carrots, and mushrooms; stir-fry until crisp-tender, about 3 minutes.

4. Add the browned chicken, the snow peas, and broth mixture. Cook, stirring constantly, until the mixture bubbles and thickens, about 2 minutes. Serve with the rice.

PER SERVING (1 cup with ½ cup rice): 345 Cal, 8 g Fat, 2 g Sat Fat, 62 mg Chol, 257 mg Sod, 38 g Carb, 6 g Fib, 30 g Prot, 59 mg Calc. *POINTS: 7.*

tip Be sure to remove and discard the tough shiitake mushroom stems.

**Lemon-Oregano Chicken
with Olives and Potatoes**

Lemon-Oregano Chicken with Olives and Potatoes

For best results, use a large roasting pan that will accommodate both the chicken and vegetables in one layer. This allows the air to circulate around the food and lets the steam escape, so the food browns nicely. If necessary, use two roasting pans for this amount of food. A lightly dressed garden salad would round out this meal.

½ cup fresh lemon juice (about 3 lemons)

1 tablespoon dried oregano

2 teaspoons extra-virgin olive oil

3 garlic cloves, minced

1 teaspoon salt

¾ teaspoon coarsely ground black pepper

6 large chicken drumsticks (about 1¾ pounds), skin removed

1¾ pounds white potatoes, cut lengthwise into 1-inch-thick wedges

1 large onion, root left intact and cut into 6 wedges

1 (10-ounce) package frozen artichoke hearts, thawed and patted dry

12 small oil-cured black olives, pitted

MAKES 6 SERVINGS

1. Preheat the oven to 425°F. Spray a large shallow roasting pan with olive-oil nonstick spray.
2. Whisk together the lemon juice, oregano, oil, garlic, salt, and pepper in a small bowl.
3. Place the chicken, potatoes, onion, artichoke hearts, and olives in the roasting pan; drizzle with the lemon mixture. Roast until the chicken is cooked through and the vegetables are tender and browned, 50–55 minutes.

PER SERVING (1 drumstick and ⅙ of vegetables): 275 Cal, 5 g Fat, 1 g Sat Fat, 45 mg Chol, 530 mg Sod, 37 g Carb, 6 g Fib, 22 g Prot, 67 mg Calc. *POINTS: 5.*

tip To further ensure that the chicken and vegetables brown nicely—and to prevent them from steaming—be sure to pat the thawed frozen artichoke hearts dry with a paper towel before using. If available, by all means, use fresh baby artichokes instead of the frozen.

Pickled-Pepper Chicken and Artichokes

Convenient canned artichoke hearts and cherry peppers from a jar make this an easy pantry-shelf supper, full of spicy, tangy flavor from the peppers. Use either mild or hot peppers according to your taste. You can substitute any fresh vegetable you have on hand, such as bell peppers or diced carrots, for the mushrooms. For an extra *2 POINTS*, serve this with ½ cup cooked brown rice or ⅔ cup cooked pasta.

MAKES 6 SERVINGS

- 6 skinless chicken thighs
- ½ teaspoon salt
- ¼ teaspoon freshly ground pepper
- 2 teaspoons canola oil
- 2 onions, sliced
- 1 (10-ounce) package fresh white mushrooms, quartered
- 1 (12-ounce) jar sliced mild pickled cherry peppers, drained
- 1 (8½-ounce) can water-packed artichoke hearts, drained and halved
- 1 cup low-sodium chicken broth
- ½ cup dry white wine
- 1 tablespoon all-purpose flour
- 2 tablespoons water
- 1 teaspoon browning and seasoning sauce

1. Sprinkle the chicken with the salt and pepper. Heat the oil in a large nonstick skillet over medium heat. Add the chicken and cook, turning occasionally, until the chicken is browned, about 15 minutes. Transfer the chicken to a plate.

2. Add the onions and mushrooms to the same skillet. Cook over medium heat, stirring occasionally, until lightly browned, about 10 minutes. Return the chicken to the skillet. Add the cherry peppers, artichoke hearts, broth, and wine; bring to a boil. Reduce the heat and simmer, covered, until the chicken is cooked through and the flavors are blended, about 20 minutes.

3. Combine the flour, water, and seasoning sauce in a small bowl until smooth; stir in about ¼ cup of the hot liquid from the skillet until blended. Add the flour mixture to the skillet and cook, stirring constantly, until the mixture bubbles and thickens, about 3 minutes.

PER SERVING (1 thigh and ⅔ cup vegetable mixture): 188 Cal, 6 g Fat, 2 g Sat Fat, 46 mg Chol, 405 mg Sod, 15 g Carb, 4 g Fib, 18 g Prot, 44 mg Calc. *POINTS: 3.*

tip Our mothers often used browning and seasoning sauce (Kitchen Bouquet or Gravy Master) to add color and flavor to gravies and sauces. Their trick, and ours, for a natural-looking, golden sauce—use it sparingly.

Stove-Top Cassoulet

Although the classic French cassoulet typically bakes in the oven for hours on end, our delicious top-of-the-stove version can be ready in under an hour.

MAKES 8 SERVINGS

2   teaspoons olive oil
1   pound skinless
    boneless chicken
    thighs, trimmed of all
    visible fat and cut into
    2-inch pieces
½   pound reduced-fat
    turkey kielbasa, sliced
3   garlic cloves, chopped
1   medium leek, cleaned
    and chopped
2   carrots, chopped
1   Granny Smith apple,
    peeled and chopped
1   (14½-ounce) can diced
    tomatoes
2   cups low-sodium
    chicken broth
¼   cup dry white wine
2   (15-ounce) cans
    cannellini (white
    kidney beans), rinsed
    and drained
½   teaspoon sugar
⅛   teaspoon ground
    allspice
1   bay leaf
2   tablespoons chopped
    parsley
1   tablespoon grated
    lemon zest

1. Heat 1 teaspoon of the oil in a nonstick Dutch oven over medium-high heat. Add the chicken and cook, turning occasionally, until browned, about 6 minutes; transfer to a bowl.

2. Add the remaining 1 teaspoon oil to the same Dutch oven, then add the kielbasa. Cook over medium-high heat until browned, about 4 minutes.

3. Add 2 of the garlic cloves, the leek, carrots, and apple, to the kielbasa in the Dutch oven. Cook, stirring, 1–2 minutes. Return the chicken to the Dutch oven. Add the tomatoes, broth, wine, beans, sugar, allspice, and bay leaf; bring to a boil. Reduce the heat and simmer, covered, until the chicken is cooked through and the vegetables are tender, about 25 minutes.

4. Combine the parsley, lemon zest, and remaining 1 chopped garlic clove in a small bowl; set aside. Discard bay leaf. Sprinkle the cassoulet with the parsley mixture just before serving.

PER SERVING (generous 1 cup). 246 Cal, 8 g Fat, 2 g Sat Fat, 55 mg Chol, 645 mg Sod, 21 g Carb, 5 g Fib, 23 g Prot, 63 mg Calc. POINTS: 5.

tip Leeks often contain sand in between their layers. Here's how to clean them: Trim away most of the dark green tops and the roots, leaving the root end intact to hold the layers together. Slice the leek lengthwise to within a half inch of the root end. Hold the leek by the root end, fan open the layers, and rinse thoroughly under cold running water.

Chicken and Sweet Potato Stew

The combination of tender Savoy cabbage and sweet potatoes says fall is in the air. If you like, use chopped fresh oregano instead of the thyme, or substitute a teaspoon of dried thyme or oregano for the fresh.

MAKES 6 SERVINGS

1 pound skinless boneless chicken thighs, trimmed of all visible fat and cut into 2-inch pieces
½ teaspoon salt
¼ teaspoon coarsely ground black pepper
2 teaspoons canola oil
1 pound Savoy cabbage, shredded (about 5 cups)
1 large onion, thinly sliced
2 garlic cloves, chopped
2 sweet potatoes, peeled and cut into 1¼-inch chunks
1¼ cups low-sodium chicken broth
¾ cup water
1 cup frozen peas
1 tablespoon chopped fresh thyme
2 tablespoons all-purpose flour

1. Sprinkle the chicken with ¼ teaspoon of the salt and the pepper.
2. Heat 1 teaspoon of the oil in a Dutch oven over medium-high heat. Add the chicken and cook, turning occasionally, until browned, about 6 minutes. Transfer to a bowl and set aside.
3. Add the remaining 1 teaspoon oil to the same Dutch oven, then add the cabbage, onion, and garlic. Cook, covered, over medium heat, stirring occasionally, until the cabbage and onion are just tender, about 8 minutes. Return the chicken to the Dutch oven; stir in the sweet potatoes, broth, ½ cup of the water and the remaining ¼ teaspoon salt; bring to a boil. Reduce the heat and simmer, covered, until the vegetables are tender and the chicken is cooked through, about 20 minutes. Stir in the peas and thyme; heat through.
4. Combine the flour and the remaining ¼ cup water in a small bowl until smooth. Add the flour mixture to the Dutch oven. Cook, stirring constantly, until the mixture bubbles and thickens, about 3 minutes.

PER SERVING (1⅓ cups): 227 Cal, 7 g Fat, 2 g Sat Fat, 51 mg Chol, 292 mg Sod, 21 g Carb, 5 g Fib, 20 g Prot, 77 mg Calc. *POINTS: 4.*

Chicken Posole

Known as the "food of all blessings," this hearty main-dish Mexican stew—made from beef, pork, or poultry and hominy—is traditionally served on New Year's Eve. Hominy is made from lime-treated whole corn kernels. Yellow or white hominy is available dried (which needs to be reconstituted before using) or in cans.

MAKES 6 SERVINGS

1¼ pounds skinless boneless chicken thighs, trimmed of all visible fat and cut into 2½-inch pieces

½ teaspoon salt

½ teaspoon freshly ground pepper

2 teaspoons olive oil

1 onion, chopped

2 garlic cloves

2 (15-ounce) cans hominy, drained

1 (14½-ounce) can stewed tomatoes, broken up

1½ cups low-sodium chicken broth

1 (8-ounce) can tomato sauce

2 teaspoons dried oregano

2 teaspoons paprika

6 tablespoons shredded reduced-fat Monterey Jack cheese

6 scallions, thinly sliced diagonally

6 radishes, finely chopped

1. Sprinkle the chicken with the salt and pepper. Heat 1 teaspoon of the oil in a nonstick Dutch oven over medium-high heat. Add the chicken and cook, turning occasionally, until browned, about 6 minutes. Transfer to a bowl and set aside.

2. Add the remaining 1 teaspoon oil to the same Dutch oven, then add the onion and garlic. Cook over medium heat, until the onion is tender, about 8 minutes.

3. Return the chicken to the Dutch oven. Stir in the hominy, tomatoes with their liquid, broth, tomato sauce, oregano, and paprika; bring to a boil. Reduce the heat and simmer, covered, until the flavors are blended and the stew thickens slightly, about 1 hour.

4. Divide the mixture among 6 bowls; sprinkle each evenly with the cheese, scallions, and radishes. Serve at once.

PER SERVING (1⅓ cups stew and 1 tablespoon cheese): 306 Cal, 10 g Fat, 3 g Sat Fat, 68 mg Chol, 959 mg Sod, 27 g Carb, 5 g Fib, 26 g Prot, 126 mg Calc. *POINTS:* 6.

Spicy Chicken with Apricot Couscous

Savory, sweet, and spicy flavors meld beautifully in this dish that's reminiscent of Moroccan cuisine. Red curry paste (a blend of chiles, garlic, onion, and spices) adds a touch of fire—you can find it in Asian groceries or substitute ¼ teaspoon crushed red pepper. Use any dried fruit you like—raisins or dried cranberries, perhaps, instead of the currants, or chopped prunes instead of the apricots.

MAKES 6 SERVINGS

2   teaspoons canola oil
1   pound skinless boneless chicken thighs, trimmed of all visible fat and cut into 2½-inch chunks
1   onion, chopped
1   tablespoon minced peeled fresh ginger
1   garlic clove, chopped
2   teaspoons cinnamon
2   teaspoons ground cumin
½   teaspoon red curry paste
1   cup low-sodium chicken broth
1   cup orange juice
1   (6-ounce) bag baby spinach, chopped
½   cup dried currants
⅓   cup dried apricots, chopped
1   tablespoon honey
½   teaspoon salt
1   cup plain couscous
3   tablespoons toasted slivered almonds

1. Heat 1 teaspoon of the oil in a Dutch oven over medium-high heat. Add the chicken and cook, turning occasionally, until browned, about 6 minutes. Transfer to a bowl and set aside.

2. Add the remaining 1 teaspoon oil to the same Dutch oven, then add the onion, ginger, and garlic. Cook over medium heat, stirring frequently, until fragrant, 3–4 minutes. Add the cinnamon, cumin, and curry paste; cook, stirring constantly, about 1 minute.

3. Stir in the broth, juice, spinach, currants, apricots, honey, and salt; bring to a boil. Return the chicken to the Dutch oven; bring to a simmer. Remove from the heat and stir in the couscous. Cover and let stand until the liquid is absorbed and the couscous is tender, about 5 minutes. Fluff the mixture with a fork, then sprinkle with the almonds just before serving.

PER SERVING (1 cup and ½ tablespoon almonds): 372 Cal, 9 g Fat, 2 g Sat Fat, 51 mg Chol, 294 mg Sod, 50 g Carb, 5 g Fib, 23 g Prot, 95 mg Calc. *POINTS: 7.*

tip To make cutting dried fruits easier, first spray your knife with a little nonstick spray—the fruit will slide right off the knife. Or use kitchen scissors to cut up the fruit.

Spicy Chicken
with Apricot Couscous

Moroccan Meatball Stew with Couscous

Fragrant and full of flavor, this comforting stew is even better the next day—which makes it well suited for entertaining, or making a double batch to enjoy again later in the week.

2 slices firm white bread

1 pound ground skinless chicken breast

¼ cup grated onion

2 tablespoons pine nuts, coarsely chopped

2 tablespoons chopped fresh parsley

1 teaspoon cinnamon

½ teaspoon ground ginger

½ teaspoon salt

2 teaspoons olive oil

1 large onion, chopped

2 garlic cloves, chopped

3 plum tomatoes, diced

½ teaspoon ground cumin

3½ cups low-sodium chicken broth

12 pitted prunes, left whole

2 carrots, cut into 1-inch chunks

1 tablespoon honey

¼ teaspoon crushed red pepper

1 (10-ounce) box plain couscous, cooked

3 tablespoons sliced almonds

MAKES 6 SERVINGS

1. Place the bread in a food processor and pulse until fine crumbs form, about 10 seconds; transfer to a large bowl. Add the chicken, onion, pine nuts, 1 tablespoon of the parsley, the cinnamon, ginger, and salt; mix well. With wet hands, shape the mixture into 12 balls.

2. Heat 1 teaspoon of the oil in a nonstick Dutch oven over medium-high heat. Add the meatballs and cook, turning occasionally, until browned, 6–8 minutes. Transfer to a plate.

3. Add the remaining 1 teaspoon oil to the Dutch oven; stir in the onion and garlic. Cook over medium heat, stirring frequently, until golden, about 8 minutes. Add the tomatoes and cumin. Cook, stirring occasionally, until the tomatoes are softened, about 5 minutes. Return the meatballs to the Dutch oven, then add the broth, prunes, carrots, honey, and crushed red pepper; bring to a boil. Reduce the heat and simmer, covered, until the flavors are blended and the meatballs are cooked through, about 20 minutes. Stir in the remaining 1 tablespoon chopped parsley.

4. Divide the couscous among 6 bowls. Spoon the meatball stew over the couscous, then sprinkle with the almonds.

PER SERVING (generous ¾ cup couscous, 2 meatballs, ½ cup sauce, and ½ tablespoon almonds): 432 Cal, 8 g Fat, 2 g Sat Fat, 41 mg Chol, 330 mg Sod, 63 g Carb, 6 g Fib, 27 g Prot, 78 mg Calc. *POINTS: 9.*

tip To make shaping the meatballs easier, dip your hands into a bowl of water before forming each meatball.

Cincinnati Chicken Chili

Spaghetti topped with chili is a kid and crowd pleaser. If you like your chili with a little more kick, substitute hot green chiles and hot salsa for the mild versions we call for.

MAKES 8 SERVINGS

- 2 teaspoons canola oil
- 1 onion, chopped
- 1 green bell pepper, seeded and chopped
- 3 garlic cloves, chopped
- 1 (4-ounce) can chopped mild green chiles
- 6 tablespoons chili powder
- 1 tablespoon unsweetened cocoa
- 2 teaspoons ground cumin
- 1 teaspoon cinnamon
- 1 teaspoon sugar
- ½ teaspoon salt
- 1 pound ground skinless chicken breast
- 1 (14½-ounce) can diced tomatoes
- 1 cup mild chunky salsa
- 1 (8-ounce) can tomato sauce
- 1 cup water
- ½ pound spaghetti, cooked according to package directions
- ½ cup shredded reduced-fat cheddar cheese
- 2 scallions, thinly sliced

1. Heat the oil in a large nonstick saucepan over medium-high heat. Add the onion, bell pepper, and garlic. Cook, stirring occasionally, until softened, about 6 minutes. Stir in the chiles, chili powder, cocoa, cumin, cinnamon, sugar, and salt. Cook until fragrant, about 1 minute. Add chicken and cook, breaking it up with a wooden spoon, until browned, about 8 minutes.

2. Add the tomatoes with their liquid, salsa, tomato sauce, and water; bring to a boil. Reduce the heat and simmer, covered, until the flavors blend and the chili thickens slightly, about 1 hour.

3. Divide the spaghetti among 8 plates. Spoon the chili on top, then sprinkle with the cheese and scallions.

PER SERVING (generous ½ cup spaghetti with 1 cup chili and 1 tablespoon cheese): 273 Cal, 6 g Fat, 2 g Sat Fat, 35 mg Chol, 737 mg Sod, 36 g Carb, 6 g Fib, 21 g Prot, 132 mg Calc. *POINTS: 5.*

Turkey Basquaise

Food prepared in the style of the Basque country—a region around the border between France and Spain—often includes tomatoes, sweet or hot red peppers, onions, and garlic. This sautéed vegetable mixture is quite versatile. You can make it (without the turkey) for a delicious filling for omelets, as a topping for sandwiches, or to toss with cooked pasta.

MAKES 4 SERVINGS

2 teaspoons olive oil
4 (4-ounce) skinless boneless turkey cutlets
2 onions, sliced
1 green bell pepper, seeded and thinly sliced
1 red bell pepper, seeded and thinly sliced
1 tomato, chopped
2 ounces fat-free ham, diced
2 garlic cloves, finely chopped
½ cup low-sodium chicken broth
¼ cup dry white wine
2 tablespoons chopped fresh thyme
½ teaspoon salt
¼ teaspoon coarsely ground black pepper
2 cups hot cooked brown rice

1. Heat 1 teaspoon of the oil in a large nonstick skillet over medium-high heat. Add the turkey cutlets and cook until browned, 2–3 minutes on each side. Transfer to a plate and set aside.

2. Add the remaining 1 teaspoon oil to the same skillet, then add the onions and green and red bell peppers. Cook over medium heat, stirring occasionally, until the onions and peppers are very tender, about 10 minutes. Add the tomato, ham, and garlic. Cook, stirring, until the tomato is softened, about 6 minutes.

3. Add the broth, wine, thyme, salt, and pepper to the skillet; bring to a boil. Reduce the heat and simmer, covered, until the flavors are blended, about 10 minutes longer. Return the turkey to the skillet and heat through. Serve with the rice.

PER SERVING (1 cutlet, ¾ cup vegetable mixture, and ½ cup rice): 331 Cal, 7 g Fat, 2 g Sat Fat, 70 mg Chol, 608 mg Sod, 32 g Carb, 4 g Fib, 34 g Prot, 52 mg Calc. *POINTS: 6.*

Turkey Kebab Wraps with Minted Yogurt Sauce

These satisfying, handheld delights celebrate the intricate flavors and aromas of Mediterranean vegetables and herbs. The refreshing yogurt sauce is not for kebabs only. Drizzle it on salad greens or sandwiches, or use it as a low-fat dip with your favorite cut-up veggies.

MAKES 4 SERVINGS

¾ cup fat-free plain yogurt

1 tablespoon fresh lemon juice

1 tablespoon chopped fresh mint

1 garlic clove, minced

¾ teaspoon salt

¼ teaspoon cayenne

1 pound turkey cutlets, cut into 12 pieces

½ pound eggplant, unpeeled and cut into 8 (2-inch) chunks

2 plum tomatoes, quartered

1 green bell pepper, seeded and cut into 8 (1½-inch) pieces

1 tablespoon extra-virgin olive oil

1 tablespoon chopped fresh rosemary

1 tablespoon chopped fresh parsley

1 tablespoon dried oregano

4 small romaine lettuce leaves, shredded

4 (6-inch) whole-wheat pocketless pita breads

1. Combine the yogurt, lemon juice, mint, garlic, ¼ teaspoon of the salt, and the cayenne in a small bowl. Cover and refrigerate until ready to use, at least 15 minutes or up to overnight.

2. Combine the turkey, eggplant, tomatoes, bell pepper, oil, rosemary, parsley, oregano, and the remaining ½ teaspoon salt in a large bowl; toss to coat.

3. Spray a broiler rack with nonstick spray. Preheat the broiler.

4. Alternately thread the turkey, eggplant, tomatoes, and bell pepper on 4 (12-inch) metal skewers. Place the kebabs on the broiler rack and broil, 4 inches from the heat, turning at least once, until the turkey is cooked through and the vegetables are tender, 12–14 minutes.

5. Divide the lettuce among the pitas. Remove the skewers from the kebabs and place the food on top of the lettuce. Drizzle with the yogurt sauce. Fold up to eat.

PER SERVING (1 wrap): 377 Cal, 9 g Fat, 2 g Sat Fat, 68 mg Chol, 830 mg Sod, 41 g Carb, 7 g Fib, 36 g Prot, 141 mg Calc. POINTS: 7.

tip To warm the pitas, place them on a microwavable plate, cover with plastic wrap, turning back one corner to vent, and microwave on High for 10 seconds. Or wrap the pitas in foil and heat them for 2 to 3 minutes on a lower rack in the oven while the kebabs are cooking.

Spanish Turkey and Rice

Annatto seasoning powder enhances the color and flavor of many Latin-inspired dishes. It can be found in the ethnic section of your supermarket.

1 pound turkey cutlets, cut into 2-inch pieces
½ teaspoon salt
¼ teaspoon freshly ground pepper
2 teaspoons olive oil
1 onion, chopped
1 green bell pepper, seeded and chopped
2 garlic cloves, chopped
1 cup long-grain white rice
1 (19-ounce) can chickpeas (garbanzo beans), rinsed and drained
15 pimiento-stuffed olives, halved
1 tablespoon chopped pimientos
1 (14-ounce) can low-sodium chicken broth
1 (8-ounce) can tomato sauce
1¼ teaspoons annatto seasoning
2 tablespoons chopped fresh parsley

1. Sprinkle the turkey with the salt and pepper.
2. Heat 1 teaspoon of the oil in a large nonstick skillet over medium-high heat. Add the turkey and cook, turning occasionally, until browned, about 8 minutes. Transfer to a bowl and set aside.
3. Add the remaining 1 teaspoon oil to the same skillet. Add the onion, bell pepper, and garlic and cook over medium heat, stirring occasionally, until lightly browned, about 8 minutes.
4. Add the rice, chickpeas, olives, pimientos, broth, tomato sauce, and annatto seasoning; bring to a boil. Return the turkey to the skillet. Reduce the heat and simmer, covered, until the liquid has evaporated, the rice is tender, and the turkey is cooked through, about 20 minutes. Fluff the mixture with a fork, then sprinkle with the parsley just before serving.

PER SERVING (1⅓ cups): 368 Cal, 7 g Fat, 1 g Sat Fat, 45 mg Chol, 870 mg Sod, 48 g Carb, 5 g Fib, 27 g Prot, 71 mg Calc. *POINTS*: 7.

tip If the onion and bell pepper seem to dry out while browning, add a little water, a tablespoon at a time, instead of more oil. Not only does this save calories, but the liquid helps to hasten the cooking time of the vegetables.

Lemon-Crumb Cornish Hens with Potatoes and Leeks

Although we remove the skin from the hens (all except the wings), the flavor is replaced with a delicious lemon-crumb topping. Cornish game hens are readily available in supermarkets, fresh or frozen. If you can't find fresh hens, simply thaw the frozen hens overnight in the refrigerator.

2 slices firm white sandwich bread, made into crumbs (1 cup)

1 tablespoon grated Parmesan cheese

1 tablespoon minced fresh parsley

1 tablespoon grated lemon zest

2 (1-pound) Cornish game hens, skinned and halved

2 tablespoons Dijon mustard

1 pound whole small red potatoes

2 cups baby carrots

2 medium leeks, cut in half lengthwise, root end intact, and cleaned

1 tablespoon extra-virgin olive oil

1 tablespoon chopped fresh thyme

½ teaspoon salt

¼ teaspoon coarsely ground black pepper

MAKES 4 SERVINGS

1. Preheat the oven to 400°F. Spray an 11 x 16-inch roasting pan with olive-oil nonstick spray.
2. Combine the bread crumbs, cheese, parsley, and lemon zest in a medium bowl; set aside.
3. Brush the top of the hens with the mustard, then top with the bread crumb mixture, pressing gently so the crumbs adhere to the hens. Place the hens in the roasting pan; spray the tops lightly with olive-oil nonstick spray.
4. Combine the potatoes, carrots, leeks, oil, thyme, salt, and pepper in a large bowl; toss to coat. Arrange the vegetables around the hens in the roasting pan. Bake until an instant-read thermometer inserted in the thigh of the hens registers 180°F and the vegetables are tender and browned, about 45 minutes.

PER SERVING (½ hen and ¼ of vegetables): 343 Cal, 9 g Fat, 2 g Sat Fat, 103 mg Chol, 581 mg Sod, 39 g Carb, 6 g Fib, 28 g Prot, 116 mg Calc. *POINTS: 7.*

Turkey Stir-fry with Asian Vegetables

Turkey Stir-fry with Asian Vegetables

Japanese eggplants—only about 4 inches long with a purple hue—have a mild, sweet flesh and a buttery texture that melts in your mouth. If you can't find them, use 1 medium regular eggplant and cut it into 2-inch chunks. Baby bok choy is a miniaturized version of bok choy. It looks like a bulb of small green leaves and is valued for its tenderness. An added benefit is that recipes often call for baby bok choy to be cooked whole, or halved, which cuts down on prep time. If you can't find the smaller variety, use regular bok choy or even napa cabbage, coarsely shredded.

MAKES 4 SERVINGS

¼ cup low-sodium chicken broth

3 tablespoons rice wine

2 tablespoons low-sodium soy sauce

1 tablespoon red-wine vinegar

1 tablespoon minced peeled fresh ginger

2 garlic cloves, minced

2 teaspoons cornstarch

1 teaspoon Asian (dark) sesame oil

1 teaspoon sugar

¼ teaspoon crushed red pepper

2 teaspoons canola oil

1 pound turkey cutlets, cut into 2-inch strips

3 (about ½ pound) Japanese eggplants

1 pound baby bok choy, cut lengthwise in half

1 (15-ounce) can enoki or straw mushrooms, drained

2 cups hot cooked basmati rice

1. Combine the broth, wine, soy sauce, vinegar, ginger, garlic, cornstarch, sesame oil, sugar, and crushed red pepper in a small bowl; set aside.

2. Heat a nonstick wok or large deep skillet over medium-high heat until a drop of water sizzles. Swirl in 1 teaspoon of the canola oil, then add the turkey. Stir-fry until just cooked through, 5–6 minutes; transfer to a plate.

3. Cut the eggplants in quarters, lengthwise. Swirl the remaining 1 teaspoon canola oil into the wok, then add the eggplant. Cook over medium heat, stirring occasionally, until the eggplant is almost tender, about 8 minutes. Add the bok choy. Cook, stirring occasionally, until tender, about 4 minutes. Return the turkey to the wok, then add the mushrooms and broth mixture. Cook, stirring constantly, until the mixture bubbles and thickens, about 2 minutes. Serve with the rice.

PER SERVING (1¼ cups stir-fry and ½ cup rice): 350 Cal, 8 g Fat, 2 g Sat Fat, 67 mg Chol, 782 mg Sod, 37 g Carb, 5 g Fib, 33 g Prot, 161 mg Calc. *POINTS:* 7.

Orange-Pineapple Duck

A sauce made colorful with pineapple, red pepper, and oranges gives this dish great eye appeal. Try it with shrimp, chicken, pork, or scallops, in place of the duck, if you prefer. It's also a great way to use leftover chicken, turkey, or pork—simply add it to the dish toward the end of the cooking time and heat through.

1 (15½-ounce) can
   pineapple chunks
   in juice
¼ cup orange juice
¼ cup rice vinegar
2 tablespoons packed
   brown sugar
2 tablespoons ketchup
1 tablespoon reduced-
   sodium soy sauce
1 teaspoon Asian (dark)
   sesame oil
1 tablespoon cornstarch
¼ teaspoon crushed
   red pepper
1 pound skinless
   boneless duck breast
½ teaspoon salt
¼ teaspoon freshly
   ground pepper
2 teaspoons canola oil
6 scallions
1 tablespoon minced
   peeled fresh ginger
2 garlic cloves, chopped
1 red bell pepper, seeded,
   cut into 1-inch pieces
2 navel oranges,
   sectioned
2 cups hot cooked rice

MAKES 6 SERVINGS

1. Drain the pineapple, reserving the liquid (about ⅓ cup). Transfer the pineapple to a small bowl; set aside. Combine the orange juice, the reserved pineapple liquid, the vinegar, sugar, ketchup, soy sauce, sesame oil, cornstarch, and crushed red pepper in a medium bowl; set aside.
2. Sprinkle the duck with the salt and pepper. Heat 1 teaspoon of the canola oil in a large nonstick skillet over medium-high heat. Add the duck and cook, turning at least once, until browned, about 8 minutes. Transfer to a cutting board, then cut into slices.
3. Cut 5 of the scallions diagonally into 2-inch pieces. Thinly slice the remaining scallion; set aside.
4. Add the remaining 1 teaspoon canola oil to the same skillet, then add the scallion pieces, ginger, and garlic. Cook, stirring constantly, until fragrant, about 1 minute. Add the bell pepper and the reserved pineapple chunks. Cook, stirring frequently, until crisp-tender, about 3 minutes. Whisk the orange juice mixture lightly with a fork. Add to the skillet and cook, stirring constantly, until the mixture bubbles and thickens. Return the duck to the skillet and add the oranges; heat through. Sprinkle with the reserved sliced scallion, then serve with the rice.

PER SERVING (¾ cup duck and sauce with ⅓ cup rice): 328 Cal, 10 g Fat, 3 g Sat Fat, 55 mg Chol, 584 mg Sod, 41 g Carb, 3 g Fib, 19 g Prot, 63 mg Calc. *POINTS:* **7.**

Turkey Sausage Gumbo

This "trinity" of celery, onions, and bell peppers is often used in Cajun and Creole cooking. A traditional gumbo starts with a slow-cooked roux, which thickens and flavors the gumbo but also uses a significant amount of oil or butter and flour. Our slimmed-down version keeps the flavor but cuts the fat.

MAKES 6 SERVINGS

2 teaspoons canola oil

1 (16-ounce) package reduced-fat turkey kielbasa, cut into ¾-inch slices

1 onion, chopped

1 celery stalk, chopped

1 green bell pepper, seeded and chopped

3 garlic cloves, chopped

2 tablespoons all-purpose flour

1 teaspoon dried thyme

½ teaspoon salt

¼ teaspoon cayenne

1 (14-ounce) can low-sodium chicken broth

1 (14½-ounce) can stewed tomatoes

1 teaspoon Worcestershire sauce

1½ cups frozen whole-kernel corn

1 tablespoon chopped fresh parsley

3 cups hot cooked white rice

1. Heat the oil in a large saucepan over medium-high heat. Add the kielbasa and cook until browned, turning occasionally, about 6 minutes. Transfer to a bowl and set aside.

2. Add the onion, celery, bell pepper, and garlic to the saucepan. Cook over medium heat, stirring frequently, until the vegetables are very tender, about 8 minutes. Stir in the flour, thyme, salt, and cayenne; cook, stirring constantly, about 1 minute. Gradually stir in the broth until the mixture is smooth.

3. Add the tomatoes, Worcestershire sauce, and bay leaf to the saucepan; bring to a boil. Reduce the heat and simmer, covered, stirring occasionally, until the flavors are well blended, about 25 minutes.

4. Stir in the browned kielbasa and corn; return to a boil. Reduce the heat and simmer, covered, until the corn is tender, about 5 minutes. Discard the bay leaf, then stir in the parsley. Serve with the rice.

PER SERVING (1 cup gumbo and ½ cup rice): 328 Cal, 9 g Fat, 2 g Sat Fat, 44 mg Chol, 1015 mg Sod, 44 g Carb, 4 g Fib, 19 g Prot, 94 mg Calc. **POINTS: 7**.

Saucy Sausage, Peppers, and Potatoes

Sausage and peppers—an all-time favorite—is made into a complete one-pot meal here by adding a few potatoes and cooking it all in a simple tomato sauce. Leftovers? Try them spooned on a crusty roll to make a hot Italian hero. Vegetarian? Use soy sausage patties (available in the freezer section of the supermarket) in place of the turkey sausage.

MAKES 6 SERVINGS

2   teaspoons olive oil
1   pound Italian turkey
    sausage, cut into
    2-inch pieces
1   green bell pepper,
    seeded and cut into
    ½-inch-wide strips
1   red bell pepper, seeded
    and cut into
    ½-inch-wide strips
1   onion, sliced
2   garlic cloves, chopped
¾   pound red potatoes,
    peeled and cut into
    1-inch cubes
1   (15-ounce) can tomato
    sauce
½   cup water
1   teaspoon dried
    oregano

1. Heat 1 teaspoon of oil in a large nonstick skillet over medium-high heat. Add the sausage and cook, turning occasionally, until browned, about 5 minutes. Transfer to a bowl and set side.

2. Add the remaining 1 teaspoon oil to the same skillet, then add the green and red bell peppers, the onion, and garlic. Cook over medium heat, stirring occasionally, until the peppers and onion begin to soften, about 8 minutes.

3. Return the sausage to the skillet. Add the potatoes, tomato sauce, water, and oregano; bring to a boil. Reduce the heat and simmer, covered, stirring occasionally, until the flavors are blended, the sausage is cooked through, and the vegetables are tender, about 25 minutes.

PER SERVING (1⅓ cups): 215 Cal, 8 g Fat, 2 g Sat Fat, 44 mg Chol, 1108 mg Sod, 21 g Carb, 3 g Fib, 15 g Prot, 37 mg Calc. *POINTS: 4.*

tip   To save prep time, use frozen, sliced, tri-color bell peppers in place of the fresh bell peppers. You may need to cook them at a slightly higher temperature with the onion in order to cook away any liquid they give off.

Fiesta Chili Cobbler

The crunchy cornbread topping makes this chili unique, as well as homey. You can make the chili, without the topping, up to two days ahead of time, and keep it in the refrigerator. Then when you're ready to serve it, reheat the chili, prepare the cornbread mixture, spoon it on top of the hot chili, and bake.

MAKES 8 SERVINGS

2 teaspoons canola oil

1 onion, chopped

1 green bell pepper, seeded and chopped

2 garlic cloves, chopped

1 pound turkey sausage, casings removed

¼ cup chili powder

2 teaspoons sugar

1 teaspoon cumin

1 teaspoon oregano

¼ teaspoon salt

1 (28-ounce) can Italian peeled tomatoes

2 (15-ounce) cans red kidney beans, drained

Cornbread Topping:

1¼ cups yellow cornmeal

1 cup all-purpose flour

2 tablespoons sugar

1 tablespoon baking powder

3 tablespoons reduced-calorie margarine

¾ cup fat-free milk

¼ cup egg substitute

½ cup shredded reduced-fat cheddar cheese

1. Heat the oil in a 3-quart Dutch oven or flameproof casserole over medium-high heat. Add the onion, bell pepper, and garlic. Cook, stirring occasionally, until softened, about 8 minutes. Add the turkey and cook, breaking up the turkey with a wooden spoon, until browned, about 8 minutes.

2. Add the chili powder, sugar, cumin, oregano, and salt. Cook, stirring constantly, 1 minute. Stir in the tomatoes with their liquid and ¾ cup water; bring to a boil. Reduce the heat and simmer, covered, until the flavors are blended and the chili thickens slightly, about 1 hour. Stir in the beans and cook until heated through.

3. Preheat the oven to 400°F.

4. To make the cornbread topping, combine the cornmeal, flour, sugar, and baking powder in a large bowl. Melt the margarine, combine with the milk and egg substitute in a small bowl. Stir the milk mixture into the cornmeal mixture until just blended. Stir in the cheese. Spoon the batter around the outer edge of the casserole. Bake until the chili is bubbly and the cornbread is golden, about 20 minutes.

PER SERVING (½ cup chili and ⅛ of cornbread): 408 Cal, 12 g Fat, 3 g Sat Fat, 35 mg Chol, 1209 mg Sod, 55 g Carb, 8 g Fib, 22 g Prot, 343 mg Calc. *POINTS: 8.*

tip Many flameproof and ovenproof casserole dishes or Dutch ovens come with colorful enameled coatings. They are great for cooking on top of the stove or baking in the oven, then for serving right from the same pot.

Seafood Specials

From sole to shrimp

Salmon en Papillote

Cooking en papillote simply means cooking food in a sealed packet—the packet is traditionally made from parchment paper, but foil is a good substitute. This technique is great for cooking fish, lean chicken, or vegetables because it keeps the food moist and—with the help of a few seasonings and vegetables—creates its own sauce. Little, if any, fat is necessary.

½ small onion, finely chopped
1 teaspoon grated lemon zest
2 tablespoons fresh lemon juice
1 tablespoon drained capers, chopped
¾ teaspoon salt
¼ teaspoon freshly ground pepper
4 (4-ounce) skinless salmon fillets
1 bunch fresh asparagus, tough ends trimmed
3 plum tomatoes, seeded and chopped
2 cups hot cooked brown rice

MAKES 4 SERVINGS

1. Preheat the oven to 450°F. Spray 4 (12 x 20-inch) sheets of foil with nonstick spray. Fold each sheet in half from one short end to mark the center line, then unfold the foil.
2. Combine the onion, lemon zest, juice, capers, ½ teaspoon of the salt, and ⅛ teaspoon of the pepper in a small bowl; set aside.
3. Sprinkle the salmon fillets with the remaining ¼ teaspoon salt and ⅛ teaspoon pepper. Place one piece of salmon in the center of the bottom half of each sheet of foil. Top each with one-fourth of the lemon mixture. Place one-fourth of the asparagus next to each piece of salmon. Sprinkle the tomatoes over the salmon. Fold the foil over the salmon and asparagus, making a tight seal.
4. Place the foil parcels on a large baking pan and bake until the salmon is just opaque in the center, 10–12 minutes. Open the parcels with care to avoid getting a steam burn. Serve the salmon and vegetables with the rice.

PER SERVING (1 salmon parcel and ½ cup rice): 300 Cal, 8 g Fat, 2 g Sat Fat, 74 mg Chol, 573 mg Sod, 29 g Carb, 4 g Fib, 29 g Prot, 42 mg Calc. POINTS: 6.

tip Although they need to be baked at the last minute, the salmon packets can be assembled several hours ahead and kept in the refrigerator until you are ready to bake them.

Salmon Strudel

Canned salmon is a wonderful convenience product that makes this a snap to put together. You can eat the soft edible bones that come in the can—they are a good source of calcium. For no extra **POINTS**, serve this with sliced red-ripe tomatoes, sprinkled with a little balsamic vinegar, salt, and chopped fresh basil.

1 (10-ounce) package frozen chopped spinach, thawed and squeezed dry

1 cup frozen peas, thawed

½ cup plain fat-free yogurt

2 ounces light cream cheese (Neufchâtel)

2 tablespoons fresh lemon juice

2 tablespoons chopped fresh dill

¼ teaspoon salt

¼ teaspoon freshly ground pepper

1 (14¾-ounce) can pink salmon, drained

4 (12 x 17-inch) sheets phyllo dough, thawed according to package directions

MAKES 4 SERVINGS

1. Preheat the oven to 350°F. Spray a baking sheet with nonstick spray; set aside.
2. Combine the spinach, peas, yogurt, cream cheese, lemon juice, dill, salt, and pepper in a large bowl until well mixed. Gently fold in the salmon so it stays in chunks.
3. Place one sheet of phyllo on a work surface with one long side nearest you. Spray lightly with nonstick spray and top with a second sheet. Repeat with the remaining 2 sheets of phyllo. Spray the top sheet lightly with nonstick spray.
4. Place the salmon mixture in a 14-inch-long cylindrical shape along the side of the phyllo nearest you leaving a 1½-inch border on the short ends and the side closest to you. Roll up jelly-roll style, folding in the short ends to seal. Transfer the roll to the baking sheet, then spray the roll lightly with nonstick spray.
5. Bake until lightly browned, 25–28 minutes. Let the strudel stand 5 minutes, then cut into 8 pieces.

PER SERVING (2 pieces): 291 Cal, 11 g Fat, 4 g Sat Fat, 69 mg Chol, 950 mg Sod, 20 g Carb, 4 g Fib, 28 g Prot, 375 mg Calc. *POINTS*: 6.

tip For a great appetizer, cut the strudel into 12 pinwheels and serve at your next cocktail party.

Salmon Strudel,
page 117

Salmon Frittata

Frittatas are an ideal weeknight supper because they're so quick and easy. Potatoes, salmon, and mushrooms add substance to our version, but if you feel you need just a little something more—for an extra *POINT*—serve each portion with 2 long breadsticks. For variety try substituting some smoked salmon for some of the regular salmon.

5   egg whites, lightly beaten
3   large eggs, lightly beaten
¼   cup fat-free milk
1   tablespoon chopped fresh dill
¾   teaspoon salt
¼   teaspoon freshly ground pepper
½   pound fresh white mushrooms, sliced
1   (14½-ounce) can sliced white potatoes, drained
1   small red bell pepper, seeded and finely chopped
2   scallions, chopped
1   (8-ounce) salmon fillet, skinned and cut into 1-inch pieces

MAKES 4 SERVINGS

1. Preheat the broiler.
2. Lightly whisk the egg whites, eggs, milk, dill, salt, and pepper in a medium bowl until well mixed.
3. Spray a 10-inch ovenproof nonstick skillet with nonstick spray and set over medium-high heat. Add the mushrooms and cook, stirring frequently, until golden brown, 5–6 minutes. Add the potatoes, red pepper, and scallions; cook, stirring frequently, until the bell pepper is softened, about 2 minutes. Add the salmon and cook, turning gently to avoid breaking it up, until the salmon is just opaque in the center, 2–3 minutes.
4. Pour the egg mixture over the salmon and vegetables in the skillet and reduce the heat to low. Cook until the eggs are set but still wet on top, 6–7 minutes. Place the skillet under the broiler, 4 inches from the heat, and cook until the top of the frittata is lightly browned, 2–3 minutes. Cut into 4 wedges and serve.

PER SERVING (1 wedge): 217 Cal, 7 g Fat, 2 g Sat Fat, 191 mg Chol, 793 mg Sod, 16 g Carb, 3 g Fib, 22 g Prot, 60 mg Calc. *POINTS: 4.*

tip If you don't have an ovenproof skillet (that is with a heat-resistant handle), simply cover the handle of your regular skillet with heavy-duty foil.

Tuna Seviche over Mixed Greens with Tortilla Chips

Seviche, raw fish marinated in citrus juice, is becoming increasingly popular in restaurants all over the country. Part of the attraction is the simple preparation of the dish, but the real draw—for home cooks and chefs alike—is the clean, refreshing flavor and the lightness of the dish.

1 pound very fresh yellowfin tuna, cut into ¼-inch dice

2 plum tomatoes, seeded and cut into ¼-inch dice

1 small red onion, finely chopped (about ⅓ cup)

1 (10½-ounce) can black beans, rinsed and drained

¾ avocado, peeled, pitted, and cut into ¼-inch dice

1 jalapeño pepper, seeded and finely chopped (wear gloves to prevent irritation)

¼ cup fresh lime juice

¼ cup fresh lemon juice

2 tablespoons chopped fresh cilantro

½ teaspoon salt

4 cups mixed baby greens

2 ounces low-fat tortilla chips (about 40)

MAKES 4 SERVINGS

1. Combine the tuna, tomatoes, onion, black beans, avocado, jalapeño pepper, lime juice, lemon juice, cilantro, and salt in a bowl; toss to coat. Refrigerate, covered, stirring once every 15 minutes for at least 1 hour or up to 2 hours.

2. Divide the greens among 4 plates. With a slotted spoon, top each plate with 1 cup of the seviche. Serve with the tortilla chips.

PER SERVING (1 salad plate and 10 chips): 378 Cal, 12 g Fat, 2 g Sat Fat, 43 mg Chol, 537 mg Sod, 35 g Carb, 9 g Fib, 35 g Prot, 99 mg Calc. *POINTS:* **8.**

tip Because the acid of the citrus juices "cooks" the fish, the dish can't be allowed to marinate for more than 2 hours before the tuna takes on a mealy consistency. To make part of this dish early in the day, however, simply combine all the chopped ingredients except the avocado and citrus juices in a bowl and refrigerate until 1 or 2 hours before serving. Then, stir in the avocado and citrus juices.

Grilled Tuna, Red Onion, and Roasted Pepper Sandwiches

Grilled Tuna, Red Onion, and Roasted Pepper Sandwiches

Fresh tuna makes an excellent filling for a sandwich. We like it cooked medium-rare—still a little pink in the center, but you can leave it on the grill a little longer if you prefer it well-cooked. To make this the perfect summertime meal, serve it with a bowl of chilled gazpacho or a crisp cucumber-dill salad.

MAKES 4 SERVINGS

- 2 tablespoons low-fat mayonnaise
- 2 tablespoons chopped fresh basil
- 2 teaspoons grated lemon zest
- 1 medium red onion, cut into 4 thick slices
- 1 red bell pepper, seeded and quartered
- 1 tablespoon extra-virgin olive oil
- ¾ teaspoon salt
- ¼ teaspoon freshly ground pepper
- 4 (6-ounce) tuna steaks (½ inch thick)
- 8 slices sourdough bread, about 3 x 5 inches
- 1 cup loosely packed arugula leaves

1. Combine the mayonnaise, basil, and lemon zest in a small bowl; set aside.

2. Spray the grill rack with nonstick spray; prepare the grill.

3. Brush the onion slices and bell pepper pieces with 1 teaspoon of the oil, then sprinkle evenly with ½ teaspoon of the salt and ⅛ teaspoon of the pepper. Place on the grill rack and cook until the vegetables are well marked and tender, 3–4 minutes on each side. Transfer the vegetables to a plate and set aside.

4. Brush the tuna with 1 teaspoon of the oil, then sprinkle with the remaining ¼ teaspoon salt and ⅛ teaspoon pepper. Place the tuna steaks on the grill and cook until browned on the outside but still a little pink in the center, 3–4 minutes on each side. Transfer the tuna to a plate and set aside.

5. Brush one side of each of the bread slices with the remaining 1 teaspoon oil and grill until lightly toasted, about 1 minute on each side.

6. Place ¼ cup arugula leaves on each of 4 slices of bread; top each with an onion slice, a piece of bell pepper, and a tuna steak. Spread one side of each of the remaining 4 bread slices with the mayonnaise mixture, then place on top of the tuna steaks.

PER SERVING (1 sandwich): 412 Cal, 14 g Fat, 3 g Sat Fat, 65 mg Chol, 806 mg Sod, 26 g Carb, 2 g Fib, 44 g Prot, 63 mg Calc. *POINTS: 9.*

Tuna Fajitas

Tuna's meaty, firm texture makes it an ideal fish to use in the popular Mexican dish of fajitas, usually reserved for chicken or beef. Serve with wedges of fresh lime for extra zing.

MAKES 4 SERVINGS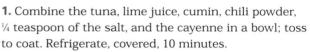

1 pound yellowfin tuna steak, cut into ½-inch-thick strips

2 tablespoons fresh lime juice

1 teaspoon ground cumin

1 teaspoon chili powder

¾ teaspoon salt

⅛ teaspoon cayenne

1 tablespoon olive oil

2 assorted-color bell peppers, seeded and sliced

1 large onion, sliced

4 (8-inch) fat-free flour tortillas

½ cup prepared salsa

¼ cup fat-free sour cream

1. Combine the tuna, lime juice, cumin, chili powder, ¼ teaspoon of the salt, and the cayenne in a bowl; toss to coat. Refrigerate, covered, 10 minutes.

2. Heat the oil in a large nonstick skillet over medium-high heat. Add the bell peppers, onion, and the remaining ½ teaspoon salt. Cook, stirring occasionally, until the vegetables begin to soften, 4–5 minutes. Stir in the tuna mixture and cook, stirring, until the tuna is just opaque in the center, 3–4 minutes.

3. Stack the tortillas on a microwavable plate. Cover with wax paper and microwave on High, 50 seconds. Spoon 1 cup of the tuna mixture onto each tortilla. Top each with 2 tablespoons salsa and 1 tablespoon sour cream. Fold to enclose the filling and serve at once.

PER SERVING (1 fajita): 356 Cal, 10 g Fat, 2 g Sat Fat, 44 mg Chol, 793 mg Sod, 33 g Carb, 4 g Fib, 33 g Prot, 129 mg Calc. *POINTS: 7.*

Greek Swordfish Kebabs

Like the classic souvlaki, but with fish instead of lamb, these marinated and skewered delights satisfy the palate with great flavors and textures.

MAKES 6 SERVINGS

1½ pounds swordfish, 1 inch thick, cut into 24 cubes

1 tablespoon grated lemon zest

2 tablespoons fresh lemon juice

1 tablespoon extra-virgin olive oil

1½ teaspoons chopped fresh oregano, or ½ teaspoon dried

24 cherry tomatoes

4 scallions, cut into 24 (1-inch) pieces

2 assorted-color bell peppers, seeded and each cut into 12 pieces

¾ teaspoon salt

¼ teaspoon freshly ground pepper

6 (6-inch) pita breads

1. Combine the swordfish, lemon zest, lemon juice, oil, and oregano in a bowl; toss well. Refrigerate, covered, at least 2 hours or up to overnight.

2. Spray the broiler rack with nonstick spray. Preheat the broiler.

3. Thread 3 swordfish cubes, 3 tomatoes, 3 scallion pieces, and 3 bell pepper pieces alternately onto each of 8 (12-inch) metal skewers. Arrange the skewers on the broiler rack. Lightly spray the food with nonstick spray, then sprinkle evenly with the salt and pepper.

4. Broil the kebabs 4 inches from the heat, turning them every 2–3 minutes, until the vegetables are crisp-tender and the fish is opaque in the center, 8–10 minutes. Serve with the pita bread.

PER SERVING (1⅓ kebabs and 1 pita): 316 Cal, 8 g Fat, 2 g Sat Fat, 60 mg Chol, 628 mg Sod, 35 g Carb, 3 g Fib, 25 g Prot, 70 mg Calc. POINTS: 6.

tip   For an extra ½ POINT per serving, serve the kebabs with a yogurt sauce made from 1 cup plain fat-free yogurt, ¼ cup chopped, peeled cucumber, a teaspoon of minced garlic, and a dash of salt.

Roasted Arctic Char with Vegetables

Arctic char is a lesser-known but readily available fish that is a relative of salmon. This farm-raised, freshwater fish has a full, rich flavor and is wonderful roasted. As with all fish, to cut the fat, be sure to remove the skin before eating.

1 medium eggplant (about 1 pound), halved lengthwise, then cut into ¼-inch slices

1 large red onion, cut into 8 wedges

1 large zucchini (about ¾ pound), halved lengthwise, then cut into ¼-inch slices

2 ears fresh corn, shucked and each cut into 4 pieces

1 tablespoon extra-virgin olive oil

1 teaspoon salt

½ teaspoon freshly ground pepper

1 pound Arctic char fillet

⅓ cup orange juice

1 tablespoon grated lemon zest

½ teaspoon dried basil

1 orange, unpeeled and thinly sliced

MAKES 4 SERVINGS

1. Preheat the oven to 450°F. Spray a large shallow baking pan with nonstick spray.

2. Combine the eggplant, onion, zucchini, and corn in a large bowl; add the oil, ½ teaspoon of the salt, and ¼ teaspoon of the pepper. Toss well to coat, then spread in a single layer in the baking pan. Roast 20 minutes.

3. Remove the baking pan from the oven; push the vegetables to the sides of the pan to create a space in the center.

4. Place the Arctic char, skin-side down, in the pan. Drizzle with the orange juice, then sprinkle with the lemon zest, basil, and the remaining ½ teaspoon salt and ¼ teaspoon pepper. Arrange the orange slices in an overlapping row across the length of the fillet. Cover the fish (not the vegetables) loosely with a sheet of foil. Return to the oven and roast, until the fish is just opaque in the center and the vegetables are tender, 20–25 minutes longer.

PER SERVING (¼ of fish and 1½ cups vegetables): 301 Cal, 11 g Fat, 2 g Sat Fat, 58 mg Chol, 648 mg Sod, 29 g Carb, 6 g Fib, 25 g Prot, 88 mg Calc. *POINTS: 6.*

Dutch-Oven Steamed Cod

Atlantic cod, once fished to near extinction, has made a marvelous recovery, thanks to strictly enforced fishing regulations. This mildly flavored fish has a very low fat content and slightly firm texture. It lends itself well to a host of sauces and methods of cooking.

MAKES 4 SERVINGS

1 tablespoon extra-virgin olive oil

4 slices turkey bacon, chopped

1 (14½-ounce) can sliced potatoes, rinsed and drained

1 Vidalia or other large sweet onion, sliced

2 garlic cloves, minced

1 large zucchini (about 12 ounces), halved lengthwise, then cut into ¼-inch slices

1 yellow squash (about 8 ounces), halved length wise, then cut into ¼-inch slices

4 plum tomatoes, chopped

⅓ cup dry white wine

¾ teaspoon salt

¼ teaspoon freshly ground pepper

4 (6-ounce) skinless cod fillets

1. Heat the oil in a Dutch oven over medium-high heat. Add the bacon and cook, stirring frequently, until lightly browned, 3–4 minutes. Stir in the potatoes, onion, and garlic. Cook, stirring frequently, until the onions soften slightly, 3–4 minutes.

2. Add the zucchini, yellow squash, and tomatoes; cook, stirring, about 4 minutes. Add the wine, ½ teaspoon of the salt, and ⅛ teaspoon of the pepper; cook about 2 minutes.

3. Sprinkle the cod with the remaining ¼ teaspoon salt and ⅛ teaspoon pepper. Place the cod in a single layer on top of the vegetables. Reduce the heat and simmer, covered, until the fish is just opaque in the center, 6–7 minutes.

4. Transfer the cod to 4 plates, then spoon the vegetables evenly around the cod.

PER SERVING (1 cod fillet and 1¼ cups vegetables): 314 Cal, 8 g Fat, 2 g Sat Fat, 102 mg Chol, 996 mg Sod, 21 g Carb, 5 g Fib, 38 g Prot, 63 mg Calc. **POINTS: 6.**

CUT*POINTS* Omit the bacon and cook the potatoes, onion, and garlic in a teaspoon of oil instead of a tablespoon and save a *POINT* per serving.

Fish and Potato Bake

What's not to like about this quick-to-throw-together dish that uses only one pan and only five simple ingredients—and delivers delicious results! Instead of cod, you could use any other moderately firm-fleshed, mild fish, such as haddock, flounder, or sole.

1 pound small white or red potatoes, scrubbed and cut into ¼-inch-thick slices

2 red onions, each cut into 8 wedges

5 teaspoons extra-virgin olive oil

1 teaspoon salt

¼ teaspoon freshly ground pepper

4 plum tomatoes, chopped

1½ pounds cod fillet

MAKES 4 SERVINGS

1. Preheat the oven to 450°F. Spray a large shallow baking pan with nonstick spray.
2. Combine the potatoes, onions, 3 teaspoons of the oil, ½ teaspoon of the salt, and ⅛ teaspoon of the pepper in a large bowl; toss well. Spread in a single layer in the baking pan. Roast, stirring occasionally, until the vegetables are slightly softened, about 20 minutes.
3. Meanwhile, combine tomatoes with remaining 2 teaspoons oil, ½ teaspoon salt, and ⅛ teaspoon pepper; set aside.
4. Remove the baking pan from the oven. Slide the potatoes and onions to one side and place the cod fillet on the other side of the baking pan. Spoon the tomato mixture on top of the cod. Roast until the fish is just opaque in the center and the potatoes are tender and lightly browned, 15–18 minutes.

PER SERVING (¼ of cod and 1 cup vegetables): 336 Cal, 8 g Fat, 1 g Sat Fat, 90 mg Chol, 735 mg Sod, 30 g Carb, 4 g Fib, 35 g Prot, 48 mg Calc. *POINTS: 7.*

tip Add pizzazz to the veggies by sprinkling chopped fresh oregano and a tablespoon of balsamic vinegar over the tomato mixture just before roasting.

Monkfish Osso Buco

Like the traditional veal osso buco, our seafood version is braised with onions, tomatoes, and wine and served with gremolada—a savory mix of parsley, lemon zest, and garlic. Monkfish—also known as anglerfish—has a firm texture and a light, sweet flavor that has been likened to lobster. It is a moderately priced fish and is often referred to as the "poor man's lobster."

MAKES 4 SERVINGS

2 tablespoons chopped fresh parsley

1 tablespoon grated lemon zest

4 garlic cloves, minced

2 teaspoons olive oil

1 onion, chopped

1 celery stalk, chopped

1 carrot, chopped

½ pound fresh white mushrooms, quartered

1 large zucchini (about 12 ounces), cut into ½-inch dice

1 tablespoon tomato paste

¾ cup dry white wine

1 (14½-ounce) can crushed tomatoes

1 cup low-sodium chicken broth

1 tablespoon fresh lemon juice

¾ teaspoon salt

¼ teaspoon freshly ground pepper

4 (6-ounce) monkfish fillets

2 cups hot cooked white rice

1. Combine the parsley, lemon zest, and 2 of the minced garlic cloves in a small bowl; set aside.

2. Heat the oil in a Dutch oven over medium-high heat. Add the remaining 2 minced garlic cloves, the onion, celery, carrot, and mushrooms. Cook, stirring frequently, until the vegetables are tender and lightly browned, about 10 minutes. Add the zucchini and tomato paste; cook, stirring, about 1 minute. Add the wine and cook, stirring occasionally, until the liquid is reduced by half, about 4 minutes.

3. Add the tomatoes, broth, lemon juice, ½ teaspoon of the salt, and ⅛ teaspoon of the pepper; bring to a boil. Reduce the heat and simmer, uncovered, until the liquid is reduced by one-third, about 20 minutes.

4. Sprinkle the fish with the remaining ¼ teaspoon salt and ⅛ teaspoon pepper; place on top of the vegetable mixture in the Dutch oven. Cook, covered, until the fish is just opaque in the center, 15–17 minutes.

5. Divide the vegetable mixture among 4 plates and top each with 1 monkfish fillet. Sprinkle the fillets with the reserved parsley mixture. Serve with the rice.

PER SERVING (1 fish fillet, 1 cup vegetable mixture, and ½ cup rice): 375 Cal, 6 g Fat, 1 g Sat Fat, 94 mg Chol, 823 mg Sod, 40 g Carb, 5 g Fib, 40 g Prot, 106 mg Calc. POINTS: 7.

tip Monkfish has a silver sinew or skin attached to its fillet. While it is edible, it is rather unattractive when cooked. You can ask your fishmonger to remove it.

Halibut Braised with Tomatoes, Capers, and Olives

Halibut has a delicate flavor that makes it well suited to the sweet tanginess of this tomato sauce. An added bonus: this ocean catch is very low in fat. Round out the dish with a mixed leafy green salad.

MAKES 4 SERVINGS

2   teaspoons olive oil
1   onion, chopped
2   garlic cloves, minced
2   celery stalks, chopped
1   teaspoon fennel seeds, lightly crushed
1   (14½-ounce) can crushed tomatoes
1¾ cups water
1   cup dry orzo (about 6 ounces)
12 pitted kalamata olives, halved
1   tablespoon drained capers
½   teaspoon salt
¼   teaspoon freshly ground pepper
1¼ pounds halibut fillet, skin removed

1. Heat the oil in a 10-inch nonstick skillet over medium-high heat. Add the onion and garlic. Cook, stirring frequently, until fragrant, about 1 minute. Add the celery and fennel seeds. Cook, stirring occasionally, until slightly softened and fragrant, about 2 minutes.
2. Stir in the tomatoes, water, orzo, olives, capers, ¼ teaspoon of the salt, and ⅛ teaspoon of the pepper; bring to a boil, stirring occasionally. Reduce the heat and simmer, covered, 5 minutes.
3. Season the halibut with the remaining ¼ teaspoon salt and ⅛ teaspoon pepper. Add the halibut to the skillet, spooning some of the tomato mixture over the fish. Cover and simmer until the fish is just opaque in the center and the orzo is tender, 10–12 minutes.

PER SERVING (¼ of halibut and 1 cup orzo mixture): 304 Cal, 6 g Fat, 1 g Sat Fat, 62 mg Chol, 734 mg Sod, 34 g Carb, 4 g Fib, 28 g Prot, 83 mg Calc. *POINTS: 6.*

tip To crush fennel seeds, place the seeds between sheets of wax paper and pound lightly with a wooden mallet or one end of a rolling pin.

Halibut Braised with
Tomatoes, Capers, and Olives

Sole Piccata

Piccata is a classic Italian dish of veal cutlets sauced with lemon juice, parsley, and capers. This brightly seasoned lemon sauce also lends itself well to the sweet, delicate taste of sole. We add zucchini to the dish and serve it with noodles to make it a complete meal.

MAKES 4 SERVINGS

3 tablespoons all-
   purpose flour
½ teaspoon salt
¼ teaspoon freshly
   ground pepper
4 (5-ounce) sole fillets
1 tablespoon olive oil
1 onion, chopped
1 large zucchini (about
   12 ounces), halved
   l engthwise, then cut
   into ¼-inch slices
¾ cup low-sodium chick
   en or vegetable broth
3 tablespoons fresh
   lemon juice
1 tablespoon drained
   capers
2 tablespoons light
   butter
4 cups hot cooked
   yokeless egg noodles
   (6 ounces dry)

1. Combine the flour with ¼ teaspoon of the salt and ⅛ teaspoon of the pepper; reserve 2 teaspoons of the flour mixture. Coat both sides of sole fillets in remaining flour mixture; set aside.
2. Heat 2 teaspoons of the oil in a large nonstick skillet over medium-high heat. Add the fillets and cook until the fish is lightly golden on the outside and just opaque in the center, 1½–2 minutes on each side. Transfer to a plate and keep warm, uncovered, in a slow oven.
3. Add the remaining 1 teaspoon oil to the skillet and heat over medium-high heat. Add the onion and cook, stirring, until slightly softened, about 2 minutes. Add the zucchini and cook until crisp-tender, 3–4 minutes. Stir in the broth, lemon juice, and capers; bring to a boil. Reduce the heat and simmer, uncovered, about 2 minutes. Remove from the heat, then stir in the butter and the remaining ¼ teaspoon salt and ⅛ teaspoon pepper, stirring until the butter melts.
4. Divide the noodles among 4 plates. Place a fish fillet on top of the noodles. Spoon the zucchini mixture over the fillets and serve at once.

PER SERVING (1 cup noodles, 1 sole fillet, and generous ½ cup vegetable mixture): 394 Cal, 10 g Fat, 3 g Sat Fat, 77 mg Chol, 493 mg Sod, 44 g Carb, 3 g Fib, 32 g Prot, 50 mg Calc. *POINTS: 8.*

Thai Steamed Snapper

Steaming—cooking on a rack over gently simmering liquid—is a good way to cook seafood, because you don't need to use any fat and the fish stays moist and succulent from the steam. You can find lemongrass, red curry paste, and fish sauce in Asian markets and some large supermarkets. One to two teaspoons of grated lemon zest makes a good substitute for the lemongrass if you can't find it.

MAKES 4 SERVINGS

2 cups water

1 onion, chopped

3 garlic cloves, minced

1 (6-inch) piece fresh lemongrass, cut into 1-inch pieces

2 tablespoons grated peeled fresh ginger

1 teaspoon Thai red curry paste

4 (6-ounce) red snapper fillets, skinned

½ pound fresh snow peas, trimmed and halved crosswise

2 tablespoons fresh lime juice

2 tablespoons chopped fresh cilantro

1 tablespoon bottled fish sauce (nam pla)

2 cups hot cooked white rice

2 scallions, chopped

1. Bring the water, onion, garlic, lemongrass, ginger, and curry paste to a boil in a steamer pot. Reduce the heat and simmer, uncovered, about 10 minutes.

2. Coat the bottom of the steamer rack with nonstick spray. Place the fish on the rack, and set the rack over the pot. Cover and cook 4 minutes. Add the snow peas and cook until the fish is just opaque in the center and the snow peas are crisp-tender, about 2 minutes longer.

3. Remove the steamer rack from the steamer pot and set aside. Then stir the lime juice, cilantro, and fish sauce into the broth. Remove from the heat and discard the lemongrass.

4. Place ½ cup of the rice in the bottom of each of 4 shallow bowls. Top each bowl with 1 fish fillet, ¼ of the snow peas, and some of the scallions. Spoon the broth over each fillet (about ⅓ cup) and serve at once.

PER SERVING (1 bowl): 290 Cal, 2 g Fat, 1 g Sat Fat, 78 mg Chol, 216 mg Sod, 33 g Carb, 3 g Fib, 33 g Prot, 71 mg Calc. POINTS: 5.

tip If you don't have a steamer, use a shallow, wide saucepan and cook the fish and snow peas directly in the simmering broth.

Coconut Shrimp

Coconut Shrimp

Thai red curry paste — made from chili peppers, lemongrass, garlic, kaffir lime leaves, shrimp paste, and cilantro, all processed into a smooth, flavorful condiment — gives this dish great flavor. The paste imparts a bit of heat, so cut back on the amount you use if you don't like spicy dishes. You can find the curry paste in small bottles in the ethnic section of most supermarkets and Asian groceries.

MAKES 6 SERVINGS

1 tablespoon peanut or canola oil

1½ pounds large shrimp, peeled and deveined

1 bunch asparagus, tough ends trimmed and cut into 1½-inch pieces

1 onion, sliced

1 red bell pepper, seeded and cut into strips

1 tablespoon grated peeled fresh ginger

3 garlic cloves, minced

1½ teaspoons Thai red curry paste

1 cup light coconut milk

2 tablespoons bottled fish sauce (nam pla)

1 tablespoon sugar

3 cups hot cooked couscous

1. Heat 1½ teaspoons of the oil in a large nonstick skillet over medium-high heat. Add the shrimp and cook until just opaque in the center, 2–3 minutes on each side. Transfer the shrimp to a plate and set aside.

2. Add the remaining 1½ teaspoons oil to the same skillet and heat over medium-high heat. Add the asparagus and cook, stirring frequently, until slightly softened, about 3 minutes. Add the onion and bell pepper; cook, stirring frequently, until softened, about 3 minutes. Stir in the ginger, garlic, and curry paste. Cook, stirring constantly, until fragrant, about 1 minute.

3. Reduce the heat to medium, then add the coconut milk, fish sauce, and sugar; bring to a simmer. Cook, stirring occasionally, until the flavors blend, about 3 minutes. Stir in the shrimp and cook 1 minute until heated through. Serve the shrimp and vegetables in bowls over the couscous.

PER SERVING (scant 1 cup shrimp and vegetable mixture and ½ cup couscous): 248 Cal, 6 g Fat, 3 g Sat Fat, 107 mg Chol, 425 mg Sod, 30 g Carb, 3 g Fib, 18 g Prot, 46 mg Calc. *POINTS: 5.*

Shrimp Risotto

The unique flavor of saffron—the most expensive spice in the world—shines in this delicately flavored dish. Saffron is hand-harvested from tiny purple crocus flowers; it takes more than 14,000 stigmas, or saffron threads, to make just 1 ounce. The good news is that a little goes a long way for both color and flavor.

5–6 cups low-sodium chicken or vegetable broth
2 tablespoons olive oil
2 shallots, chopped
1½ cups Arborio rice
½ cup dry white wine
½ teaspoon saffron threads, lightly crushed
1 pound medium shrimp, peeled and deveined
3 plum tomatoes, seeded and chopped
¾ teaspoon salt
¼ teaspoon freshly ground pepper
½ cup chopped fresh basil

MAKES 6 SERVINGS

1. Pour the broth into a large measuring cup and microwave on High until very hot.

2. Heat the oil in a large Dutch oven over medium heat. Add the shallots and cook, stirring occasionally, until softened, about 3 minutes. Add the rice and cook, stirring, until the outer shell is translucent, about 1 minute.

3. Add the wine and saffron and cook, stirring constantly, until the liquid is almost completely absorbed, 1–2 minutes. Add 1 cup of the hot broth and cook, stirring constantly, until the liquid is almost completely absorbed. Continue to add broth, 1 cup at a time, stirring until it is absorbed before adding more, until the rice is just tender. The cooking time from the first addition of broth should be 20–22 minutes.

4. Stir in the shrimp, tomatoes, salt, and pepper. Cook, stirring, until the shrimp are just opaque in the center, 2–3 minutes. Remove from the heat and stir in the basil. Serve at once.

PER SERVING (generous 1 cup): 294 Cal, 6 g Fat, 1 g Sat Fat, 71 mg Chol, 426 mg Sod, 44 g Carb, 1 g Fib, 14 g Prot, 53 mg Calc. *POINTS: 6.*

tip Turn risotto leftovers into delicious risotto cakes. For every 2 cups of leftover risotto, add 1 lightly beaten egg white. Mix well, then shape into 4 patties. Coat each patty in dry bread crumbs and refrigerate 15 minutes. Heat 2 teaspoons of olive oil in a large nonstick skillet and cook the risotto cakes until lightly golden and heated through, about 3 minutes on each side. Serve with lemon wedges and a simple green salad.

Spicy Orange Shrimp with Broccoli

Spicy orange beef is a favorite in many Asian restaurants. Our seafood version, with the addition of a few broccoli florets, will please family or friends just as much. For diehard beef lovers, substitute 12 ounces of thinly sliced beef top round or boneless sirloin for the shrimp.

MAKES 4 SERVINGS

1 pound extra-large shrimp, peeled and deveined
2 tablespoons cornstarch
1 tablespoon grated peeled fresh ginger
2 teaspoons grated orange zest
½ cup low-sodium chicken or vegetable broth
¼ cup orange juice
2 tablespoons reduced-sodium soy sauce
1 tablespoon sugar
¼ teaspoon crushed red pepper
1 (12-ounce) bag fresh broccoli florets
¼ cup water
2 cups hot cooked white rice

1. Combine the shrimp, 1 tablespoon of the cornstarch, the ginger, and orange zest in a medium bowl; toss to coat.
2. Combine the remaining 1 tablespoon cornstarch, the broth, orange juice, soy sauce, sugar, and crushed red pepper in a small bowl; set aside.
3. Spray a large nonstick skillet with nonstick spray and set over medium-high heat. Add the shrimp mixture and cook, stirring occasionally, until the shrimp are just opaque in the center, 3–4 minutes. Transfer the shrimp to a plate.
4. Add the broccoli and water to the skillet. Cook, stirring occasionally, until crisp-tender and the water evaporates, about 3 minutes. Add the broth mixture and cook, stirring constantly, until the mixture bubbles and thickens. Add the cooked shrimp and heat through, about 1 minute. Serve over the rice.

PER SERVING (1¼ cups shrimp mixture and ½ cup rice): 228 Cal, 1 g Fat, 0 g Sat Fat, 107 mg Chol, 455 mg Sod, 37 g Carb, 3 g Fib, 17 g Prot, 76 mg Calc. *POINTS: 4.*

tip It's often convenient to buy shrimp frozen and keep it on hand in the freezer. When ready to use, thaw the shrimp overnight in the refrigerator. Or run under cold running water until defrosted, then drain well and pat dry on several layers of paper towels.

Shrimp and Sausage Jambalaya

Jambalaya is a Creole dish made from cooked rice, tomatoes, onions, and green bell peppers with a variety of other interchangeable ingredients. Small chunks of skinless boneless chicken breast can easily be substituted for the shrimp and/or the kielbasa, and a cup of thawed frozen peas can be added with the shrimp.

MAKES 6 SERVINGS

1   tablespoon butter
1   large onion, chopped
1   green bell pepper, seeded and chopped
2   celery stalks, chopped
3   garlic cloves, minced
6   ounces turkey kielbasa, halved lengthwise and cut into ¼-inch slices
1½ cups long-grain white rice
1   (28-ounce) can whole peeled tomatoes, broken up
1   (14½-ounce) can reduced-sodium, fat-free chicken broth
¾   teaspoon dried thyme
¼   teaspoon cayenne
1   pound medium shrimp, peeled and deveined

1. Melt the butter in a Dutch oven over medium heat. Add the onion, bell pepper, celery, and garlic. Cook, stirring occasionally, until softened, 7–8 minutes. Add the kielbasa and cook, stirring, 3 minutes longer.

2. Add the rice and cook, stirring frequently, until lightly toasted, about 2 minutes. Add the tomatoes and their liquid, the broth, thyme, and cayenne; bring to a boil. Reduce the heat and simmer, covered, until the rice is tender, about 30 minutes.

3. Add the shrimp to the mixture and cook until just opaque in the center and all the liquid has been absorbed, 5–7 minutes longer.

PER SERVING (1⅓ cups): 338 Cal, 6 g Fat, 2 g Sat Fat, 93 mg Chol, 718 mg Sod, 51 g Carb, 3 g Fib, 20 g Prot, 87 mg Calc. *POINTS:* 7.

Shrimp Quesadillas

Here's a family-friendly solution when you need to have dinner on the table fast. For an even speedier alternative, buy precooked shrimp.

MAKES 4 SERVINGS

¾ pound large shrimp, peeled and deveined

½ teaspoon salt

1 small onion, thinly sliced

1 garlic clove, minced

1 jalapeño pepper, seeded and finely chopped (wear gloves to prevent irritation)

½ teaspoon ground cumin

½ pound fresh white mushrooms, sliced

1 tablespoon chopped fresh cilantro

4 (8-inch) fat-free flour tortillas

1 cup (4 ounces) reduced-fat shredded Monterey Jack cheese

1. Spray a large nonstick skillet with nonstick spray and set over medium-high heat. Season the shrimp with ¼ teaspoon of the salt and add to the skillet. Cook, turning occasionally, until just opaque in the center, about 3 minutes. Transfer to a plate and set aside.

2. Spray the same skillet with nonstick spray and set over medium-high heat. Add the onion, garlic, jalapeño pepper, cumin, and the remaining ¼ teaspoon salt. Cook, stirring occasionally, until fragrant, about 1 minute. Stir in the mushrooms and cook, stirring frequently, until softened, 3–5 minutes. Remove from the heat, then stir in the shrimp and cilantro.

3. Place a tortilla on a work surface. Top half the tortilla with 2 tablespoons of the cheese, one-fourth of the shrimp mixture, then 2 tablespoons more cheese. Fold the top half of the tortilla over the filling to form a semicircle, lightly pressing the edges to seal. Repeat with the remaining ingredients, making 4 quesadillas.

4. Wipe the skillet clean, spray with nonstick spray, and set over medium heat. Add 2 quesadillas and cook until the cheese melts and the outsides of the tortillas are lightly browned, about 4 minutes on each side. Transfer the quesadillas to a plate and keep warm. Repeat with the remaining 2 quesadillas.

PER SERVING (1 quesadilla): 263 Cal, 6 g Fat, 3 g Sat Fat, 95 mg Chol, 739 mg Sod, 30 g Carb, 3 g Fib, 22 g Prot, 288 mg Calc. *POINTS: 5.*

tip To make this recipe ahead, simply cook the filling as directed, let cool to room temperature, then refrigerate overnight in an airtight container. You can then assemble the quesadillas without cooking them, keep them covered with plastic wrap in the refrigerator for up to 3 hours, and cook them when you're ready.

Hoisin-Glazed Scallops

The sweet, rich flavor of scallops lends a great deal to the success of this dish. The hoisin sauce (made from soybeans, garlic, chili peppers, and sweet spices), mixed with honey, makes a perfect complementary sauce.

⅓ cup bottled hoisin sauce

2 teaspoons honey

3 tablespoons water

1 tablespoon peanut or canola oil

1 pound sea scallops (16–18)

2 teaspoons grated peeled fresh ginger

2 garlic cloves, minced

1 (12-ounce) bag fresh vegetables for stir-fry (broccoli, snow peas, baby carrots)

1 (8-ounce) can sliced water chestnuts, drained

3 scallions, chopped

2 cups hot cooked brown rice

MAKES 4 SERVINGS

1. Combine the hoisin sauce, honey, and water in a small bowl, set aside.

2. Heat 1 teaspoon of the oil in a large nonstick skillet or wok over medium-high heat until a drop of water sizzles. Add the scallops and stir-fry until just opaque in the center, about 5 minutes. Transfer the scallops to a plate and set aside.

3. Heat the remaining 2 teaspoons oil in the same skillet over medium-high heat. Add ginger and garlic; stir-fry until fragrant, about 30 seconds. Add the vegetables and water chestnuts; stir-fry until the vegetables are crisp-tender, 2–3 minutes. Add the hoisin sauce mixture and cook, stirring constantly, about 1 minute. Add the scallops and scallions; cook, stirring constantly, until heated through, about 1 minute. Serve with the rice.

PER SERVING (1 cup scallop and vegetable mixture and ½ cup rice): 323 Cal, 6 g Fat, 1 g Sat Fat, 23 mg Chol, 226 mg Sod, 46 g Carb, 6 g Fib, 23 g Prot, 159 mg Calc. *POINTS: 6.*

Vietnamese Scallop Fried Rice

This recipe uses fish sauce, which is the Vietnamese equivalent of soy sauce. If you are unable to find it, substitute an equal amount of reduced-sodium soy sauce. We call for cold cooked rice (preferably one day old) when making fried-rice recipes, because the cold rice is drier than freshly cooked rice and this helps keep the rice grains separate.

MAKES 6 SERVINGS

3 tablespoons Asian fish sauce (nam pla)
2 teaspoons rice vinegar
2 teaspoons sugar
¼ teaspoon crushed red pepper
4 teaspoons canola oil
1 pound sea scallops
3 large eggs, lightly beaten
4 scallions, cut into ¼-inch pieces
1 tablespoon minced peeled fresh ginger
1 (10-ounce) package frozen peas and carrots
4 cups cold cooked rice
3 tablespoons chopped fresh cilantro

1. Combine the fish sauce, vinegar, sugar, and crushed red pepper in a small bowl; set aside.
2. Heat 1 teaspoon of the oil in a large nonstick skillet over medium-high heat. Add the scallops and cook until lightly browned, 2–3 minutes on each side. Transfer to a plate.
3. Heat another 1 teaspoon of the oil in the skillet, then add the eggs. Cook, stirring occasionally, until the eggs are scrambled and cooked through, about 2 minutes. Transfer the eggs to the plate with the scallops.
4. Heat the remaining 2 teaspoons oil in the skillet, then add the scallions and ginger. Cook, stirring, until fragrant, about 30 seconds. Add the peas and carrots; cook, stirring occasionally, until hot, 3–4 minutes. Stir in the rice and fish sauce mixture. Cook, stirring often, until heated through, 3–4 minutes. Add the scallops and eggs; cook until heated through, about 1 minute. Remove from the heat, then stir in the cilantro.

PER SERVING (1⅓ cups): 300 Cal, 7 g Fat, 1 g Sat Fat, 121 mg Chol, 538 mg Sod, 40 g Carb, 2 g Fib, 19 g Prot, 97 mg Calc. *POINTS:* 6.

Cioppino Stew

Cioppino is the West Coast's answer to Provence's bouillabaisse. Created by San Francisco's Italian immigrant population, this delectable seafood stew is made with a base of fresh fish, shellfish, tomatoes, onions, and garlic—just as bouillabaisse is.

1 tablespoon olive oil

1 large onion, chopped

2 garlic cloves, minced

¼ teaspoon crushed red pepper

2 assorted-color bell peppers, seeded and chopped

2 tablespoons tomato paste

1 cup dry white wine

1¼ pounds small red potatoes, quartered

2 (14½-ounce) cans Italian-seasoned diced tomatoes

1 (8-ounce) bottle clam juice

½ cup water

18 littleneck clams, scrubbed

¾ pound cod fillet, cut into 2-inch pieces

¾ pound large shrimp, peeled and deveined

¾ pound sea scallops

¼ cup chopped fresh basil

MAKES 6 SERVINGS

1. Heat the oil in a large nonstick pot over medium-high heat. Add the onion, garlic, and crushed red pepper; cook, stirring frequently, until the onions are softened, 4–5 minutes. Add the bell peppers and tomato paste; cook, stirring, 1 minute. Stir in the wine; bring to a boil. Cook rapidly until the mixture is reduced by one-third, about 4 minutes.

2. Stir in the potatoes, tomatoes, clam juice, and water; bring to a boil. Reduce the heat and simmer, covered, until the potatoes are just tender, about 30 minutes.

3. Add the clams to the pot and simmer, covered, until they open, 12–15 minutes. Discard any clams that do not open. Transfer the clams to 6 serving bowls; cover with foil to keep warm.

4. Stir the cod, shrimp, and scallops into the pot and return to a simmer. Simmer, covered, until the fish is just opaque in the center, 7–8 minutes. Ladle the stew into the bowls over the clams, then sprinkle with the basil.

PER SERVING (2 cups): 322 Cal, 5 g Fat, 1 g Sat Fat, 109 mg Chol, 750 mg Sod, 37 g Carb, 4 g Fib, 33 g Prot, 139 mg Calc. *POINTS: 6.*

tip To make this ahead, cook the recipe through step 2, let it cool to room temperature and store in the refrigerator overnight or freeze it for up to one month. When ready to use, heat the broth to a simmer, then proceed from step 3.

Seafood Pot-au-Feu

Pot-au-feu, literally meaning "pot on the fire," is a French dish of meat and vegetables, simmered in water to create a rich broth. We've taken liberties with this dish to create a light and flavorful seafood stew, using clam juice and chicken broth to maximize the flavor.

MAKES 6 SERVINGS

2 (8-ounce) bottles clam juice

2 cups low-sodium chicken or vegetable broth

½ cup dry white wine

2 carrots, cut into matchstick-thin strips

2 celery stalks, cut into matchstick-thin strips

1 small fennel bulb, cored and cut into matchstick-thin strips

1 medium white turnip, peeled and cut into matchstick-thin strips

1 small onion, finely chopped

1 (¾-pound) salmon fillet, skinned and cut into 6 pieces

½ pound large shrimp, peeled and deveined

½ pound squid bodies, cut into ½-inch rings

6 ounces French baguette, cut into 6 slices

1. Bring the clam juice, chicken broth, wine, carrots, celery, fennel, turnip, and onion to a boil in a Dutch oven. Reduce the heat and simmer, covered, until the vegetables are tender, 5–6 minutes.

2. Add the salmon and shrimp; return to a simmer. Cover and gently poach about 5 minutes. Add the squid and poach until the salmon, shrimp, and squid are just opaque in the center, 2–3 minutes longer. Remove from the heat. Ladle evenly into 6 bowls. Serve with the baguette slices.

PER SERVING (1⅓ cups and 1 baguette slice): 245 Cal, 5 g Fat, 1 g Sat Fat, 174 mg Chol, 485 mg Sod, 24 g Carb, 3 g Fib, 25 g Prot, 99 mg Calc. *POINTS: 5.*

tip Save the feathery green leaves—sometimes called fronds—from the fennel bulb to garnish the dish.

Seafood Tagine

In Morocco, many stew-like dishes are cooked in an earthenware vessel called a tagine. Although we cook this dish in a Dutch oven, it uses many of the same sweet spices and citrus flavors that define what a tagine stew is.

MAKES 4 SERVINGS

2 teaspoons olive oil

2 onions, chopped

1 red bell pepper, seeded and chopped

1 jalapeño pepper, seeded and chopped (wear gloves to prevent irritation)

3 garlic cloves, minced

½ teaspoon ground ginger

½ teaspoon cinnamon

¼ teaspoon saffron threads

1 (8-ounce) bottle clam juice

¼ cup fresh lemon juice

¾ teaspoon salt

¼ teaspoon freshly ground pepper

1 pound tilapia fillet, cut into 1 x 2-inch strips

¾ pound extra-large shrimp, peeled and deveined

⅓ cup chopped fresh cilantro

10 pitted kalamata olives, halved

2 cups hot cooked couscous

1. Heat the oil in a Dutch oven over medium-high heat. Add the onions, bell pepper, jalapeño pepper, garlic, ginger, cinnamon, and saffron. Cook, stirring frequently, until the vegetables begin to soften, 4–5 minutes.

2. Add the clam juice, lemon juice, salt, and pepper to the pot; bring to a boil. Reduce the heat and simmer, covered, until the vegetables are completely softened, about 10 minutes.

3. Add the tilapia and shrimp to the pot; simmer, covered, until just opaque in the center, 6–7 minutes. Remove from the heat, then stir in the cilantro and olives. Serve over the couscous.

PER SERVING (1¼ cups fish mixture and ½ cup couscous): 317 Cal, 6 g Fat, 1 g Sat Fat, 142 mg Chol, 840 mg Sod, 31 g Carb, 4 g Fib, 35 g Prot, 83 mg Calc. *POINTS: 6.*

Grilled Shellfish Bake

If you can't get to the beach to dig a pit for your next seafood bake, don't fret: Our easy technique requires only a backyard grill and pan.

¾ pound small red
   potatoes, scrubbed
   and quartered
4 ears fresh corn,
   shucked and each cut
   into thirds
2 medium red onions,
   each cut into 8 wedges
10 garlic cloves
8 parsley sprigs
1 (8-ounce) bottle clam
   juice
4 sprigs fresh thyme or
   ½ teaspoon dried
¼ cup fresh lemon juice
1 tablespoon extra-virgin
   olive oil
½ teaspoon salt
¼ teaspoon freshly
   ground pepper
24 littleneck clams,
   scrubbed
2 pounds mussels,
   scrubbed and debearded
1 pound extra-large
   shrimp, unpeeled
1 bunch asparagus,
   tough ends trimmed

MAKES 6 SERVINGS

1. Prepare the grill.
2. Combine the potatoes, corn, onions, garlic, parsley, clam juice, thyme, lemon juice, oil, salt, and pepper in a large, deep disposable aluminum pan. Cover the pan tightly with foil and place on the grill. Close the grill cover and cook 25 minutes.
3. Remove the pan from the grill and carefully remove the foil. Place the clams and mussels in a single layer on top of the potato mixture. Reseal the pan with foil and return to the grill. Close the grill cover and cook 10 minutes.
4. Remove the pan from the grill and carefully remove the foil. Add the shrimp and asparagus, reseal the pan with foil, and return to the grill. Close the grill cover and cook until the clams and mussels open, the shrimp are just opaque in the center, and the vegetables are tender, 10–15 minutes longer. Discard any clams or mussels that do not open.

PER SERVING (⅙ of seafood and vegetable mixture): 265 Cal, 5 g Fat, 1 g Sat Fat, 103 mg Chol, 447 mg Sod, 34 g Carb, 4 g Fib, 24 g Prot, 92 mg Calc. *POINTS*: 5.

tip When buying clams and mussels, look for tightly closed shells or shells that close when lightly tapped. Discard any with shells that remain open. To help rid the clams and mussels of any sand they may have in their shells, place them in a large bowl with cold water and ¼ cup of cornmeal. Refrigerate 30 minutes, pour off the water, then scrub them with a stiff brush under cold running water.

Vegetarian Entrées

Tofu, bean, and cheese favorites

Thai Curry Stir-fry

If you're looking for a recipe to hook someone on tofu, this one—with its rich, spicy flavors and crunchy textures—might just be it. Tofu is available in cakes of firm, extra-firm, soft, and silken textures. Generally, we use firm and extra-firm for making stir-fries, while soft and silken tofu are good in soups, sauces, and smoothies. Purple basil is frequently used in Thai cooking. If you can't find it, substitute fresh green basil.

MAKES 6 SERVINGS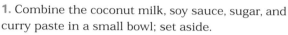

1	cup light coconut milk
1	tablespoon reduced-sodium soy sauce
1	tablespoon packed brown sugar
1	teaspoon Thai red curry paste
2	teaspoons canola oil
2	garlic cloves, finely chopped
1	tablespoon minced peeled fresh ginger
2	red bell peppers, seeded and cut into 1-inch pieces
6	scallions, cut into 2-inch pieces
¾	pound bok choy, chopped (about 5 cups)
¼	pound fresh snow peas
1	(7-ounce) can baby corn, drained
½	pound firm tofu, cut into 1-inch cubes
¼	cup chopped fresh purple basil
2	cups hot cooked brown rice

1. Combine the coconut milk, soy sauce, sugar, and curry paste in a small bowl; set aside.

2. Heat the oil in a large nonstick skillet over medium-high heat. Add the garlic and ginger. Cook, stirring frequently, until fragrant, about 30 seconds. Add the bell peppers and scallions; cook, stirring occasionally, until crisp-tender, about 5 minutes. Stir in the bok choy and cook until tender, about 5 minutes.

3. Add the snow peas, corn, and coconut-milk mixture to the skillet; bring to a boil. Reduce the heat and simmer, uncovered, until the snow peas begin to turn bright green, about 2 minutes. Gently stir in the tofu and basil; cook until heated through, about 3 minutes. Serve with the rice.

PER SERVING (1⅓ cups stir-fry and ⅓ cup rice): 229 Cal, 9 g Fat, 3 g Sat Fat, 0 mg Chol, 231 mg Sod, 29 g Carb, 4 g Fib, 11 g Prot, 174 mg Calc. *POINTS: 5.*

Thai Curry Stir-fry

Hot-and-Sour Tofu Stew

Tofu (soybean curd) provides high-quality protein, and though it contains a fair amount of fat, it has very little saturated fat and no cholesterol. Wood-ear mushrooms, also known as cloud-ear mushrooms, can be found in the produce department of most supermarkets. For a heartier meal, stir 1½ cups of cooked rice into the stew and add an extra *2 POINTS* per serving.

MAKES 3 SERVINGS

1 (¾-ounce) package dried wood-ear mushrooms
2 teaspoons peanut oil
4 scallions, chopped
2 garlic cloves, minced
1 teaspoon minced peeled fresh ginger
½ pound fresh shiitake mushrooms, stems discarded, caps sliced
2 carrots, cut into matchstick-thin strips
4 cups reduced-sodium vegetable broth
3 tablespoons rice vinegar
2 tablespoons reduced-sodium soy sauce
1 teaspoon Asian (dark) sesame oil
½ pound reduced-fat soft tofu, drained and cut into½-inch cubes
¼ teaspoon crushed red pepper
1 (6-ounce) bag fresh baby spinach, chopped
2 tablespoons cornstarch
1 large egg

1. Combine the dried mushrooms with enough hot water to cover by about 2 inches in a bowl. Let stand 15 minutes, then drain and coarsely chop.

2. Meanwhile, heat the peanut oil in a large nonstick saucepan over medium heat. Add the scallions, garlic, and ginger. Cook, stirring frequently, until fragrant and the scallions just begin to wilt, about 30 seconds. Add the shiitake mushrooms and carrots. Cook, stirring, until the vegetables are tender, about 6 minutes. Stir in the broth, vinegar, soy sauce, and sesame oil; bring to a boil. Add the drained dried mushrooms, tofu, and crushed red pepper. Reduce the heat and simmer about 6 minutes. Stir in the spinach and cook until it just begins to wilt, about 1 minute.

3. Combine the cornstarch and 3 tablespoons water in a small bowl; stir in about ¼ cup of the hot liquid, then return to the pan. Cook, stirring constantly, until the mixture bubbles and thickens slightly, about 1 minute; remove from the heat. Lightly beat the egg with 1 tablespoon water; slowly pour in a stream into the stew while stirring constantly, until the egg sets in shreds. Serve at once.

PER SERVING (2½ cups): 212 Cal, 8 g Fat, 2 g Sat Fat, 71 mg Chol, 852 mg Sod, 26 g Carb, 6 g Fib, 14 g Prot, 193 mg Calc. *POINTS: 4.*

Spicy Tofu and Eggplant Kebabs

This Asian-inspired marinade gets its zesty flavor from chili sauce, pickled ginger, and chili paste—look for them in jars in the ethnic section of the supermarket. Be sure to drain the tofu well and pat dry with paper towels before cutting into cubes. This helps the tofu brown nicely when being broiled.

MAKES 4 SERVINGS

¼ cup rice wine

2 tablespoons bottled hoisin sauce

2 tablespoons reduced-sodium soy sauce

2 tablespoons chili sauce

1 tablespoon sugar

1 tablespoon pickled ginger, finely chopped

1 teaspoon chili paste

1 teaspoon Asian (dark) sesame oil

½ pound extra-firm tofu, cut into 12 cubes

½ pound eggplant, unpeeled and cut into 12 chunks

1 red bell pepper, seeded and cut into 12 pieces

8 medium fresh white mushrooms

4 scallions, each cut in thirds

2 cups hot cooked rice

1. Combine the rice wine, hoisin sauce, soy sauce, chili sauce, sugar, ginger, chili paste, and sesame oil in an extra-large zip-close plastic bag. Add tofu, eggplant, bell pepper, mushrooms, and scallions. Squeeze out the air and seal the bag; turn to coat the tofu and vegetables. Refrigerate, turning the bag occasionally, at least 20 minutes or up to 8 hours.

2. Spray the broiler pan with nonstick spray; preheat the broiler.

3. Thread 3 tofu pieces, 3 eggplant pieces, 3 bell pepper pieces, 2 mushrooms, and 3 scallion pieces onto each of 4 (12-inch) metal skewers, alternating the ingredients. Place the skewers on the boiler pan.

4. Broil the skewers 4 inches from the heat, carefully turning at least once, and brushing occasionally with the marinade, until the vegetables are tender and the tofu is lightly browned, 8–10 minutes. Serve with the rice.

PER SERVING (1 kebab and ½ cup rice): 252 Cal, 7 g Fat, 1 g Sat Fat, 0 mg Chol, 214 mg Sod, 37 g Carb, 5 g Fib, 14 g Prot, 151 mg Calc. *POINTS: 5.*

Tempeh, Mushroom, and Sweet Onion Chili

Tempeh—the soyfood that most resembles meat in texture—is a fermented soybean cake that is very high in protein. It is available in 8-ounce vacuum-sealed packages and can be found in most supermarkets next to the tofu, or in health-food stores. It makes a great substitute for ground beef in this perfect-for-a-blustery-day chili.

1 (3.5-ounce) package dried porcini mushrooms
1 tablespoon olive oil
2 Vidalia or other large sweet onions, chopped
1 green bell pepper, seeded and chopped
2 garlic cloves, chopped
3 tablespoons chili powder
2 teaspoons ground cumin
1 teaspoon cinnamon
¾ pound fresh shiitake mushrooms, stems discarded, caps sliced
1 (8-ounce) package tempeh, crumbled
1 (14-ounce) can peeled tomatoes, broken up
2 cups vegetable broth
1 (15½-ounce) can cannellini (white kidney) beans, rinsed and drained
6 tablespoons shredded reduced-fat Monterey Jack cheese
½ cup chopped scallions

MAKES 6 SERVINGS

1. Combine the dried mushrooms with enough boiling water to cover by about 2 inches in a small bowl. Let stand 15 minutes, then drain (reserving 1 cup of the liquid) and coarsely chop the mushrooms.
2. Meanwhile, heat the oil in a large nonstick saucepan over medium-high heat. Add the onion, bell pepper, and garlic. Cook, stirring occasionally, until golden, about 8 minutes. Stir in the chili powder, cumin, and cinnamon. Cook, stirring constantly, until fragrant, about 1 minute. Add the shiitake mushrooms and cook, stirring occasionally, until tender, about 8 minutes.
3. Stir the tempeh, tomatoes, broth, the reconstituted dried mushrooms, and their reserved liquid into the saucepan; bring to a boil. Reduce the heat and simmer, covered, until the flavors are blended and the mixture thickens slightly, about 45 minutes.
4. Add the beans and cook, stirring occasionally, until heated through, about 3 minutes. Serve the chili in bowls, sprinkled with the cheese and scallions.

PER SERVING (1½ cups chili and 1 tablespoon cheese): 247 Cal, 8 g Fat, 2 g Sat Fat, 4 mg Chol, 695 mg Sod, 33 g Carb, 11 g Fib, 17 g Prot, 163 mg Calc. *POINTS: 5.*

"Soysage" and Potato Stew

If meatless soy products are new to you, you are in for a treat. Not only are these meatless sausages high in protein, the texture and flavor is almost identical to Italian sausage—without all the saturated fat.

MAKES 4 SERVINGS

1 teaspoon olive oil
1 (10-ounce) package frozen Italian meatless sausage links, thawed and each cut diagonally into 4 pieces
1 onion, thinly sliced
½ fennel bulb, cored and thinly sliced
3 plum tomatoes, chopped
5 kalamata olives, pitted and chopped
1 tablespoon chopped fresh thyme, or 1 teaspoon dried
¼ cup dry white wine
2 baking potatoes, peeled and cut into 1-inch chunks
2 cups reduced-sodium vegetable broth
1 bay leaf
2 tablespoons all-purpose flour
3 tablespoons cold water

1. Heat ½ teaspoon of the oil in a large nonstick Dutch oven over medium-high heat. Add the meatless sausage and cook, turning occasionally, until browned, about 5 minutes; transfer to a bowl.

2. Heat the remaining ½ teaspoon oil in the same Dutch oven. Add the onion and fennel. Cook, stirring frequently, until golden, 8–10 minutes. Add the tomatoes, olives, and thyme. Cook, stirring occasionally, until the tomatoes are softened, about 10 minutes. Stir in the wine and cook over high heat until the wine evaporates, about 3 minutes.

3. Add the potatoes, broth, bay leaf, and the browned meatless sausage to the Dutch oven; bring to a boil. Reduce the heat and simmer, covered, until the potatoes are tender, about 20 minutes.

4. Combine the flour and water in a small bowl until smooth; stir in about ½ cup of the hot liquid from the Dutch oven until blended. Stir the flour mixture into the simmering stew and cook, stirring constantly, until the mixture bubbles and thickens, about 3 minutes. Discard the bay leaf.

PER SERVING (1⅓ cups): 301 Cal, 15 g Fat, 2 g Sat Fat, 0 mg Chol, 823 mg Sod, 31 g Carb, 5 g Fib, 16 g Prot, 84 mg Calc. *POINTS*: 6.

tip For added zest, sprinkle the stew with a basil gremolada topping made from ¼ cup chopped fresh basil, 1 tablespoon grated lemon zest, and 2 minced garlic cloves. Chop the basil at the very last minute to keep it from darkening. To save time, buy pitted kalamata olives from the supermarket's salad bar.

Tempeh Chili Verde

Tempeh Chili Verde

Tomatillos (green tomatoes), chipotle chiles (smoked jalapeño peppers), and salsa verde (green salsa) are available in most supermarkets today, making it a cinch to produce this authentically flavored chili. You'll find tomatillos in the produce section and chipotle chiles in adobo sauce in cans in the ethnic section. Green salsa gives a unique flavor, so avoid substituting red salsa here.

MAKES 4 SERVINGS

2   teaspoons olive oil
1   onion, chopped
1   (8-ounce) package
    tempeh (fermented
    soybean cake)
1   tablespoon ground
    cumin
1   teaspoon sugar
¾   teaspoon salt
4   fresh tomatillos,
    husks removed,
    quartered
6   scallions, chopped
1   green bell pepper,
    seeded and quartered
½   cup cilantro leaves
1   (4-ounce) can chopped
    green chiles
3   garlic cloves
1   chipotle chile en adobo
1¾ cups water
1   cup mild or medium
    green salsa
6   tablespoons shredded
    reduced-fat cheddar
    cheese
6   tablespoons light sour
    cream
Cilantro sprigs, for
    garnish

1. Heat the oil in a large saucepan over medium-high heat. Add the onion and crumble the tempeh into the pan. Cook, stirring frequently, until browned, about 6 minutes. Stir in the cumin, sugar, and salt. Cook until fragrant, about 1 minute.
2. Meanwhile, puree the tomatillos, scallions, bell pepper, cilantro leaves, green chiles, garlic, and chipotle chile in a food processor.
3. Stir the tomatillo mixture, the water, and salsa into the saucepan; bring to a boil. Reduce the heat and simmer, covered, until the flavors are blended and the chili thickens slightly, about 40 minutes.
4. Serve the chili in bowls, topped with the cheese, sour cream, and cilantro sprigs.

PER SERVING (2 cups chili and 1½ tablespoons each cheese and sour cream): 262 Cal, 11 g Fat, 3 g Sat Fat, 13 mg Chol, 1062 mg Sod, 28 g Carb, 10 g Fib, 18 g Prot, 241 mg Calc. *POINTS: 5.*

White Lasagna

Refrigerated and frozen soymeats come in a variety of forms, from chicken-like cutlets to "meatballs" to "sausage" links and patties. They need only brief cooking and offer good flavor and high protein with little or no fat. If you can't find the particular sausage we call for in this recipe, any other soy-based sausage will do. Oven-ready, no-boil lasagna noodles are widely available and are a boon for making speedy lasagnas.

MAKES 8 SERVINGS

1 (26-ounce) can condensed fat-free cream of mushroom soup
1 cup fat-free milk
1 cup water
1 (10-ounce) package frozen chopped spinach, thawed and squeezed dry
½ (14-ounce) package frozen fat-free soy sausage, thawed and crumbled
1 cup fat-free ricotta cheese
1 cup shredded part-skim mozzarella cheese
9 oven-ready no-boil lasagna noodles
8 whole flat-leaf parsley leaves

1. Preheat the oven to 375°F. Spray a 9 x 13-inch baking pan with nonstick spray.
2. To make the sauce, whisk together the mushroom soup, milk, and water in a large bowl; set aside.
3. Combine the spinach, sausage, ricotta, mozzarella, and 1 cup of the sauce in a large bowl.
4. Spoon 1 cup of the remaining sauce into the bottom of the baking dish. Arrange 3 of the lasagna noodles over the sauce. Spoon half of the spinach mixture over the noodles; top with one-third of the remaining sauce. Repeat layering once with the noodles, spinach mixture, and sauce. Top with the remaining noodles and remaining sauce.
5. Arrange parsley leaves on the sauce in a decorative pattern. Cover the lasagna loosely with foil and bake until hot and bubbly, about 50 minutes. Let the lasagna stand about 10 minutes before serving.

PER SERVING (⅛ of lasagna): 240 Cal, 3 g Fat, 2 g Sat Fat, 11 mg Chol, 1100 mg Sod, 33 g Carb, 2 g Fib, 14 g Prot, 256 mg Calc. *POINTS: 5.*

Caraway Cabbage with "Sausage" and Noodles

Inspired by German cuisine, this hearty skillet dinner is easy to make. The crinkle-leafed savoy cabbage is mellow and goes well with the aromatic caraway and tart Granny Smith apple. The flavor of the soy sausage links is so good, the meat-eater in the family won't be able to tell the difference. Yogurt spread comes in tubs and can be found near the butter in the supermarket.

MAKES 6 SERVINGS

2 teaspoons canola oil

½ (11.2-ounce) package frozen soy sausage links (4 links), thawed and cut into 1½-inch chunks

1 Granny Smith apple, peeled, cored, and cut into 1-inch chunks

1 onion, chopped

½ pound savoy cabbage, thinly sliced (about 4 cups)

1 cup vegetable broth

2 teaspoons caraway seeds

4 cups cooked broad no-yolk noodles (about ½ pound dry)

2 tablespoons reduced-calorie yogurt spread

½ teaspoon salt

½ teaspoon freshly ground pepper

1. Heat the oil in a large nonstick skillet over medium-high heat. Add soy sausage, apple, and onion. Cook, stirring occasionally, until browned, about 8 minutes.
2. Stir the cabbage, broth, and caraway seeds into the skillet; bring to a boil. Reduce the heat and simmer, covered, until the cabbage is very tender and the liquid is almost evaporated, about 25 minutes.
3. Stir the noodles, yogurt spread, salt, and pepper into the skillet. Cook over low heat, stirring occasionally, until the noodles are heated through, about 3 minutes. Serve at once.

PER SERVING (1⅓ cups): 271 Cal, 10 g Fat, 2 g Sat Fat, 3 mg Chol, 638 mg Sod, 37 g Carb, 4 g Fib, 11 g Prot, 59 mg Calc. *POINTS: 5.*

Curried Eggplant and Chickpea Stew with Tangy Yogurt Sauce

The spicy Middle Eastern flavors in this stew are tamed by a cool and refreshing yogurt sauce. If you prefer, serve it with basmati or jasmine rice instead of the brown rice.

MAKES 4 SERVINGS

2   teaspoons olive oil
2   garlic cloves, chopped
1   tablespoon minced peeled fresh ginger
2   bell peppers, seeded and chopped
1   onion, chopped
1   tablespoon curry powder
2   teaspoons cumin
1   teaspoon cinnamon
⅛   teaspoon cayenne
1   (1¼-pound) eggplant, unpeeled and cut into 1-inch cubes
1   (19-ounce) can chickpeas, drained
2   cups reduced-sodium vegetable broth
1   cup canned diced tomatoes, drained
½   teaspoon salt
¾   teaspoon sugar
¼   cup chopped cilantro
2   cups cooked brown rice

Tangy Yogurt Sauce:
1   (8-ounce) container plain fat-free yogurt
1   teaspoon lemon juice
1   garlic clove, minced
½   teaspoon ground cumin

1. Heat the oil in a large nonstick saucepan over medium-high heat. Add the garlic and ginger. Cook, stirring constantly, until fragrant, about 30 seconds. Add the bell peppers and onion. Cook, stirring occasionally, until softened, about 8 minutes. Add the curry powder, cumin, cinnamon, and cayenne; cook, stirring, until fragrant, about 1 minute. Add the eggplant and cook until slightly softened, about 10 minutes.

2. Stir the chickpeas, broth, tomatoes, salt, and sugar into the saucepan; bring to a boil. Reduce the heat and simmer, covered, until the flavors are blended, about 30 minutes. Uncover and cook until the mixture thickens slightly, about 10 minutes longer. Remove from the heat and stir in the cilantro.

3. Meanwhile, to prepare the yogurt sauce, whisk together the yogurt, mint, lemon juice, garlic, and cumin in a medium bowl.

4. Serve the stew with the rice and yogurt sauce.

PER SERVING (1½ cups stew, ½ cup rice, and ¼ cup sauce): 399 Cal, 7 g Fat, 1 g Sat Fat, 1 mg Chol, 783 mg Sod, 72 g Carb, 13 g Fib, 17 g Prot, 235 mg Calc. *POINTS: 8.*

tip In summertime, when fresh mint is abundant, add a tablespoon or two to the yogurt sauce.

Kale, Sweet Potato, and Chickpea Ragout

Kale is a powerhouse of vitamins and minerals and a valuable addition to any healthy diet. This savory stew is perfect for supper on a cold winter's night.

2 teaspoons olive oil

1 onion, chopped

1 tablespoon grated peeled fresh ginger

1 garlic clove, finely chopped

½ teaspoon cinnamon

½ teaspoon ground cumin

¼ teaspoon cayenne

1½ cups baby carrots

1 sweet potato (about ¾ pound), peeled and cut into 1-inch chunks

1 (14-ounce) can vegetable broth

½ cup orange juice

2 teaspoons honey

½ cup dried currants

1 bunch kale (about ¾ pound), tough stems removed, leaves coarsely chopped

1 (15½-ounce) can chickpeas (garbanzo beans), rinsed and drained

½ teaspoon salt

2 cups hot cooked couscous

4 teaspoons toasted slivered almonds

MAKES 6 SERVINGS

1. Heat the oil in a nonstick Dutch oven over medium-high heat. Add the onion and cook, stirring frequently, until golden, about 8 minutes. Add the ginger, garlic, cinnamon, cumin, and cayenne. Cook, stirring constantly, until fragrant, about 1 minute.

2. Stir the carrots, sweet potato, broth, orange juice, honey, and currants into the Dutch oven; bring to a boil. Reduce the heat and simmer, covered, until the vegetables are almost tender, about 10 minutes.

3. Stir the kale, chickpeas, and salt into the Dutch oven; bring to boil, stirring occasionally, until the kale wilts. Reduce the heat and simmer, covered, until the kale and vegetables are tender, about 15 minutes. Serve the stew with the couscous and sprinkle with the almonds.

PER SERVING (1 cup stew, ⅓ cup couscous, and scant teaspoon almonds): 304 Cal, 4 g Fat, 1 g Sat Fat, 0 mg Chol, 611 mg Sod, 60 g Carb, 8 g Fib, 10 g Prot, 124 mg Calc. *POINTS*: 6.

tip For an easy kale side dish, first remove the kale's tough stems, rinse, then chop the leaves. Next, cook it in a base of sautéed garlic and onions, a touch of broth, and a few raisins. Cook the kale long enough to tenderize it, at least 15 minutes.

Tamale Casserole

Want an easy weeknight casserole that even the kids can throw together? This is it. To make it even easier—especially if your kids don't like spicy dishes—leave out the chipotle chiles and use a can of Mexican-style stewed tomatoes instead of the regular stewed tomatoes. While it bakes, someone can easily put a bagged salad in a bowl and toss it with a dash of olive oil, a squeeze of fresh lime juice, and a shake of salt and pepper.

MAKES 4 SERVINGS

1   (16-ounce) can fat-free refried beans
6   scallions, finely chopped
¼   cup fat-free sour cream
2   tablespoons chopped fresh cilantro
1   chipotle chile en adobo, chopped (about 2 teaspoons)
1   (14½-ounce can) stewed tomatoes, broken up
1   (16-ounce) tube refrigerated fat-free plain polenta, cut into 12 rounds
¾   cup shredded reduced-fat Monterey Jack cheese
3   tablespoons sliced pitted ripe olives

1. Preheat the oven to 375°F. Spray a 9 x 13-inch baking pan with nonstick spray.
2. Combine the beans, scallions, sour cream, cilantro, and chipotle in a medium bowl; set aside.
3. Spoon half of the stewed tomatoes into the bottom of the pan. Arrange the polenta rounds in one layer over the sauce. Spoon the bean mixture on top of each round. Top with the remaining stewed tomatoes. Sprinkle with the cheese and olives. Bake, uncovered, until heated through and the cheese melts, about 25 minutes. Let stand 5 minutes before serving.

PER SERVING (¼ of casserole): 264 Cal, 5 g Fat, 3 g Sat Fat, 12 mg Chol, 1078 mg Sod, 40 g Carb, 9 g Fib, 15 g Prot, 278 mg Calc. *POINTS: 5.*

tip Use kitchen scissors or a long, sharp knife to break up the tomatoes right in the can.

Vegetable and Black-Bean Paella

If you have leftovers, refrigerate them overnight (or for up to three nights), then shape into patties for a delicious veggie burger. Simply brush the patties lightly with oil, top with a slice of reduced-fat cheddar cheese, and broil. Serve on a whole-wheat roll with lettuce and tomato and you've got lunch.

2 teaspoons olive oil
1 onion, chopped
1 green bell pepper, seeded and chopped
1 tomato, chopped
2 garlic cloves, finely chopped
½ teaspoon salt
½ teaspoon freshly ground pepper
¼ cup dry white wine
1 cup short-grain white rice
2 cups vegetable broth
1 (19-ounce) can black beans, rinsed and drained
Pinch saffron threads
1 cup frozen peas
3 tablespoons pimiento strips
2 tablespoons chopped fresh parsley

MAKES 4 SERVINGS

1. Heat the oil in a large nonstick skillet over medium heat. Add the onion and bell pepper. Cook, stirring occasionally, until softened, about 8 minutes. If the mixture is too dry, add ¼ cup water, stirring, until the water evaporates, about 2 minutes.
2. Stir the tomato, garlic, salt, and pepper into the skillet. Cook, stirring occasionally, until the tomato is softened, about 6 minutes. Stir in the wine and cook until it evaporates, about 2 minutes. Add the rice, stirring until well coated. Stir in the broth, beans, and saffron; bring to a boil. Reduce the heat and simmer, covered, until all the liquid is absorbed and the rice is tender, about 20 minutes.
3. Stir in peas, pimiento, and parsley. Cook, stirring occasionally, until heated through, about 2 minutes. Serve at once.

PER SERVING (1¼ cups): 382 Cal, 3 g Fat, 1 g Sat Fat, 0 mg Chol, 1038 mg Sod, 74 g Carb, 10 g Fib, 14 g Prot, 104 mg Calc. POINTS: 7.

tip For extra texture, nutrients, and color, add 2 cups chopped fresh spinach when you add the peas.

Southern Italian Stew

Simple, inexpensive peasant fare makes a hearty, nourishing, and flavorful stew. It's a snap to put together and the kind of recipe you can easily double for a crowd or freeze half of for another day. If you're pressed for time, or fresh green beans aren't available, use a 10-ounce package of frozen cut green beans.

MAKES 4 SERVINGS

2   teaspoons olive oil
1   onion, chopped
2   garlic cloves, finely chopped
1   tomato, chopped
4   cups reduced-sodium vegetable broth
2   cups water
2   medium red potatoes, scrubbed and cut into 1-inch cubes
1   cup tubetti or elbow macaroni
½   pound fresh green beans, trimmed and cut into 1-inch pieces
1   (15½-ounce) can red kidney beans, rinsed and drained
1   (6-ounce) bag baby spinach
¼   cup grated Parmesan cheese

1. Heat the oil in a large saucepan over medium-high heat. Add the onion and garlic. Cook, stirring frequently, until softened, about 3 minutes. Add the tomato and cook, stirring, until softened, about 2 minutes.

2. Stir the broth, water, potatoes, and pasta into the saucepan; bring to a boil. Reduce the heat and simmer, covered, until the potatoes and pasta are tender, about 10 minutes. Add the green beans; return to a boil. Reduce the heat and simmer, covered, until the green beans are crisp-tender, about 5 minutes.

3. Stir the kidney beans and spinach into the saucepan. Cook, stirring occasionally, until heated through and the spinach just wilts, about 2 minutes longer. Serve with the cheese.

PER SERVING (2¼ cups stew and 1 tablespoon cheese): 354 Cal, 5 g Fat, 2 g Sat Fat, 5 mg Chol, 663 mg Sod, 63 g Carb, 9 g Fib, 15 g Prot, 197 mg Calc. *POINTS: 7.*

Mediterranean Portobello, Escarole, and Bean Toss

Vibrant with the distinctive flavors of fresh thyme and basil, this popular beans-and-greens combination comes alive. You can substitute spinach for the escarole and red kidney beans for the white—and if you like a little kick, stir in ¼ teaspoon of crushed red pepper.

MAKES 4 SERVINGS

2 teaspoons olive oil

6 ounces (4 medium) Portobello mushrooms, cleaned and coarsely chopped

1 large onion, sliced

2 plum tomatoes, chopped

2 garlic cloves, minced

¼ cup dry white wine

1 tablespoon chopped fresh thyme, or 1 teaspoon dried

1 bunch escarole (about ¾ pound), cleaned and coarsely chopped

1 (19-ounce) can cannellini (white kidney) beans, rinsed and drained

1 cup vegetable broth

¼ cup chopped fresh basil

2 cups hot cooked orzo (about 6 ounces dry)

2 tablespoons grated Parmesan cheese

1. Heat the oil in a large nonstick skillet over medium-high heat. Add the mushrooms and onion. Cook, stirring occasionally, until softened, about 8 minutes.

2. Add the tomatoes, garlic, wine, and thyme to the skillet; bring to a boil. Reduce the heat and simmer, uncovered, until the tomatoes are soft and the wine evaporates, about 5 minutes.

3. Add the escarole, beans, and broth; bring to a boil, stirring to help wilt the escarole. Reduce the heat and simmer, covered, until the escarole is just tender, about 5 minutes. Remove from the heat and stir in the basil. Serve with the orzo and sprinkle with the cheese.

PER SERVING (1 cup stew, ½ cup orzo, and ½ tablespoon cheese): 314 Cal, 5 g Fat, 1 g Sat Fat, 2 mg Chol, 551 mg Sod, 55 g Carb, 13 g Fib, 15 g Prot, 160 mg Calc. POINTS: 6.

Pasta e Fagioli

Serve this one-pot favorite with crusty Italian bread to sop up the juices—a half-ounce slice will add a *POINT*. Leftovers? No problem: It's even better reheated the next day after the flavors have had a chance to develop and the stew has thickened slightly.

MAKES 6 SERVING

- 2 teaspoons olive oil
- 1 onion, finely chopped
- 1 carrot, finely chopped
- 1 celery stalk, finely chopped
- 1 plum tomato, coarsely chopped
- 2 garlic cloves, finely chopped
- 4 cups vegetable broth
- 1 cup ditalini or elbow macaroni
- 2 (15½-ounce) cans pinto beans, rinsed and drained
- 1 (5-ounce) bag baby spinach, coarsely chopped
- 2 tablespoons grated Parmesan cheese

1. Heat the oil in a Dutch oven over medium-high heat. Add the onion, carrot, and celery. Cook, stirring frequently, until very tender, about 8 minutes. Add the tomato and garlic. Cook, stirring occasionally, until the tomato softens, about 6 minutes.

2. Stir the broth and pasta into the Dutch oven; bring to a boil. Reduce the heat to a low boil and cook, uncovered, until the pasta is tender, about 8 minutes. Stir in the beans and the spinach. Cook until the beans are heated through and the spinach begins to wilt, about 2 minutes. Serve with the cheese.

PER SERVING (1½ cups and 2 teaspoons cheese): 274 Cal, 3 g Fat, 1 g Sat Fat, 2 mg Chol, 967 mg Sod, 49 g Carb, 11 g Fib, 13 g Prot, 121 mg Calc. *POINTS: 5.*

Garlicky Broccoli and Cauliflower Pasta

Not a soup and not exactly a stew—more like pasta and vegetables in a light broth—this makes a warming winter lunch or easy-to-digest late-night supper. If you like, you can use spaghetti (break it up into 3-inch pieces) or egg noodles instead of the farfalle.

1 tablespoon olive oil

6 garlic cloves, thinly sliced

1 (14-ounce) can whole tomatoes, broken up

¼ teaspoon salt

¼ teaspoon crushed red pepper

2 (14-ounce) cans reduced-sodium vegetable broth

3 cups fresh broccoli florets

3 cups fresh cauliflower florets

2 cups (about ¼ pound) farfalle (bow tie) pasta

1 cup frozen peas

¼ cup grated Parmesan cheese

MAKES 4 SERVINGS

1. Heat the oil in a large nonstick saucepan over low heat. Add the garlic and cook, stirring occasionally, until just golden, about 2 minutes. Stir in the tomatoes, salt, and crushed red pepper; bring to a boil. Reduce the heat and simmer, uncovered, until the tomatoes have softened, about 5 minutes.

2. Stir the broth, broccoli, cauliflower, and pasta into the saucepan; return to a boil. Reduce the heat and simmer, covered, stirring occasionally, until the vegetables and pasta are tender, about 10 minutes.

3. Stir in the peas; cook until heated through, about 2 minutes. Remove from the heat and serve sprinkled with the cheese.

PER SERVING (2 cups and 1 tablespoon cheese): 296 Cal, 7 g Fat, 2 g Sat Fat, 5 mg Chol, 701 mg Sod, 48 g Carb, 8 g Fib, 13 g Prot, 183 mg Calc. POINTS: 6.

Creamy Polenta Casserole

Almost like a spoon bread but creamier, this comforting casserole takes minutes to prepare, thanks to the food processor and prepared polenta. There are many flavors of prepared polenta, such as Italian herb and wild mushroom. We recommend using plain polenta for this recipe. Serve with your favorite salsa, a few baked tortilla chips (6 chips for a *POINT*), and a green salad.

MAKES 3 SERVINGS

1 (16-ounce) tube refrigerated fat-free plain polenta, cut into 2-inch pieces

½ cup fat-free milk

1 (11-ounce) can Mexican-style corn, drained

½ cup shredded reduced-fat cheddar cheese

2 egg yolks

2 tablespoons chopped green chiles

2 tablespoons chopped fresh chives

1 teaspoon sugar

¼ teaspoon salt

4 drops hot pepper sauce

3 egg whites, at room temperature

1. Preheat the oven to 375°F. Spray a 2-quart round baking dish with nonstick spray.

2. Place the polenta and the milk in a food processor. Pulse until smooth, about 10 seconds. Transfer the polenta mixture to a large bowl. Stir in the corn, cheese, egg yolks, chiles, chives, sugar, salt, and hot pepper sauce.

3. Whisk the egg whites in a large bowl until soft peaks form. Stir one-quarter of the egg whites into the polenta mixture to lighten. Gently fold in the remaining egg whites until blended. Spoon the polenta into the baking dish.

4. Bake until slightly puffed and golden, about 45 minutes. Serve at once.

PER SERVING (⅓ of casserole): 275 Cal, 7 g Fat, 3 g Sat Fat, 153 mg Chol, 763 mg Sod, 38 g Carb, 4 g Fib, 16 g Prot, 216 mg Calc. *POINTS: 5.*

**Creamy Polenta
Casserole**

Spicy Hominy and Squash Stew

Poblanos are dark green chili peppers, almost as big as green bell peppers but more triangular in shape and more flavorful. The darker the poblano, the richer the flavor. If you can't find poblanos, use a green bell pepper. Canned hominy (dried yellow or white corn kernels) can be found in the ethnic aisle of the supermarket.

MAKES 4 SERVINGS

2 teaspoons canola oil
1 red onion, finely chopped
1 poblano chile pepper, seeded and chopped
2 garlic cloves, finely chopped
1 teaspoon Thai red curry paste
1 tomato, coarsely chopped
1 (15-ounce) can hominy, drained
1 (14-ounce) can vegetable broth
1 zucchini, halved lengthwise, then cut crosswise into ½-inch-thick slices
1 yellow squash, halved lengthwise, then cut crosswise into ½-inch-thick slices
2 cups hot cooked rice
½ cup shredded reduced-fat cheddar cheese
¼ cup whole cilantro leaves

1. Heat the oil in a nonstick Dutch oven over medium-high heat. Add onion, chile pepper, garlic, and curry paste. Cook, stirring occasionally, until tender and fragrant, about 8 minutes. Add the tomato and cook, stirring, until softened, about 6 minutes.
2. Stir the hominy and broth into the Dutch oven; bring to a boil. Reduce the heat and simmer, covered, until the flavors are blended and the mixture thickens slightly, about 15 minutes.
3. Stir in the zucchini and yellow squash; return to a boil. Reduce the heat and simmer, covered, until the zucchini and squash are just tender, about 6 minutes. Serve with the rice and sprinkle with the cheese and cilantro leaves.

PER SERVING (1½ cups stew, ½ cup rice, and 2 tablespoons cheese): 261 Cal, 6 g Fat, 2 g Sat Fat, 8 mg Chol, 695 mg Sod, 43 g Carb, 5 g Fib, 9 g Prot, 149 mg Calc. POINTS: 5.

Mexican Rice, Corn, and Cheese Casserole

You can find a variety of colorful, enamel-coated cast-iron pots that are both flameproof and ovenproof on the market. They are perfect for this dish, which cooks first on top of the stove, then in the oven, and then can be taken directly to the table for serving—all in the same pot.

MAKES 6 SERVINGS

2 teaspoons canola oil

1 green bell pepper, seeded and chopped

6 scallions, chopped

2 garlic cloves, finely chopped

1 tablespoon Cajun seasoning

1 cup long-grain white rice

1 (14½-ounce) can stewed tomatoes, chopped

1 (14-ounce) can vegetable broth

2 cups frozen small whole white onions

1½ cups frozen whole-kernel corn

2 tablespoons chopped mild green chiles

1 tomato, finely diced

¾ cup shredded reduced-fat cheddar cheese

¼ cup chopped fresh cilantro

1. Preheat the oven to 350°F.

2. Heat the oil in a large Dutch oven or flameproof and ovenproof casserole over medium-high heat. Add the bell pepper and cook, stirring occasionally, until tender, about 5 minutes. Add the scallions, garlic, and Cajun seasoning. Cook, stirring occasionally, until the scallions are soft, about 2 minutes. Add the rice, stirring until well coated.

3. Stir the tomatoes, broth, onions, corn, and chiles into the casserole; bring to a boil. Remove from the heat and cover. Bake until most of the liquid is absorbed and the rice and vegetables are tender, about 20 minutes.

4. Remove the cover, then sprinkle the casserole with the tomato and cheese. Return to the oven and bake, uncovered, until the cheese melts, about 5 minutes longer. Serve the casserole sprinkled with the cilantro.

PER SERVING (generous 1 cup): 256 Cal, 5 g Fat, 2 g Sat Fat, 8 mg Chol, 818 mg Sod, 46 g Carb, 3 g Fib, 9 g Prot, 156 mg Calc. POINTS: 5.

tip There is no need to thaw the corn or onions. Simply add them to the mixture frozen (step 3).

Spring Vegetable Ragout

Spring Vegetable Ragout

Although there are lots of vegetables in this colorful light ragout, the prep time is minimal. The potatoes need no peeling; the carrots are prepackaged, the onions frozen, and the artichoke hearts canned. Even the fresh asparagus is easy to prepare. The seasoning sauce is vegetarian and gives the ragout a rich, deep color—find it in the gravy section of supermarkets. Try serving the ragout with a slice of crusty French baguette on the side; a 1-ounce slice will add *2 POINTS*.

MAKES 4 SERVINGS

2 teaspoons olive oil

1 shallot, minced

2 garlic cloves, minced

½ pound small white potatoes, scrubbed and halved

1 cup baby carrots

1 cup frozen whole small white onions

2 tablespoons all-purpose flour

1 cup vegetable broth

1 cup water

¼ cup dry white wine

1 teaspoon vegetarian browning and seasoning sauce

1 teaspoon sugar

½ teaspoon salt

1 bay leaf

1 (14-ounce) can water-packed artichoke hearts, drained and cut in half

¾ pound fresh asparagus, trimmed and cut diagonally into 2-inch pieces

1. Heat the oil in a nonstick Dutch oven over medium heat. Add the shallot and garlic. Cook, stirring constantly, until softened, about 2 minutes. Add the potatoes, carrots, and onions. Cook, stirring occasionally, 2–3 minutes.

2. Sprinkle the flour over the vegetables, stirring to coat the vegetables. Stir in the broth, water, wine, seasoning sauce, sugar, salt, and bay leaf; bring to a boil. Reduce the heat and simmer, covered, stirring occasionally, until the vegetables are almost tender, about 15 minutes.

3. Add the artichoke hearts, and asparagus; return to a boil. Reduce the heat and simmer, uncovered, until the asparagus is tender, about 5 minutes longer. Remove from the heat and discard the bay leaf.

PER SERVING (2 cups): 185 Cal, 3 g Fat, 0 g Sat Fat, 0 mg Chol, 781 mg Sod, 36 g Carb, 8 g Fib, 7 g Prot, 84 mg Calc. *POINTS: 3.*

tip If you have time, and for extra flavor, stir in 1 or 2 tablespoons of chopped parsley and a tablespoon of grated lemon zest just before serving.

Main-Dish Salads

Refreshing and satisfying weeknight meals

Simple Steak Salad

Set the steak to marinate in the dressing the night before or early in the morning before leaving for work. When you get home, all you need do is broil the steak and toss the salad and you'll have this one-bowl dinner on the table in minutes.

1 (12-ounce) boneless sirloin steak, ¾-inch thick, trimmed of all visible fat

½ cup fat-free bottled Italian dressing

¼ teaspoon freshly ground pepper

1 (16-ounce) bag prepared iceberg salad

¼ cup reduced-fat feta cheese, crumbled

½ cup fat-free seasoned croutons

MAKES 2 SERVINGS

1. Combine the steak with ¼ cup of the dressing in a zip-close plastic bag. Squeeze out the air and seal the bag; turn to coat the steak. Refrigerate, turning the bag occasionally, at least 30 minutes or up to overnight.
2. Spray the broiler rack with nonstick spray. Preheat the broiler.
3. Remove the steak from the marinade; discard the marinade. Sprinkle the steak with the pepper and place on the broiler rack. Broil 4 inches from the heat until an instant-read thermometer inserted in the center of the steak registers 145°F for medium-rare, 3–4 minutes on each side. Let stand 2–3 minutes, then thinly slice.
4. Meanwhile, combine the iceberg salad, cheese, and croutons in a large bowl. Add the remaining ¼ cup dressing; toss to coat. Serve the sliced steak with the salad.

PER SERVING (½ of steak and 3 cups salad): 289 Cal, 8 g Fat, 3 g Sat Fat, 102 mg Chol, 635 mg Sod, 14 g Carb, 4 g Fib, 39 g Prot, 128 mg Calc. *POINTS:* 6.

tip If you prefer your steak cooked to medium, leave it under the broiler until the instant-read thermometer inserted in the center of the steak registers 160°F, about 3 minutes longer. After each use, be sure to wash the stem section of the meat thermometer thoroughly in hot, soapy water.

Simple Steak Salad

Roasted Pork Panzanella Salad

When the tomatoes are ripe and the bread is crusty and slightly stale (one or two days old), the time is right for making this traditional Italian bread salad. The dry bread soaks up the tomato juices and dressing, while the cucumber and red onion add crunch. We add chunks of succulent, fresh-roasted pork tenderloin and voilà—a complete dinner.

MAKES 6 SERVINGS

1 (1-pound) pork tenderloin, trimmed of all visible fat
¼ teaspoon salt
⅛ teaspoon freshly ground pepper
8 ounces day-old Italian or French bread, cut into 1-inch cubes
3 large ripe tomatoes, each cut into 12 wedges
½ seedless cucumber, peeled and cut into scant ¼-inch-thick slices
1 small red onion, thinly sliced
½ cup fat-free red-wine vinaigrette
⅓ cup chopped fresh basil
1 tablespoon drained capers

1. Preheat the oven to 425°F. Spray a shallow roasting pan with nonstick spray.
2. Sprinkle the pork with the salt and pepper; place in the pan. Roast until an instant-read thermometer inserted in the center of the pork registers 160°F for medium, 20–25 minutes. Let stand 5 minutes, then cut into 12 chunks.
3. Meanwhile, combine the bread, tomatoes, cucumber, onion, vinaigrette, basil, and capers in a large bowl. Toss well and let stand until the bread soaks up the juices, about 20 minutes. Divide the salad evenly between 6 plates. Top each salad with 2 chunks of the pork and serve at once.

PER SERVING (1 salad): 237 Cal, 5 g Fat, 1 g Sat Fat, 48 mg Chol, 579 mg Sod, 27 g Carb, 3 g Fib, 22 g Prot, 49 mg Calc. POINTS: 5.

tip Harmful bacteria are destroyed when food is cooked to the proper temperature. A meat thermometer is the only reliable way to determine that safe temperature. The U.S. Department of Agriculture recommends that pork (roasts, steaks, and chops) be cooked to at least 160°F. This produces medium-cooked meat. For well-done, cook the meat to 170°F.

Greek Lamb Salad

To put on some speed, buy precut vegetables from your favorite salad bar on the way home. Then you just have to broil the lamb and toss the veggies with the dressing.

MAKES 4 SERVINGS

4 (4-ounce) loin lamb
    chops, trimmed of all
    visible fat
½ teaspoon salt
¼ teaspoon freshly
    ground pepper
2 large tomatoes, each
    cut into 12 wedges
1 green bell pepper,
    seeded and cut into
    thin strips
1 cucumber, peeled,
    halved lengthwise,
    seeded, and cut into
    ¼-inch slices
1 small onion, thinly
    sliced
1 tablespoon red-wine
    vinegar
2 teaspoons extra-virgin
    olive oil
1 teaspoon dried
    oregano
4 (6-inch) pita breads

1. Spray the broiler rack with nonstick spray. Preheat the broiler.

2. Sprinkle the lamb with ¼ teaspoon of the salt and ⅛ teaspoon of the pepper; place on the broiler pan. Broil 4 inches from the heat until an instant-read thermometer inserted in the center of the lamb chops registers 145°F for medium-rare, 2–3 minutes on each side. Let stand 5 minutes, then thinly slice the lamb away from the bone.

3. Combine the tomatoes, bell pepper, cucumber, onion, vinegar, oil, oregano, and the remaining ¼ teaspoon salt and ⅛ teaspoon pepper; toss well.

4. Divide the tomato mixture among 4 plates, then top each with a sliced lamb chop. Serve with the pita bread.

PER SERVING (1 chop, 1½ cups salad, and 1 pita): 292 Cal, 7 g Fat, 2 g Sat Fat, 41 mg Chol, 607 mg Sod, 37 g Carb, 3 g Fib, 19 g Prot, 69 mg Calc. *POINTS: 6.*

Chef Salad Pizza

Chef Salad Pizza

This recipe takes advantage of prebaked pizza crusts and packaged sliced ham, cheese, and turkey from the supermarket. We make pinwheels out of the cold cuts, but you can also simply chop the cold cuts and toss with the spinach, vinegar, oil, tomatoes, and onion in a large bowl. Spread the mixture over the crust and bake as directed.

MAKES 6 SERVINGS

1 (10-ounce) thin
   prebaked pizza crust
4 ounces (4 slices)
   deli-sliced ham
4 ounces (4 slices)
   low-fat deli-sliced
   Swiss cheese
4 ounces (4 slices)
   fat-free deli-sliced
   turkey breast
4 cups fresh baby
   spinach leaves
5 teaspoons balsamic
   vinegar
4 teaspoons extra-virgin
   olive oil
2 medium tomatoes, cut
   into ¼-inch-thick slices
1 small Vidalia or other
   sweet onion, thinly
   sliced
¼ cup fresh basil leaves

1. Preheat the oven to 450°F. Place pizza crust on a baking sheet.

2. On a cutting board, arrange the ham slices next to each other in a single layer with the short ends closest to you. Top each ham slice with a slice of cheese, then a slice of turkey. Roll up each stack of cold cuts jelly-roll style, then cut each roll into 6 pinwheels, making a total of 24 pinwheels.

3. Combine the spinach with 2 teaspoons of the vinegar and 2 teaspoons of the oil in a large bowl; toss to coat. Top the pizza crust with the spinach. Arrange the tomato slices and onion slices over the spinach. Top with the cold-cut pinwheels, cut-side up. Drizzle the pizza with the remaining 3 teaspoons vinegar and 2 teaspoons oil. Bake until the crust and toppings are heated through, 8–10 minutes.

4. Sprinkle the pizza with the basil and cut into 6 slices.

PER SERVING (1 slice): 258 Cal, 8 g Fat, 2 g Sat Fat, 21 mg Chol, 902 mg Sod, 29 g Carb, 3 g Fib, 17 g Prot, 186 mg Calc. *POINTS: 5.*

 **tip** If you prefer, you can sprinkle the pizza with thinly sliced basil. Simply stack several basil leaves on top of one another, roll up, and cut crosswise into thin strips.

Warm Barley, Chicken, and Stone Fruit Mélange

This wonderful salad takes full advantage of summer's abundance of juicy peaches, nectarines, and plums. Look for fragrant fruit that gives slightly to pressure but with no bruises or soft spots. Freestone fruit is what we find most in supermarkets starting from early to mid-June. They are easy to prepare because the pit releases easily from the fruit.

1 cup quick-cooking barley
¼ cup chopped fresh mint
1½ tablespoons raspberry vinegar
1 tablespoon walnut or canola oil
¾ teaspoon salt
¼ teaspoon freshly ground pepper
¾ pound cooked skinless boneless chicken breast, cut into ½-inch pieces
2 fresh ripe peaches, pitted and chopped
2 fresh ripe nectarines, pitted and chopped
2 fresh ripe plums, pitted and chopped
2 celery stalks, chopped
2 scallions, chopped

MAKES 6 SERVINGS

1. Cook barley according to package directions; drain and set aside.
2. Meanwhile, combine the mint, vinegar, oil, salt, and pepper in a small bowl.
3. Combine the chicken, peaches, nectarines, plums, celery, and scallions in a large bowl. Add the mint mixture and barley to the chicken mixture; mix well. Serve at once.

PER SERVING (1⅓ cups): 283 Cal, 5 g Fat, 1 g Sat Fat, 44 mg Chol, 346 mg Sod, 39 g Carb, 7 g Fib, 22 g Prot, 36 mg Calc. POINTS: 5.

tip For best flavor, use peaches, nectarines, and plums at room temperature in this recipe and stir the barley into the salad mixture while still warm. The salad is even better if the chicken is freshly cooked and not chilled. If you don't get to serve this salad right away while still warm, don't let it sit at room temperature for more than an hour or so. Cover it and pop it in the refrigerator until mealtime, then let it come to room temperature for about 30 minutes before serving.

Roast Vegetable and Chicken Salad

While homemade roasted garlic offers wonderful flavor, if you are pressed for time, you can substitute one tablespoon of the prepared kind in a jar. To keep the chicken extra-moist and to add depth of flavor, we roasted it with the bone in.

MAKES 4 SERVINGS

1   whole garlic bulb
¾   pound baby white or red potatoes, scrubbed and quartered
1   medium fennel bulb, cored and cut into ¼-inch-thick strips
3   carrots, cut into 1-inch pieces
1   red onion, cut into 8 wedges
2   teaspoons olive oil
4   (4-ounce) skinless chicken thighs, all visible fat removed
¼   cup low-fat mayonnaise
1   tablespoon fresh lemon juice
½   teaspoon dried tarragon
½   teaspoon salt
¼   teaspoon freshly ground pepper

1. Preheat the oven to 425°F. Slice the top third from the garlic bulb. Wrap the garlic in foil and place in the center of the oven. Bake 15 minutes, then move to the side of the oven.

2. Combine the potatoes, fennel, carrots, onion, and oil in a large bowl; toss to coat. Arrange the vegetables in one layer in a large baking or shallow roasting pan. Bake until the vegetables are slightly softened, about 15 minutes. Add the chicken to the pan and roast, until the vegetables are tender and the juices run clear when the chicken is pierced with a fork, 30–35 minutes longer. Remove the baking pan and the garlic from the oven and let cool about 15 minutes.

3. Remove the bones from the chicken and cut the meat into ½-inch cubes. Transfer the chicken and vegetables to a large bowl.

4. Squeeze the roasted garlic out of the skin and combine in a small bowl with the mayonnaise, lemon juice, tarragon, salt, and pepper. Add to the chicken mixture and toss well. Serve at once.

PER SERVING (1 chicken thigh and ⅔ cup vegetables): 295 Cal, 8 g Fat, 2 g Sat Fat, 50 mg Chol, 537 mg Sod, 37 g Carb, 6 g Fib, 20 g Prot, 89 mg Calc. *POINTS: 6.*

tip This salad is also good chilled (and the flavors have more of a chance to develop). To serve it cold, make sure that the chicken and vegetables are allowed to cool to room temperature before tossing with the mayonnaise mixture. Then store it up to 24 hours in an airtight container in the coldest section of your refrigerator.

Thai Chicken Salad

Cellophane noodles—also known as bean threads, glass noodles, or saifun—are made from the starch of green mung beans. The noodles are sold dried, needing only a brief soaking in hot water before being ready to use. They can be found in the ethnic section of supermarkets and in Asian markets.

MAKES 6 SERVINGS

2　tablespoons canola oil

3　garlic cloves, minced

1　pound ground skinless chicken breast

2　cups cellophane noodles

1　red bell pepper, seeded and chopped

1　red onion, chopped

1　cucumber, peeled, seeded, and chopped

1　cup shredded carrots

¼　cup chopped fresh mint

5　tablespoons rice vinegar

3　tablespoons bottled fish sauce (nam pla)

3　tablespoons sugar

1　serrano pepper, seeded and chopped (wear gloves to prevent irritation)

12　Boston lettuce leaves

1. Heat the oil in a large nonstick skillet over medium-high heat. Add the garlic and cook until fragrant, about 30 seconds. Add the chicken and cook, breaking up the chicken with a wooden spoon until lightly browned, 5–6 minutes. Remove from the heat and let cool 5 minutes.

2. Place the cellophane noodles in a large bowl. Add enough boiling water to cover. Let stand until softened, about 5 minutes. Drain and coarsely chop the noodles.

3. Combine the bell pepper, onion, cucumber, carrots, mint, vinegar, fish sauce, sugar, and serrano pepper in a large bowl. Add the browned chicken and softened noodles; toss well.

4. Arrange 2 lettuce leaves on each of 6 plates. Fill each lettuce leaf with ½ cup chicken mixture. Serve at once.

PER SERVING (2 filled lettuce leaves): 227 Cal, 7 g Fat, 1 g Sat Fat, 41 mg Chol, 394 mg Sod, 23 g Carb, 2 g Fib, 19 g Prot, 37 mg Calc. *POINTS: 5.*

Caribbean Chicken Salad

This easy-to-make salad has a refreshing tropical taste. Pick up the pineapple and mango from the salad bar if you want the convenience. Or substitute any other favorite fruits, such as orange segments, papaya wedges, or fresh grapefruit segments, if they're more readily available.

MAKES 4 SERVINGS

1 large sweet potato (1 pound), peeled and cut into 1-inch chunks

⅓ cup low-fat mayonnaise

¼ cup plain fat-free yogurt

1 tablespoon fresh lime juice

2 teaspoons curry powder

½ teaspoon salt

¼ teaspoon freshly ground pepper

1 (10-ounce) package carved roasted skinless chicken breasts

2 cups fresh pineapple chunks

2 cups seedless red grapes, halved

1 mango, peeled, seeded, and cut into ¾-inch chunks

1 small red onion, chopped

4 romaine lettuce leaves

1. Bring the sweet potato, with enough cold water to cover, to a boil in a medium saucepan. Reduce the heat and simmer, covered, until tender, about 10 minutes. Drain, then rinse the potato under cold water.

2. Meanwhile, combine the mayonnaise, yogurt, lime juice, curry powder, salt, and pepper in a small bowl; mix well.

3. Combine the chicken, pineapple, grapes, mango, and onion in a large bowl. Add the mayonnaise mixture and sweet potato to the chicken mixture; toss to coat.

4. Place a lettuce leaf on each of 4 plates. Top each lettuce leaf with 2 cups of the salad. Serve at once.

PER SERVING (1 filled lettuce leaf): 346 Cal, 5 g Fat, 1 g Sat Fat, 55 mg Chol, 549 mg Sod, 53 g Carb, 5 g Fib, 25 g Prot, 92 mg Calc. *POINTS: 7.*

tip For an easy seafood version of this recipe, substitute ½ pound of cooked small shrimp for the chicken.

Chicken, Dried Fruit, and Rice Salad

For a nuttier flavor, a slightly chewier texture, and extra fiber, substitute uncooked brown rice for the white rice. Be sure to increase the water to 2½ cups and cook for 20 minutes longer to fully cook the brown rice.

1¾ cups water

1 teaspoon salt

1 teaspoon ground cumin

½ teaspoon saffron threads, lightly crushed

¼ teaspoon ground cinnamon

¾ cup long-grain white rice

¼ cup golden raisins

¼ cup dried apricots, sliced

1 (10-ounce) package carved roasted skinless chicken breasts

1 small red onion, chopped

1 small red bell pepper, seeded and cut into ¼-inch dice

⅓ cup chopped fresh parsley

3 tablespoons sliced almonds

3 tablespoons raspberry vinegar

1 tablespoon olive oil

MAKES 4 SERVINGS

1. Bring the water, ½ teaspoon of the salt, the cumin, saffron, and cinnamon to a boil in a medium saucepan. Add the rice, raisins, and apricots, then reduce the heat to medium-low. Cover and simmer until the rice is tender and all of the liquid is absorbed, about 20 minutes.

2. Remove the saucepan from the heat and let stand 5 minutes. Spread the rice mixture on a baking sheet and let cool to room temperature, about 20 minutes.

3. Transfer the rice mixture to a large bowl, then stir in the chicken, onion, bell pepper, parsley, almonds, vinegar, oil, and the remaining ½ teaspoon salt. Mix well and serve at once, or cover and refrigerate for up to 24 hours and serve chilled.

PER SERVING (1½ cups): 368 Cal, 9 g Fat, 2 g Sat Fat, 55 mg Chol, 640 mg Sod, 46 g Carb, 3 g Fib, 26 g Prot, 64 mg Calc. *POINTS: 8.*

tip Cooked chicken breast pieces are available packaged in many flavors: plain roasted (as we use here), Italian, mesquite, and lemon are some of them. For this recipe, you can substitute any cooked lean chicken you have on hand—leftover or other.

Mexican Turkey Salad Platter

The look of this salad is reminiscent of seven-layer dip. We call for arranging the colorful chopped vegetables in neat rows on top of the lettuce and turkey, but you can simply sprinkle the veggies and cheese on top of the turkey mixture, spoon the salsa and sour cream on top, then dig in with the chips.

1 pound ground skinless turkey breast

1 (1¼-ounce) packet reduced-sodium taco seasoning

⅔ cup water

½ medium head iceberg lettuce, shredded

2 medium tomatoes, seeded and chopped

1 Vidalia or other sweet onion, chopped

1 cucumber, peeled, seeded, and sliced

1 cup shredded reduced-fat sharp cheddar cheese

¾ cup fat-free prepared salsa

½ cup light sour cream

4 ounces low-fat tortilla chips (about 80 chips)

MAKES 6 SERVINGS

1. Spray a large nonstick skillet with nonstick spray and set over medium-high heat. Add the turkey and cook, breaking up the turkey with a wooden spoon, until lightly browned, 3–4 minutes. Stir in the seasoning packet and the water. Cook, stirring occasionally, until the turkey is cooked through, about 3 minutes. Remove from the heat.

2. Arrange the lettuce over a large platter and top with the turkey mixture. Top the turkey with the tomatoes, onion, cucumber, and cheese, arranging them in 4 rows. Serve with the salsa, sour cream, and chips on the side.

PER SERVING (⅙ of platter, 2 tablespoons salsa, generous tablespoon sour cream, and 13 chips): 307 Cal, 9 g Fat, 4 g Sat Fat, 62 mg Chol, 537 mg Sod, 28 g Carb, 5 g Fib, 28 g Prot, 231 mg Calc. *POINTS: 6.*

Grilled Tuna and Vegetable Salad

Redolent of homemade pesto, and full of flavor from just-grilled fresh vegetables and meaty tuna steaks, this elegant salad is sure to please. If you own a mini food processor, use it for making this small amount of pesto.

1 cup packed fresh basil leaves
1 garlic clove
1 tablespoon pine nuts
2 tablespoons olive oil
2 tablespoons fresh lemon juice
1 teaspoon salt
6 (4-ounce) tuna steaks, about ½-inch thick
1 pound fresh asparagus, trimmed
1 large zucchini (about ¾ pound), cut on an angle into ¼-inch-thick slices
1 yellow onion, cut into ¼-inch-thick rounds
1 small head radicchio, cut into 8 wedges
¼ teaspoon freshly ground pepper

MAKES 6 SERVINGS

1. Combine the basil, garlic, pine nuts, oil, lemon juice, and ½ teaspoon of the salt in a food processor or blender; process until smooth. Transfer to a small bowl and set aside.
2. Spray the grill rack with nonstick spray. Prepare the grill.
3. Lightly spray the tuna, asparagus, zucchini, onion, and radicchio with nonstick spray, then sprinkle with the remaining ½ teaspoon salt and the pepper.
4. Place the tuna on the grill rack and grill 4 inches from the heat, 2–3 minutes on each side for medium-rare. Transfer the tuna to a plate. Next grill the asparagus and zucchini until crisp tender, 3–4 minutes on each side; the onion until well marked and tender, 5–6 minutes on each side; and the radicchio until slightly wilted, 2 minutes on each side.
5. Arrange the tuna steaks and vegetables on a large platter. Drizzle with the pesto and serve at once.

PER SERVING (1 tuna steak, ⅙ of vegetables, and scant tablespoon pesto): 251 Cal, 12 g Fat, 2 g Sat Fat, 43 mg Chol, 444 mg Sod, 7 g Carb, 3 g Fib, 29 g Prot, 48 mg Calc. *POINTS: 5.*

tip A grill basket—usually rectangular with tightly spaced grids or small perforations—works wonders when grilling smaller items, such as the asparagus and sliced zucchini, that might otherwise fall through the spaces in the grill rack.

Crab-Stuffed Tomatoes

For a fun take on a northeast favorite—the lobster or crab roll—simply leave out the orzo and stuff the crab filling in 4 toasted hot dog rolls. You'll be adding *2 POINTS* per serving for the roll version.

MAKES 4 SERVINGS

½ cup uncooked orzo

8 medium tomatoes

¾ pound cooked lump crabmeat, picked over for pieces of shell

1 celery stalk, chopped

½ small red bell pepper, seeded and chopped

½ small onion, chopped

⅓ cup low-fat mayonnaise

1 tablespoon Dijon mustard

1 tablespoon chopped fresh parsley

½ teaspoon Old Bay seasoning

1. Cook the orzo according to package directions; drain and rinse under cold water.

2. Slice off the top fourth of each tomato and reserve. Using a spoon, scoop out the pulp from each tomato. Place the tomato shells upside down on a layer of paper towels to drain; set aside. (Save the pulp for use in stews and soups.)

3. Combine the orzo, crabmeat, celery, bell pepper, onion, mayonnaise, mustard, parsley, and Old Bay seasoning in a bowl; mix well.

4. Fill each tomato shell with about ½ cup of the crab mixture, mounding if necessary. Replace the reserved tomato tops.

PER SERVING (2 stuffed tomatoes): 243 Cal, 4 g Fat, 1 g Sat Fat, 85 mg Chol, 583 mg Sod, 31 g Carb, 4 g Fib, 22 g Prot, 115 mg Calc. *POINTS: 4.*

Teriyaki Scallop and Spinach Salad

The key to this salad is getting the freshest scallops you can find. Scallops should have a slightly sweet smell of the sea and not be at all fishy-smelling. Rice crackers add a wonderful crisp texture and Japanese flavor here. If you want extra, add a *POINT* for every 8 rice crackers.

1	tablespoon Asian (dark) sesame oil
1½	pounds sea scallops
1	tablespoon minced peeled fresh ginger
2	scallions, chopped
½	cup orange juice
¼	cup teriyaki sauce
2	tablespoons honey
8	cups baby spinach leaves
1	small red bell pepper, seeded and diced
32	(about 2 ounces) Japanese rice crackers

MAKES 4 SERVINGS

1. Heat 2 teaspoons of the oil in a very large nonstick skillet over medium-high heat. Add the scallops and cook until lightly browned on the outside and opaque in the center, 2–3 minutes on each side. Transfer to a plate and set aside.

2. Wipe out the skillet with a paper towel, add the remaining 1 teaspoon oil, and set over medium-high heat. Add the ginger and scallions; cook, stirring, until fragrant, about 30 seconds. Add the orange juice, teriyaki sauce, and honey; cook, stirring, until slightly thickened, 1½–2 minutes.

3. Divide the spinach among 4 plates. Top each plate evenly with the scallops and the bell pepper. Drizzle each salad with about 3 tablespoons of the orange mixture. Serve with the rice crackers.

PER SERVING (1 salad and 8 rice crackers): 303 Cal, 6 g Fat, 1 g Sat Fat, 34 mg Chol, 1154 mg Sod, 36 g Carb, 4 g Fib, 30 g Prot, 252 mg Calc. *POINTS*: 6.

tip To get nicely browned scallops, it's best to cook them in one layer in the skillet. If your skillet is not big enough, cook the scallops in two batches.

**Teriyaki Scallop and
Spinach Salad**

Mixed Seafood Salad

This restaurant classic is a breeze to make at home and packs a lot of flavor. Try serving it with a warm piece of crusty French baguette—a 1-ounce slice will cost you *2 POINTS*.

MAKES 6 SERVINGS

½ pound baby white
    potatoes, scrubbed
¾ pound large shrimp,
    peeled and deveined
¾ pound bay scallops
¾ pound squid bodies,
    cut into ½-inch-thick
    rings
2 celery stalks, chopped
1 small fennel bulb,
    cored and chopped
1 carrot, chopped
1 small red onion,
    chopped
3 tablespoons chopped
    fresh parsley
2 tablespoons fresh
    lemon juice
2 tablespoons
    extra-virgin olive oil
½ teaspoon salt
¼ teaspoon freshly
    ground pepper
6 romaine lettuce leaves

1. Bring a large pot, two-thirds full of water, to a boil. Add the potatoes and simmer until just tender, 12–15 minutes. With a slotted spoon, transfer to a cutting board and let stand until cool enough to handle. Cut the potatoes into thin slices and set aside.

2. Return the water in the pot to a gentle simmer. Add the shrimp and cook until just opaque in the center, 2–3 minutes. With a slotted spoon, transfer the shrimp to a bowl of iced water. Add the scallops to the pot and simmer until just opaque in the center, 2–3 minutes. With a slotted spoon, transfer the scallops to the bowl with the shrimp. Add the squid to the pot and simmer until tender but still slightly firm, about 2 minutes. Drain the squid and transfer to the bowl with the shrimp and scallops.

3. Combine the celery, fennel, carrot, onion, parsley, lemon juice, oil, salt, and pepper in a large bowl. Add the potatoes, shrimp, scallops, and squid; toss to coat.

4. Place a lettuce leaf on each of 6 plates. Spoon about 1⅓ cups salad onto each lettuce leaf and serve at once.

PER SERVING (1 salad): 214 Cal, 6 g Fat, 1 g Sat Fat, 220 mg Chol, 398 mg Sod, 17 g Carb, 3 g Fib, 23 g Prot, 103 mg Calc. *POINTS: 4.*

Tuna Salad Niçoise

The term niçoise refers to the cuisine of Nice, in southern France. Foods of that region often include tomatoes, garlic, fresh herbs, and olives. The olives are niçoise olives—tiny, black, and tender—grown around the area of Provence. Use Greek kalamata olives if you can't find niçoise olives. For an extra *POINT*, serve with 2 long sesame breadsticks.

MAKES 4 SERVINGS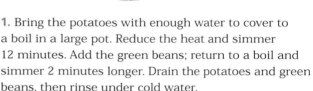

½ pound small red or
    white potatoes,
    scrubbed and
    quartered
½ pound fresh green
    beans, trimmed
4 cups mixed baby
    greens
2 (6-ounce) cans solid
    white tuna in water,
    drained
1 (7-ounce) jar roasted
    red peppers, drained
    and cut into strips
1 pint cherry tomatoes
12 niçoise olives
⅓ cup fat-free red-wine
    vinaigrette
2 tablespoons chopped
    fresh basil
1 tablespoon drained
    capers

1. Bring the potatoes with enough water to cover to a boil in a large pot. Reduce the heat and simmer 12 minutes. Add the green beans; return to a boil and simmer 2 minutes longer. Drain the potatoes and green beans, then rinse under cold water.

2. Arrange the baby greens on a large platter. Pull the tuna into large chunks and place in the center of the platter. Arrange the potatoes, green beans, roasted red peppers, cherry tomatoes, and olives in clusters around the tuna. Drizzle with the vinaigrette, then sprinkle with the basil and capers.

PER SERVING (¼ of salad): 208 Cal, 3 g Fat, 0 g Sat Fat, 23 mg Chol, 730 mg Sod, 25 g Carb, 5 g Fib, 23 g Prot, 84 mg Calc. *POINTS: 4.*

tip For a speedier weeknight version, use drained canned potatoes and frozen green beans that you can quickly cook in the microwave, then chill in ice water.

Tuscan White Bean and Tuna Salad

Great Northern beans take center stage in this recipe—their delicate flavor enhanced by a zippy vinaigrette and aromatic sage. Similarly, the mild-tasting tuna is balanced by the peppery arugula. Feel free to substitute cannellini (white kidney) beans for the great Northern beans, if you like.

MAKES 4 SERVINGS

1　onion, chopped

1　carrot, chopped

3　tablespoons chopped fresh parsley

2　tablespoons drained capers

2　tablespoons extra-virgin olive oil

1　tablespoon white-wine vinegar

1　tablespoon chopped fresh sage, or ¾ teaspoon dried

¼　teaspoon freshly ground pepper

1　(6-ounce) can solid white tuna in water, drained

1　(15½-ounce) can great Northern beans, rinsed and drained

1　bunch arugula, cleaned and coarsely chopped (about 3 cups)

1. Combine the onion, carrot, parsley, capers, oil, vinegar, sage, and pepper in a large bowl; toss to coat.
2. Break the tuna into large chunks and gently stir into the onion mixture. Gently stir in the beans.
3. Divide the arugula among 4 plates. Spoon about 1 cup of the bean salad on each plate. Serve at once.

PER SERVING (1 salad): 233 Cal, 8 g Fat, 1 g Sat Fat, 11 mg Chol, 434 mg Sod, 24 g Carb, 6 g Fib, 18 g Prot, 112 mg Calc. *POINTS: 5.*

Malaysian Tofu, Cucumber, and Peanut Salad

Asian sesame oil, also called dark sesame oil, can be found in the ethnic section of most supermarkets. It differs from regular sesame oil in that it has a deeper, nuttier flavor, because it is made from toasted sesame seeds. To save time, use preshredded carrots, available in 12-ounce bags in the produce section of the supermarket.

MAKES 2 SERVINGS

¾ pound low-fat firm tofu
2 teaspoons Asian (dark) sesame oil
1 tablespoon minced peeled fresh ginger
2 garlic cloves, minced
1 cucumber, peeled, seeded, and sliced
1 red bell pepper, seeded and thinly sliced
1 cup shredded carrots
2 scallions, finely chopped
3 tablespoons honey
2 tablespoons rice vinegar
2 tablespoons bottled fish sauce (nam pla)
2 tablespoons chopped fresh cilantro
2 tablespoons chopped lightly salted dry-roasted peanuts

1. Wrap the tofu in paper towels and place on a plate. Top with a heavy saucepan and let it stand for 20 minutes to press out the excess liquid. Cut the tofu into ½-inch cubes.

2. Meanwhile, heat 1 teaspoon of the oil in a large nonstick skillet over medium-high heat. Add the ginger and garlic; cook, stirring, until fragrant, about 30 seconds. Add the tofu and cook, turning occasionally, until browned, 3–4 minutes. Transfer to a large bowl.

3. Add the cucumber, bell pepper, carrots, scallions, honey, vinegar, fish sauce, cilantro, and the remaining 1 teaspoon oil to the browned tofu; toss well. Serve at once, sprinkled with the peanuts.

PER SERVING (generous 2 cups tofu mixture and 1 tablespoon peanuts): 332 Cal, 11 g Fat, 2 g Sat Fat, 0 mg Chol, 832 mg Sod, 49 g Carb, 6 g Fib, 17 g Prot, 100 mg Calc. POINTS: 7.

tip To turn this main dish salad into a side dish, omit the tofu and 1 teaspoon of the sesame oil. Then add 4 cups of shredded napa cabbage, toss, and let stand 1 hour—and you've got Malaysian coleslaw.

Chickpea, Orange, and Couscous Salad

Sweet and spicy Middle Eastern flavors shout from this exotic and healthy salad. With the simple addition of ¼ teaspoon cinnamon, ¼ teaspoon ground ginger, and a touch of cayenne to the liquid that cooks the couscous, you could have an even more intense, North African tasting experience.

MAKES 6 SERVINGS

¾ cup orange juice

½ cup water

1 teaspoon ground coriander

¾ teaspoon salt

1 cup couscous

1 (15½-ounce) can chickpeas (garbanzo beans), rinsed and drained

2 oranges, peeled, cut into segments, and coarsely chopped

½ bunch watercress, trimmed and torn into small pieces (about 2 cups)

¼ cup dried cranberries

¼ cup slivered almonds

2 tablespoons chopped fresh mint

2 tablespoons fresh lemon juice

1 tablespoon extra-virgin olive oil

1. Bring the orange juice, water, coriander, and salt to a boil in a small saucepan. Add the couscous, cover, and remove from the heat. Let stand 5 minutes, then fluff with a fork.

2. Combine the chickpeas, oranges, watercress, cranberries, almonds, mint, lemon juice, and oil in a large bowl. Add the couscous and mix well. Serve at once while still warm, or let cool for about 1 hour and serve at room temperature.

PER SERVING (1 cup): 293 Cal, 6 g Fat, 1 g Sat Fat, 0 mg Chol, 415 mg Sod, 51 g Carb, 6 g Fib, 10 g Prot, 82 mg Calc. POINTS: 6.

tip To make the salad ahead, prepare it without the watercress and refrigerate in an airtight container for up to two days. Serve chilled or allow it to come to room temperature for about one hour. Stir in the watercress just before serving.

Three-Bean-Salad Tortillas

We've put a distinctive southwestern twist on this traditional summer salad. For a flavor boost and an extra ½ *POINT*, garnish each tortilla with 1½ tablespoons light sour cream.

MAKES 6 SERVINGS

½ pound fresh green beans, trimmed and cut crosswise into thirds

1 (15½-ounce) can black beans, rinsed and drained

1 (15½-ounce) can red kidney beans, rinsed and drained

2 medium tomatoes, seeded and chopped

1 small red onion, chopped

1 jalapeño pepper, seeded and finely chopped (wear gloves to prevent irritation)

¼ cup chopped fresh cilantro

3 tablespoons cider vinegar

1 tablespoon olive oil

1½ teaspoons chili powder

1½ teaspoons ground cumin

½ teaspoon salt

6 (6-inch) fat-free flour tortillas

¾ cup shredded reduced-fat Monterey Jack cheese

1. Bring a large pot of lightly salted water to a boil. Add the green beans, return to a boil, and cook 2 minutes. Drain and rinse under cold water.

2. Combine the green beans, black beans, kidney beans, tomatoes, onion, jalapeño pepper, cilantro, vinegar, oil, chili powder, cumin, and salt in a large bowl; mix well.

3. Arrange a flour tortilla on each of 6 plates. Top each tortilla with 1 generous cup of salad. Sprinkle each with 2 tablespoons of cheese.

PER SERVING (1 tortilla): 232 Cal, 4 g Fat, 1 g Sat Fat, 0 mg Chol, 648 mg Sod, 41 g Carb, 8 g Fib, 11 g Prot, 103 mg Calc. *POINTS: 4.*

Tortellini Salad

Tortellini Salad

A terrific summertime dinner or anytime lunch, this colorful, hearty salad is also perfect for making ahead—for any day or for a party. During the late summer months, substitute your favorite local tomatoes for the plum tomatoes and add some chopped fresh basil. For an extra splash of color, try using tri-color tortellini.

MAKES 8 SERVINGS

1 package (1 pound) frozen spinach tortellini
1 (15½-ounce) can small red beans, rinsed and drained
1 (14-ounce) can artichoke hearts, drained and quartered
4 ripe plum tomatoes, seeded and coarsely chopped
½ small head radicchio, shredded
1 medium yellow bell pepper, seeded and thinly sliced
2 scallions, chopped
⅔ cup bottled Parmesan-basil Italian dressing
3 tablespoons grated Parmesan cheese
½ teaspoon salt

1. Cook the tortellini according to package directions; drain and rinse under cold water.

2. Meanwhile, combine the beans, artichoke hearts, tomatoes, radicchio, bell pepper, scallions, dressing, Parmesan cheese, and salt in a large bowl. Add the tortellini and toss well to coat.

PER SERVING (1¼ cups): 264 Cal, 13 g Fat, 3 g Sat Fat, 80 mg Chol, 704 mg Sod, 27 g Carb, 5 g Fib, 10 g Prot, 132 mg Calc. *POINTS:* 6.

tip To make ahead, combine all the salad ingredients, except the dressing, cheese, and salt, then store in an airtight container in the refrigerator overnight. Just before serving, toss the salad with the dressing, cheese, and salt.

Pasta Meals

So filling and so good

Rigatoni and Fennel Bolognese

Bolognese is a rich, thick meat-and-vegetable sauce, most often served over pasta. This lightened version still has a good helping of lean ground beef *and* a big boost of flavor from bacon, fennel, and Parmesan cheese. You can serve the Parmesan cheese on the side instead of stirring it into the sauce, if you prefer. You'll need about ½ pound dry rigatoni to get 4 cups cooked.

MAKES 6 SERVINGS

¾ pound lean ground beef (10% or less fat)
3 slices turkey bacon, chopped
1 onion, chopped
1 small fennel bulb, cored and chopped
1 carrot, chopped
2 garlic cloves, minced
1 teaspoon fennel seeds, lightly crushed
1 (28-ounce) can crushed tomatoes
½ cup dry white wine
¼ cup grated Parmesan cheese
¼ teaspoon freshly ground pepper
4 cups hot cooked rigatoni

1. Heat a large nonstick skillet over medium-high heat. Add the beef and bacon. Cook, breaking the beef up with a spoon, until the beef and bacon brown, 4–6 minutes. Add the onion, fennel, carrot, garlic, and fennel seeds. Cook, stirring frequently, until the vegetables are slightly softened, 5–6 minutes.

2. Stir the tomatoes and wine into the skillet; bring to a boil. Reduce the heat to medium and simmer, stirring occasionally, until slightly thickened, 12–15 minutes. Remove from the heat, then stir in the Parmesan cheese and pepper. Serve over the rigatoni.

PER SERVING (⅔ cup sauce and ⅔ cup rigatoni): 322 Cal, 7 g Fat, 3 g Sat Fat, 43 mg Chol, 599 mg Sod, 42 g Carb, 4 g Fib, 23 g Prot, 135 mg Calc. *POINTS:* 6.

tip Crushing fennel seeds releases their rich, aromatic flavor. To crush them, place the fennel seeds between sheets of wax paper and pound with a wooden mallet or the end of a rolling pin.

Rigatoni and Fennel
Bolognese

Mediterranean Three-Cheese Lasagna

A hint of sweet spices (cinnamon and nutmeg) and a generous amount of feta cheese give this vegetarian lasagna a distinctly Greek air, while no-boil lasagna noodles and jarred sauce make it decidedly easy. You can even make it ahead. Simply assemble the lasagna (don't bake it), cover it with foil, and refrigerate for up to two days or freeze for up to three months. Then bake as directed (if frozen, first thaw in the refrigerator overnight), adding a few minutes to the cooking time to compensate for starting with a chilled dish.

MAKES 8 SERVINGS

1 (15-ounce) container fat-free ricotta cheese

1 (10-ounce) package frozen chopped spinach, thawed and squeezed dry

2 cups shredded fat-free mozzarella cheese

4 ounces crumbled reduced-fat feta cheese (about 1 cup)

1 large egg, lightly beaten

1 teaspoon dried oregano

¼ teaspoon cinnamon

⅛ teaspoon ground nutmeg

1 (26-ounce) jar mushroom and ripe-olive tomato sauce

9 oven-ready no-boil lasagna noodles

1. Preheat the oven to 375°F. Spray a 9 x 13-inch baking dish with nonstick spray.
2. Combine the ricotta cheese, spinach, 1 cup of the mozzarella cheese, the feta cheese, egg, oregano, cinnamon, and nutmeg in a large bowl; mix well.
3. Spread one-fourth (about ¾ cup) of the tomato sauce over the bottom of the baking pan. Top with 3 of the lasagna noodles. Spread half (about 2 cups) of the ricotta mixture over the noodles. Spread with one-fourth more tomato sauce. Repeat the layering once more with 3 noodles, the remaining half of the ricotta mixture, and one-fourth more tomato sauce. Top with the remaining 3 noodles, one-fourth sauce, and 1 cup mozzarella cheese.
4. Cover the lasagna with foil and bake 30 minutes. Uncover and bake until the cheese melts and the lasagna is heated through and bubbling, 10–15 minutes longer.

PER SERVING (⅛ of lasagna): 234 Cal, 5 g Fat, 3 g Sat Fat, 44 mg Chol, 518 mg Sod, 25 g Carb, 2 g Fib, 22 g Prot, 410 mg Calc. *POINTS: 5.*

tip To prevent the lasagna from sticking to the foil, spray the foil with nonstick spray before using it to cover the dish.

Four-Way Cincinnati Chili

In Cincinnati, chili is usually made without beans, ordered by the number, and served over spaghetti. Basic chili is called one-way chili, and four-way chili is basic chili served with three garnishes—over spaghetti, with shredded cheese, and with chopped onion. Five-way chili is four-way chili plus a foundation of kidney beans and sometimes with sour cream. Sweet spices, such as cinnamon, nutmeg, allspice, or cloves, and sometimes chocolate are added to Cincinnati chili. You'll need about 6 ounces dry spaghetti to get 3 cups cooked.

MAKES 6 SERVINGS

2 teaspoons canola oil
1 pound ground skinless turkey breast
2 onions, chopped
2 garlic cloves, minced
1 tablespoon chili powder
½ teaspoon cinnamon
1 (14½-ounce) can diced tomatoes with jalapeño peppers
¼ cup water
½ ounce semisweet chocolate, chopped
½ teaspoon salt
¼ teaspoon freshly ground pepper
3 cups hot cooked spaghetti
½ cup shredded reduced-fat sharp cheddar cheese

1. Heat the oil in a Dutch oven over medium-high heat. Add the turkey and cook, breaking it up with a spoon, until the meat browns, 3–4 minutes. Add 1½ onions, the garlic, chili powder, and cinnamon. Cook, stirring occasionally, until fragrant and the onions begin to soften slightly, about 2 minutes.
2. Stir the tomatoes and water into the Dutch oven; bring to a boil. Reduce the heat and simmer, covered, until slightly thickened, about 20 minutes. Remove from the heat, then stir in the chocolate, salt, and pepper until the chocolate melts.
3. Divide the spaghetti among 6 plates. Spoon the chili (about ⅔ cup) over each plate of spaghetti. Sprinkle each with a generous tablespoon of the cheese and the remaining chopped onion.

PER SERVING (1 plate): 301 Cal, 7 g Fat, 2 g Sat Fat, 50 mg Chol, 608 mg Sod, 34 g Carb, 3 g Fib, 25 g Prot, 117 mg Calc. POINTS: 6.

tip This chili recipe is great to make ahead to have on hand for an easy weeknight dinner. Prepare the recipe, excluding the spaghetti, cheese, and onion garnish. Let the chili cool to room temperature, transfer to a freezer container, and freeze for up to three months. Or refrigerate the chili for up to two days.

Fusilli with Tomato, Basil, and Shrimp

Fusilli (pronounced foo-ZEE-lee) pasta looks like corkscrews. It is available long or cut into short pieces. We use cut fusilli here. If you can't find it in your supermarket, substitute spiralini or rotini, which are a similar shape and size.

10 ounces cut fusilli pasta

1 pound large shrimp, peeled and deveined

3 large tomatoes, chopped

¼ cup chopped fresh basil

¼ cup chopped fresh parsley

1 garlic clove, minced

2 scallions, chopped

1 tablespoon balsamic vinegar

1 tablespoon extra-virgin olive oil

2 tablespoon grated Romano cheese

1 teaspoon salt

¼ teaspoon freshly ground pepper

MAKES 6 SERVINGS

1. Bring a large pot of lightly salted water to a boil. Add the pasta and cook according to package directions, adding the shrimp during the last 2 minutes of cooking. Drain, then return the pasta and shrimp to the pot.
2. Add the tomatoes, basil, parsley, garlic, scallions, vinegar, oil, cheese, salt, and pepper to the pasta and shrimp; mix well. Serve at once while still warm or cover and refrigerate for up to 8 hours and serve chilled.

PER SERVING (1⅓ cups): 270 Cal, 4 g Fat, 1 g Sat Fat, 73 mg Chol, 684 mg Sod, 42 g Carb, 3 g Fib, 15 g Prot, 55 mg Calc. *POINTS: 5.*

tip To save time, have your fishmonger peel and devein the shrimp for you. This service is available at most fish shops or supermarket seafood counters.

Spaghetti alla Carbonara

Alla carbonara is an Italian phrase that describes a creamy pasta sauce made from eggs, grated Parmesan or Romano cheese, and bacon. The version made in the United States tends to be much heavier than its Northern Italian cousin, because of the addition of heavy cream. We stick with the lighter, traditional Italian style, and also add spinach to make it a complete meal. You'll need about ½ pound dry spaghetti to get 4 cups cooked.

MAKES 4 SERVINGS

- 1 (10-ounce) package frozen chopped spinach, thawed and squeezed dry
- ¾ cup low-fat (1%) milk
- 2 large eggs, lightly beaten
- ½ cup grated Romano cheese
- 1 teaspoon butter
- 3 garlic cloves, minced
- 2 ounces thinly sliced prosciutto, cut into strips
- 3 tablespoons dry vermouth
- 4 cups cooked spaghetti
- ¼ teaspoon freshly ground pepper

1. Combine the spinach, milk, eggs, and cheese in a bowl.
2. Melt the butter in a large nonstick skillet over medium heat. Add the garlic and cook, stirring constantly, until fragrant and light golden, 1–2 minutes. Add the prosciutto and cook until lightly browned, about 2 minutes. Pour in the vermouth and cook until it almost evaporates, about 30 seconds.
3. Reduce the heat to medium-low, then add the spaghetti and the spinach mixture. Cook, tossing constantly, until the mixture is just thickened and creamy and the eggs are cooked, about 3 minutes. Remove from the heat and season with the pepper.

PER SERVING (1 cup): 386 Cal, 10 g Fat, 5 g Sat Fat, 129 mg Chol, 561 mg Sod, 53 g Carb, 4 g Fib, 19 g Prot, 247 mg Calc. POINTS: 8.

tip We use prosciutto instead of bacon, because a small amount adds full, rich flavor and little fat to the carbonara. For best flavor, choose prosciutto imported from Italy, such as prosciutto di Parma (also called Parma ham).

Spaghetti alla
Carbonara, page 205

Penne with Chicken, Artichokes, and Peppers

If you don't feel like slicing chicken breasts for this recipe, buy chicken tenders—bite-size pieces of skinless boneless chicken breast. Although slightly more expensive, they help save time. You'll need about ¾ pound dry penne to get 6 cups cooked.

MAKES 6 SERVINGS

2 tablespoons extra-virgin olive oil
¾ pound skinless boneless chicken breast halves, cut into 1-inch chunks
½ teaspoon salt
¼ teaspoon freshly ground pepper
1 onion, sliced
3 garlic cloves, minced
1 (14-ounce) can artichoke hearts, drained, patted dry, and quartered
1 (12-ounce) jar roasted red peppers, drained, patted dry, and cut into strips
⅓ cup dry white wine
1 cup reduced-sodium fat-free chicken broth
6 cups cooked penne pasta
¼ cup grated Romano cheese
¼ cup chopped fresh parsley

1. Heat 1 tablespoon of the oil in a large nonstick skillet over medium-high heat. Add chicken and sprinkle with ¼ teaspoon of the salt and ⅛ teaspoon of the pepper. Cook, turning occasionally, until lightly browned and just cooked through, 3–4 minutes. Transfer to a plate and set aside.

2. Heat the remaining 1 tablespoon oil in the same skillet over medium-high heat. Add the onion and garlic. Cook, stirring occasionally, until the onion begins to soften, about 2 minutes. Stir in the artichoke hearts and roasted peppers. Cook, stirring, about 1 minute. Add the wine and cook until the liquid is reduced by half, about 1 minute. Stir in the broth and bring to a simmer.

3. Add the pasta to the skillet and cook, tossing occasionally, until heated through and the liquid thickens slightly, about 2 minutes. Add the chicken and the remaining ¼ teaspoon salt and ⅛ teaspoon pepper. Cook until the chicken is heated through, about 1 minute. Remove from the heat, then stir in the cheese and parsley.

PER SERVING (1½ cups): 397 Cal, 9 g Fat, 2 g Sat Fat, 35 mg Chol, 830 mg Sod, 55 g Carb, 6 g Fib, 24 g Prot, 87 mg Calc. *POINTS: 8.*

tip This speedy recipe calls for canned artichoke hearts and jarred roasted red peppers. Be sure to drain them well and, for best results, pat them dry with paper towels before using.

Stir-Fried Pork with Shiitake Mushrooms and Penne

Since today's pork is bred to be very lean, it can easily dry out if overcooked. Stir-frying is an ideal cooking method for boneless pork pieces, because the meat is seared quickly over high heat, helping to keep it moist. You'll need about ¼ pound dry penne to get 2 cups cooked.

MAKES 4 SERVINGS

1 cup reduced-sodium fat-free chicken broth

3 tablespoons reduced-sodium soy sauce

2 tablespoons dry sherry wine

2 tablespoons cornstarch

¾ pound pork tenderloin, trimmed of all visible fat and cut into 2 x ¼-inch strips

1 tablespoon canola oil

1 bunch asparagus, tough ends trimmed and cut into 1½-inch pieces

⅓ pound fresh shiitake mushrooms, stems discarded and caps sliced

1 tablespoon grated peeled fresh ginger

2 garlic cloves, minced

2 cups cooked penne pasta

1. Combine broth, 2 tablespoons of the soy sauce, 1 tablespoon of the sherry, and 1 tablespoon of the cornstarch in a small bowl; set aside.

2. Combine the pork with the remaining 1 tablespoon soy sauce, 1 tablespoon sherry, and 1 tablespoon cornstarch in a medium bowl; set aside.

3. Heat 2 teaspoons of the oil in a large nonstick skillet over medium-high heat. Add the pork mixture and cook, turning occasionally, until the pork is just cooked through, 2–3 minutes. Transfer the pork to a plate and set aside.

4. Heat the remaining 1 teaspoon oil in the same skillet. Add the asparagus and mushrooms. Cook, stirring, until slightly softened, about 4 minutes. Add the ginger and garlic. Cook, stirring, until fragrant and vegetables are tender, 1–2 minutes. Add the broth mixture and cook, stirring constantly, until the mixture bubbles and thickens. Add the pork and pasta. Cook, stirring occasionally, until heated through, about 2 minutes.

PER SERVING (1½ cups): 322 Cal, 8 g Fat, 2 g Sat Fat, 54 mg Chol, 726 mg Sod, 35 g Carb, 3 g Fib, 28 g Prot, 34 mg Calc. *POINTS: 7.*

tip To maximize the amount of flavor the pork absorbs, marinate it in the soy sauce mixture in the refrigerator for several hours or up to overnight.

Pasta with Escarole,
Sausage, and Beans

Pasta with Escarole, Sausage, and Beans

Escarole is a somewhat bitter green in the endive family. While it is mostly used in salads in this country, the Italians have perfected the art of cooking it in soups, in pasta dishes, and as a side dish. Orecchiette (pronounced oh-reck-ee-ET-tay) are pieces of pasta shaped like little ears. If you can't find them, substitute cut fusilli or tubettini.

¾ pound orecchiette pasta

1 medium head escarole, trimmed and torn into bite-size pieces

1 tablespoon extra-virgin olive oil

4 garlic cloves, sliced

½ pound sweet Italian turkey sausage, casings removed

4 plum tomatoes, seeded and chopped

1 (15½-ounce) can cannellini (white kidney) beans, rinsed and drained

¼ teaspoon crushed red pepper

1¼ cups reduced-sodium fat-free chicken broth

3 tablespoons grated Parmesan cheese

1. Bring a large pot of lightly salted water to a boil. Add the pasta, return to a boil, and cook until the pasta is almost tender, about 9 minutes. Stir in the escarole and cook until the pasta is cooked through and the escarole is tender, about 4 minutes longer. Drain the pasta and escarole and set aside in the colander.

2. Heat the oil in the same pot over medium-high heat. Add the garlic and cook, stirring, until fragrant, about 30 seconds. Add the sausage and cook, breaking up the sausage with a spoon, until lightly browned, 2–3 minutes. Add the tomatoes, beans, and crushed red pepper. Cook, stirring, until the tomatoes begin to soften, about 2 minutes.

3. Add the broth to the pot and bring to a simmer. Stir in the pasta and escarole and cook until heated through, 2–3 minutes. Serve in bowls with the Parmesan cheese.

PER SERVING (1⅓ cups pasta and ½ tablespoon cheese): 379 Cal, 8 g Fat, 2 g Sat Fat, 23 mg Chol, 844 mg Sod, 56 g Carb, 6 g Fib, 20 g Prot, 98 mg Calc. *POINTS: 7.*

tip A way to eliminate some of endive's bitter edge in cooked dishes is to blanch it briefly in boiling water before using it. We cook it for a few minutes in the boiling water with the pasta, which does the trick here.

Sausage, Golden Onion, and Apple Pasta

Pappardelle are ribbon noodles about ¾-inch wide and are perfect for carrying the large chunks of sausages, onions, mushrooms, and apples in this dish. If you can't find pappardelle in your supermarket, try substituting extra-wide egg noodles or fettuccine. You'll need about ½ pound dry pappardelle pasta to get 4½ cups cooked.

MAKES 6 SERVINGS

¾ pound sweet Italian turkey sausage, cut into 1-inch pieces
½ cup water
1 tablespoon butter
3 onions, thinly sliced
1 (8-ounce) package sliced fresh white mushrooms
½ teaspoon dried thyme
2 Granny Smith apples, peeled, cored, and cut into ¼-inch-thick slices
⅔ cup dry Marsala wine
⅔ cup reduced-sodium fat-free chicken broth
2 teaspoons cornstarch
½ teaspoon salt
¼ teaspoon freshly ground pepper
4½ cups cooked pappardelle pasta or extra-wide egg noodles
3 tablespoons grated Romano cheese

1. Heat a large nonstick skillet over medium-high heat. Add the sausage and water; cook, stirring occasionally, until the water evaporates and the sausage browns, 6–8 minutes.
2. Add the butter to the skillet and heat 30 seconds. Stir in the onions, mushrooms, and thyme. Cook, stirring occasionally, until the onions are golden, 7–9 minutes. Add the apples and cook until softened, about 2 minutes.
3. Combine the Marsala, broth, cornstarch, salt, and pepper in a bowl. Pour into the skillet and cook, stirring constantly, until the mixture bubbles and thickens. Add the pasta and cook until heated through, about 2 minutes. Serve sprinkled with the cheese.

PER SERVING (1⅓ cups pasta and ½ tablespoon cheese): 322 Cal, 9 g Fat, 4 g Sat Fat, 71 mg Chol, 872 mg Sod, 42 g Carb, 3 g Fib, 17 g Prot, 64 mg Calc. POINTS: 7.

Kielbasa Baked Ziti

What can turn a humdrum dish into a special, crowd-pleasing favorite? Sometimes just one ingredient, such as this smoky kielbasa, will do it. If traditional Italian flavor is what you're after, substitute Italian turkey sausage for the kielbasa.

10 ounces ziti
½ pound turkey kielbasa, cut into ¼-inch-thick slices
1 cup shredded part-skim mozzarella cheese
2 cups jarred fat-free basil tomato sauce
1 (10-ounce) package frozen peas, thawed
3 tablespoons grated Parmesan cheese

MAKES 6 SERVINGS

1. Preheat the oven to 350°F. Spray a 7 x 11-inch baking dish with nonstick spray.
2. Bring a large pot of lightly salted water to a boil. Cook the ziti according to package directions; drain and return to the pot.
3. Add the kielbasa, ½cup of the mozzarella cheese, 1 cup of the sauce, the peas, and 1 tablespoon of the Parmesan cheese to the pot with the ziti; toss well. Pour into the baking dish and spread smooth. Spoon the remaining sauce over the top of the ziti mixture, then sprinkle with the remaining ½ cup mozzarella cheese and 2 tablespoons Parmesan cheese.
4. Lightly spray a sheet of foil with nonstick spray, then place it over the baking dish. Bake 20 minutes, then uncover and bake until the cheese melts and the ziti is heated through, about 10 minutes longer.

PER SERVING (⅙ of casserole): 368 Cal, 9 g Fat, 4 g Sat Fat, 34 mg Chol, 1210 mg Sod, 50 g Carb, 5 g Fib, 22 g Prot, 217 mg Calc. *POINTS:* 7.

tip Canned and jarred tomato products can be high in sodium. If you are concerned about your sodium intake, use a low-sodium or no-salt-added tomato sauce. Or you can substitute low-sodium canned tomatoes, such as crushed or diced tomatoes, for the tomato sauce.

Stove-Top Macaroni and Cheese

This comfort-food favorite takes on a new look and new taste with the addition of tomatoes. The sauce is made in one skillet, and if you have any leftover pasta in the refrigerator, you won't need to dirty a second pot to cook the pasta. Leftover spaghetti works best if cut into 1- to 2-inch lengths, and leftover large pasta, such as rigatoni or ziti, could be cut in half. You'll need about ½ pound dry macaroni to get 4 cups cooked.

MAKES 6 SERVINGS

1 tablespoon butter

2 tablespoons all-purpose flour

1 (14½-ounce) can diced tomatoes

1½ cups shredded reduced-fat mild cheddar cheese

½ cup low-fat (1%) milk

2 tablespoons grated Parmesan cheese

½ teaspoon dry mustard

½ teaspoon salt

4 cups cooked elbow macaroni

1. Melt the butter in a large nonstick skillet over medium-high heat. Add the flour and cook, stirring constantly, until golden, about 1 minute. Add the tomatoes and cook, stirring constantly, until the mixture bubbles and thickens slightly, 2–3 minutes.
2. Stir the cheddar cheese, milk, Parmesan cheese, mustard, and salt into the skillet. Cook, stirring constantly, until the cheese melts and the mixture is smooth, 2–3 minutes.
3. Stir the pasta into the skillet and cook until heated through and well coated, 1–2 minutes. Let stand 2 minutes before serving.

PER SERVING (scant 1 cup): 285 Cal, 9 g Fat, 5 g Sat Fat, 23 mg Chol, 665 mg Sod, 36 g Carb, 2 g Fib, 15 g Prot, 288 mg Calc. *POINTS:* 6.

tip If you want a slightly crunchy texture, sprinkle each portion with a few toasted bread crumbs.

**Stove-Top Macaroni
and Cheese**

Southwestern Black Beans with Wagon Wheels

Wagon-wheel pasta, or ruote (pronounced ro-OH-tay), is a whimsical way to add great fun to a dish—and great for carrying chunky sauces such as this. For a nonvegetarian version, add 1½ cups cooked chicken breast chunks to the sauce and heat through with the cooked pasta. You'll be adding a *POINT* per serving, as well as an extra dose of lean protein.

½ pound wagon-wheel pasta
1 tablespoon olive oil
1 onion, chopped
2 assorted-color bell peppers, seeded and chopped
1 teaspoon dried oregano
1 teaspoon ground cumin
1 (14½-ounce) can diced tomatoes with green chiles
1 (15½-ounce) can black beans, rinsed and drained
1 (7-ounce) can corn kernels, drained
1 cup (4 ounces) shredded reduced-fat Mexican 4-cheese blend (cheddar, Monterey Jack, asadero, and queso blanco)

MAKES 6 SERVINGS

1. In a large pot of lightly salted boiling water, cook the pasta according to package directions; drain.
2. Heat the oil in the same pot over medium-high heat. Add the onion and bell peppers. Cook until the vegetables just begin to soften, about 3 minutes. Stir in the oregano and cumin. Cook, stirring frequently, until fragrant, about 30 seconds.
3. Add the tomatoes, beans, and corn to the pot; bring to a boil. Reduce the heat and simmer until the flavors are blended, about 5 minutes. Return the pasta to the pot and simmer until heated through, about 1 minute. Serve the pasta in bowls, sprinkled with the cheese.

PER SERVING (1⅓ cups pasta and scant 3 tablespoons cheese): 347 Cal, 7 g Fat, 3 g Sat Fat, 10 mg Chol, 648 mg Sod, 56 g Carb, 7 g Fib, 16 g Prot, 208 mg Calc. *POINTS: 7.*

tip This is a great "sauce" to make ahead. Simply prepare the recipe (omitting the pasta and cheese), let cool to room temperature, then refrigerate for up to three days or freeze for up to six months.

Thai Curried Tofu and Bowties

Coconut milk, fresh ginger, and red curry paste (a blend of chiles, garlic, onion, lemongrass, and spices) are staples in Thai cuisine. The light coconut milk adds sweetness (with little fat) and the ginger and curry paste add fire. Look for coconut milk and red curry paste in the ethnic section of your supermarket. You'll need about 6 ounces dry bowtie pasta to get 3 cups cooked.

1 (15-ounce) package low-fat firm tofu
1 tablespoon canola oil
1 tablespoon grated peeled fresh ginger
2 garlic cloves, minced
1½ teaspoons Thai red curry paste
1 onion, chopped
1 (14½-ounce) can diced tomatoes
1 cup light coconut milk
1 tablespoon sugar
1 (12-ounce) bag fresh broccoli, cauliflower, and carrots
1 tablespoon chopped fresh cilantro
¾ teaspoon salt
3 cups hot cooked bowtie pasta

MAKES 4 SERVINGS

1. Wrap the tofu in paper towels and place on a plate. Place a heavy saucepan on top and let it stand for 20 minutes to press out the excess liquid. Cut the tofu into ¼-inch cubes.
2. Heat 1½ teaspoons of the oil in a large nonstick skillet over medium-high heat. Add the tofu and cook, turning occasionally, until golden, about 2 minutes. Transfer the tofu to a plate.
3. Heat the remaining 1½ teaspoons oil in the same skillet over medium-high heat. Add the ginger, garlic, and curry paste. Cook, stirring frequently, until fragrant, about 20 seconds. Add the onion, reduce heat to medium, and cook, stirring occasionally, until the onion is softened, about 5 minutes.
4. Add the tomatoes, coconut milk, and sugar; bring to a boil. Reduce the heat to medium-low and cook, stirring occasionally, until slightly thickened, 5–6 minutes. Add the bag of broccoli, cauliflower, and carrots and the tofu. Cook, covered, until the vegetables are tender, 18–20 minutes.
5. Remove the skillet from the heat, then stir in the cilantro and salt. Serve with the bowties.

PER SERVING (1¼ cups sauce and ¾ cup pasta): 355 Cal, 10 g Fat, 4 g Sat Fat, 0 mg Chol, 900 mg Sod, 52 g Carb, 6 g Fib, 17 g Prot, 109 mg Calc. *POINTS: 7.*

Peanutty Noodles
with Tofu and Snow Peas

What could be easier? The spaghetti, tofu, and snow peas are cooked quickly in one pot, the peanut sauce ingredients are simply mixed, then everything is stirred together for this flavorful Asian-American favorite. If you prefer, substitute ¾ pound of cooked medium shrimp for the tofu and add some chopped fresh mint, cilantro, or basil.

6 tablespoons
   reduced-fat chunky
   peanut butter
6 tablespoons bottled
   hoisin sauce
2 tablespoons water
1 tablespoon packed
   dark brown sugar
1 tablespoon reduced-
   sodium soy sauce
1 teaspoon rice vinegar
½ pound spaghetti,
   broken in half
1 (15-ounce) package
   low-fat firm tofu, cut
   into ½-inch pieces
½ pound fresh snow
   peas, trimmed
2 scallions, chopped

MAKES 6 SERVINGS

1. Combine the peanut butter, hoisin sauce, water, sugar, soy sauce, and vinegar in a small bowl; mix well until smooth.
2. Bring a large pot of lightly salted water to a boil. Add the spaghetti and cook until almost done, about 10 minutes. Add the tofu and snow peas; cook until the pasta is cooked through and the snow peas are crisp-tender, about 2 minutes longer; drain.
3. Return the spaghetti, tofu, and snow peas to the pot. Add the peanut butter mixture and toss well to coat. Stir in the scallions just before serving.

PER SERVING (1 cup): 327 Cal, 8 g Fat, 1 g Sat Fat, 0 mg Chol, 389 mg Sod, 48 g Carb, 4 g Fib, 17 g Prot, 69 mg Calc. *POINTS:* 6.

tip You can serve this dish hot or at room temperature. If you have leftovers, refrigerate for up to two days, then let come to room temperature or gently reheat before serving.

Creamy Orzo with Chicken and Mushrooms

Rice-shaped orzo and a light cream sauce make this dish similar to a risotto, without all the stirring. To save some time, look for presliced shiitake mushrooms in your supermarket's produce section. You'll need about 1 cup dry orzo to get 2½ cups cooked.

MAKES 6 SERVINGS

1½ tablespoons extra-virgin olive oil
1 onion, chopped
1 garlic clove, minced
¾ pound fresh shiitake mushrooms, stems discarded, caps sliced
⅓ cup dry sherry
1½ cups low-fat (1%) milk
4 teaspoons cornstarch
¼ teaspoon salt
¼ teaspoon freshly ground pepper
⅛ teaspoon ground nutmeg
2½ cups cooked orzo
1 (10-ounce) package carved roasted skinless chicken breasts
¼ cup chopped fresh parsley

1. Heat the oil in a large nonstick skillet over medium-high heat. Add the onion and garlic. Cook, stirring, until softened, about 3 minutes. Add the mushrooms and cook, stirring occasionally, until tender and lightly browned, 4–5 minutes. Add the sherry and cook until it evaporates, about 1 minute.

2. Combine the milk, cornstarch, salt, pepper, and nutmeg in a bowl until smooth. Add the milk mixture to the skillet and cook over medium-low heat, stirring constantly, until the mixture bubbles and thickens, about 3 minutes. Stir in the orzo and chicken. Cook, stirring occasionally, until heated through, about 1 minute. Remove from the heat and stir in the parsley.

PER SERVING (1 cup): 254 Cal, 7 g Fat, 2 g Sat Fat, 39 mg Chol, 249 mg Sod, 27 g Carb, 2 g Fib, 21 g Prot, 100 mg Calc. *POINTS: 5.*

Grain Mains

Barley, bulgur, and more

Beef, Bulgur, and Eggplant Pilaf

Bulgur wheat—steamed, dried, and crushed wheat kernels—can be found in health-food stores and some supermarkets. This tasty grain is used as the main ingredient in many vegetarian dishes, such as tabbouleh (see recipe opposite page), pilafs, and casseroles, and as a nutritious extender for meat dishes. Bulgur can be used in place of rice in just about any recipe.

2 teaspoons olive oil

1 onion, chopped

2 garlic cloves, minced

½ pound ground lean beef (10% or less fat)

1 tablespoon tomato paste

1 teaspoon red curry paste

1 teaspoon cinnamon

1 teaspoon ground cumin

1 teaspoon ground allspice

¾ teaspoon salt

½ pound eggplant, unpeeled and cut into ½-inch cubes

3 plum tomatoes, chopped

4 cups low-sodium chicken broth

1 cup bulgur wheat

1 cup frozen peas

¼ cup chopped fresh parsley

MAKES 4 SERVINGS

1. Heat the oil in a nonstick Dutch oven over medium-high heat. Add the onion and garlic. Cook, stirring occasionally, until the onion is very tender, about 8 minutes. Add the beef and cook, breaking up the meat with a wooden spoon, until browned, about 8 minutes.

2. Stir the tomato paste, curry paste, cinnamon, cumin, allspice, and salt into the Dutch oven. Cook, stirring constantly, until fragrant, about 1 minute. Add the eggplant and tomatoes. Cook, stirring occasionally, over medium heat, until the eggplant and tomatoes begin to soften, about 5 minutes. Stir in the broth and bulgur; bring to a boil. Reduce the heat and simmer, covered, until the mixture thickens and the liquid is almost absorbed, about 25 minutes. Stir in the peas and heat through. Remove from the heat and stir in the parsley. Serve at once.

PER SERVING (2 cups): 322 Cal, 8 g Fat, 2 g Sat Fat, 32 mg Chol, 628 mg Sod, 44 g Carb, 11 g Fib, 22 g Prot, 70 mg Calc. *POINTS: 6.*

Minted Tabbouleh with Tofu

Bulgur is the grain of choice in this no-cook Middle Eastern favorite. The nutty flavor and chewy texture of the bulgur contrast well with the crisp, fresh vegetables. Substitute a cup of drained canned chickpeas (garbanzo beans) for the tofu, if you prefer.

MAKES 4 SERVINGS

1¼ cups water
1 cup bulgur wheat
2 tomatoes, diced
½ cucumber, peeled, seeded, and diced
6 scallions, finely chopped
½ cup chopped fresh mint
¼ cup chopped flat-leaf parsley
¼ cup fresh lemon juice
2 teaspoons extra-virgin olive oil
¾ teaspoon salt
½ teaspoon freshly ground pepper
½ pound firm tofu, cut into ¼-inch dice

1. Bring the water to a boil in a large saucepan. Stir in the bulgur, then remove from the heat. Cover and let stand until the water is absorbed, 25–30 minutes.
2. Meanwhile, combine the tomatoes, cucumber, scallions, mint, parsley, lemon juice, oil, salt, and pepper in a large bowl. Add the bulgur; toss to combine. Gently fold in the tofu and serve at once. Or refrigerate the dish, covered, until well chilled, at least 2 hours. Let stand at room temperature about 10 minutes before serving.

PER SERVING (2¼ cups): 256 Cal, 9 g Fat, 1 g Sat Fat, 0 mg Chol, 466 mg Sod, 36 g Carb, 10 g Fib, 15 g Prot, 173 mg Calc. *POINTS: 5.*

tip This portable main-dish salad is great for taking to potluck dinners. You can make it up to one to two days ahead and store it in the refrigerator until ready to serve.

Wheat Berry Waldorf Salad with Ham

The wheat berry is a whole unprocessed wheat kernel that adds fabulous crunch and texture to salads or cooked dishes such as pilafs and casseroles. Uncooked wheat berries (available at health-food stores) keep for up to one year stored in an airtight container in the pantry. If you prefer, you can substitute cubed cooked chicken or turkey for the ham.

2¼ cups water
1 cup wheat berries
½ pound piece fat-free fully cooked honey ham, cut into ½-inch cubes
1 Granny Smith apple, cored and cubed
1 red onion, finely chopped
1 cup golden raisins
2 celery stalks, finely chopped
¼ cup chopped walnuts
¼ cup chopped fresh parsley
2 tablespoons cider vinegar
2 tablespoons orange juice
1 tablespoon honey
1 tablespoon olive oil
1 tablespoon minced peeled fresh ginger
1 teaspoon Dijon mustard
¼ teaspoon salt
6 Boston or Bibb lettuce leaves

MAKES 6 SERVINGS

1. Bring the water to a boil in a medium saucepan; stir in the wheat berries. Reduce the heat and simmer, covered, until the wheat berries are tender and liquid is absorbed, about 1 hour.
2. Combine the ham, apple, onion, raisins, celery, walnuts, and parsley in a large bowl.
3. Whisk together the vinegar, orange juice, honey, oil, ginger, mustard, and salt in a small bowl. Stir the vinegar mixture into ham mixture until blended. Add the wheat berries; toss well.
4. Arrange the lettuce leaves in each of 6 bowls. Spoon the wheat-berry mixture (about 1 cup) on top of each. Serve at once.

PER SERVING (1 salad): 280 Cal, 7 g Fat, 1 g Sat Fat, 20 mg Chol, 583 mg Sod, 47 g Carb, 5 g Fib, 13 g Prot, 47 mg Calc. *POINTS: 5.*

tip Since wheat berries take an hour to cook, you may want to cook them ahead and store them in a zip-close plastic bag in the refrigerator—they will keep for up to three days. Toss them with the remaining ingredients just before serving.

Wheat Berry Waldorf
Salad with Ham

Sausage and Spinach Couscous

Couscous is a coarse-ground wheat grain (similar to semolina) and a staple of North African cuisine. It is sometimes referred to as Moroccan-style pasta and can be substituted as a quick alternative to rice in many recipes—it cooks in only 5 minutes.

1 teaspoon olive oil

1 pound Italian chicken sausage, cut into 2-inch chunks

1 onion, chopped

1 red bell pepper, seeded and chopped

2 garlic cloves, minced

¾ cup low-sodium chicken broth

½ cup jarred marinara sauce

1 (5-ounce) bag baby spinach, coarsely chopped

1 cup plain couscous

MAKES 6 SERVINGS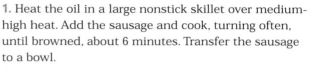

1. Heat the oil in a large nonstick skillet over medium-high heat. Add the sausage and cook, turning often, until browned, about 6 minutes. Transfer the sausage to a bowl.

2. Add the onion, bell pepper, and garlic to the skillet. Cook, over medium-low heat, stirring occasionally, until the vegetables are softened, about 5 minutes. If the mixture seems dry, add about ¼ cup water to the skillet while the vegetables are cooking.

3. Return the sausage to the skillet. Add the broth and marinara sauce; bring to a boil. Reduce the heat and simmer, covered, until the sausage is cooked through, about 8 minutes longer. Stir in the spinach. Cook, stirring occasionally, until the spinach just begins to wilt, about 2 minutes. Stir in the couscous. Cover and remove from the heat. Let stand until the liquid is absorbed and the couscous is tender, about 5 minutes. Fluff the mixture lightly with a fork just before serving.

PER SERVING (generous 1 cup): 272 Cal, 9 g Fat, 2 g Sat Fat, 44 mg Chol, 711 mg Sod, 29 g Carb, 3 g Fib, 19 g Prot, 56 mg Calc. POINTS: 6.

tip Couscous is available boxed in a variety of flavors, such as roasted garlic and olive oil or Parmesan, as well as the most commonly used plain couscous. Be sure to use the plain variety in this and the Turkey Couscous with Dried Fruit and Pine Nuts, on the following page.

Turkey Couscous with Dried Fruit and Pine Nuts

This tasty couscous salad of smoked turkey, currants, dates, and grapes, drizzled with a honey-balsamic vinaigrette, is full of great flavor and texture. Be as creative as you like by using your own favorite dried fruits—dried cranberries, chopped dried apricots, or figs work well.

2 cups low-sodium chicken broth
1 cup plain couscous
3 tablespoons orange juice
2 tablespoons balsamic vinegar
1 tablespoon olive oil
1 teaspoon honey
1 teaspoon Dijon mustard
½ teaspoon salt
¼ teaspoon ground cumin
½ pound smoked turkey in one piece, cut into ½-inch cubes
1 cup seedless red grapes
1 red onion, finely chopped
⅓ cup currants
10 pitted dates, chopped
¼ cup pine nuts
3 tablespoons chopped flat-leaf parsley

MAKES 6 SERVINGS

1. Bring the broth to a boil in a medium saucepan; stir in the couscous. Cover and remove from the heat; let stand 5 minutes. Gently fluff the couscous with a fork and transfer to a bowl. Let cool slightly.
2. Meanwhile, whisk together the orange juice, vinegar, oil, honey, mustard, salt, and cumin in a small bowl. Blend the orange-juice mixture into the couscous..
3. Add the turkey, grapes, onion, currants, dates, pine nuts, and parsley to the couscous mixture; toss well to combine. Serve at once while still warm.

PER SERVING (generous 1 cup): 309 Cal, 7 g Fat, 1 g Sat Fat, 16 mg Chol, 696 mg Sod, 51 g Carb, 4 g Fib, 13 g Prot, 36 mg Calc. *POINTS: 6.*

tip If you'd like to make this salad ahead and serve it cold, toss the cooked couscous with the orange-juice mixture and refrigerate until chilled. Add the turkey and the remaining ingredients just before serving.

Couscous Tuna Niçoise

Couscous comes in a variety of sizes—fine, medium, and large pearls that resemble tapioca. The largest size, often referred to as Israeli couscous or Mediterranean couscous, is packaged in boxes of about 5 ounces. If you buy a brand that has a flavor packet inside, don't use the seasonings to make this recipe. Use orzo or quick-cooking barley if you can't find Israeli couscous.

MAKES 4 SERVINGS

2¼ cups water
1 (5-ounce) box Israeli couscous
1 red onion, diced
12 kalamata olives, pitted and chopped
½ cup chopped fresh basil
2 tablespoons drained capers, rinsed
1 tablespoon grated lemon zest
2 tablespoons fresh lemon juice
1 tablespoon extra-virgin olive oil
1 teaspoon Dijon mustard
¼ teaspoon salt
1 (12-ounce) can solid white tuna, packed in water, drained
1 cup cherry tomatoes, halved
2 ounces reduced-fat goat cheese, crumbled

1. Bring the water to a boil in a medium saucepan; add the couscous. Reduce the heat and simmer, covered, until most of the liquid is absorbed and the couscous is tender, about 15 minutes. Drain; run the couscous under cold running water and drain well. Transfer the couscous to a large bowl.
2. Add the onion, olives, basil, capers, lemon zest, lemon juice, oil, mustard, and salt to the couscous; toss well to combine.
3. Break the tuna into large chunks. Add the tuna and tomatoes to the couscous mixture and toss gently to combine. Sprinkle the salad with the goat cheese and serve at once.

PER SERVING (1¼ cups): 329 Cal, 9 g Fat, 3 g Sat Fat, 36 mg Chol, 697 mg Sod, 34 g Carb, 3 g Fib, 27 g Prot, 119 mg Calc. *POINTS: 7.*

tip Aromatic oils in lemon zest give much flavor to food. The zest of the lemon is the thin outermost yellow layer of the skin (without any of the bitter white part underneath). To remove the zest, rub the whole lemon against the fine side of a grater until the zest is grated away. You can get 1 to 2 teaspoons of grated lemon zest from 1 lemon.

Kasha Varnishkes

Kasha varnishkes is an Eastern European classic. Kasha is the Russian name for roasted buckwheat groats, and varnishkes are thick bowtie egg noodles. You can find kasha and varnishkes in the kosher section of large supermarkets or in health-food stores. We use farfalle instead of the varnishkes, but you can use whichever is available. Stirring an egg white into the kasha before adding any liquid helps make this dish a little fluffy.

MAKES 3 SERVINGS

1 tablespoon canola oil
2 large sweet onions, such as Vidalia, chopped
½ teaspoon salt
¼ teaspoon freshly ground pepper
½ cup kasha or buckwheat groats
1 egg white, lightly beaten
1½ cups water
2 cups cooked farfalle (bowtie) pasta (about 4 ounces dry)
2 tablespoons chopped fresh parsley

1. Heat 2 teaspoons of the oil in a large nonstick skillet over medium heat. Add the onions, salt, and pepper. Cook, stirring occasionally, until the onions are very tender, about 10 minutes; transfer to a bowl.
2. Meanwhile, combine the kasha and egg white in a small bowl, stirring with a fork until the kasha is well coated. Set aside.
3. Heat the remaining 1 teaspoon oil in the same skillet, then add the kasha mixture. Cook, over medium-high heat, stirring frequently, until the egg is cooked and the kasha kernels have separated, about 5 minutes. Stir in the water; bring to a boil. Reduce the heat and simmer, covered, until the kasha is tender and the liquid is absorbed, about 6 minutes. Stir in the onion mixture, cooked pasta, and parsley. Serve at once.

PER SERVING (1⅓ cups): 293 Cal, 6 g Fat, 1 g Sat Fat, 0 mg Chol, 561 mg Sod, 52 g Carb, 4 g Fib, 9 g Prot, 39 mg Calc. *POINTS: 6.*

tip This recipe, made without the pasta, makes an excellent vegetarian stuffing for cabbage, bell peppers, or eggplant.

Posole with Ham and Vegetables

The unique flavor of posole (hominy) is the same as the flavor in tamales and corn tortillas—earthy, sweet, and mellow. It pairs well with the smokiness of the chipotle chiles and the ham in this simple stew.

MAKES 4 SERVINGS

2 teaspoons canola oil
1 onion, coarsely chopped
1 green bell pepper, seeded and cut into ½-inch pieces
2 celery stalks, chopped
2 chipotle chiles en adobo, chopped
2 garlic cloves, minced
1 (14½-ounce) can diced tomatoes, drained
1 (15-ounce) can hominy, drained
1 cup water
½ pound cooked ham in one piece, cut into ½-inch pieces
1 cup whole baby carrots
1 medium zucchini, cut into ½-inch dice
¼ cup chopped fresh cilantro
¼ cup shredded reduced-fat Monterey Jack cheese

1. Heat the oil in a large nonstick saucepan over medium-high heat. Add the onion, bell pepper, celery, chiles, and garlic. Cook, stirring occasionally, until the vegetables are very tender and golden, about 12 minutes.

2. Add the tomatoes to the saucepan and cook until softened, about 5 minutes. Stir in the hominy, water, ham, and carrots; bring to a boil. Reduce the heat and simmer, covered, until the flavors blend and sauce thickens slightly, about 30 minutes.

3. Add the zucchini to the saucepan and cook until crisp-tender, about 6 minutes. Remove from the heat, then stir in the cilantro. Serve the stew sprinkled with the cheese.

PER SERVING (1½ cups stew and 1 tablespoon cheese): 268 Cal, 10 g Fat, 3 g Sat Fat, 37 mg Chol, 1174 mg Sod, 27 g Carb, 6 g Fib, 19 g Prot, 128 mg Calc. *POINTS: 5.*

Polenta Lasagna with Olives and Sun-Dried Tomatoes

Packaged polenta, available in a 16-ounce tube in the refrigerator section of most supermarkets, makes this creamy lasagna a breeze to assemble. Jarred marinara sauce and preshredded cheese also help keep preparation time to a minimum.

MAKES 4 SERVINGS

1 cup fat-free ricotta cheese

2 tablespoons grated Parmesan cheese

2 tablespoons chopped flat-leaf parsley

1 oil-packed sun-dried tomato, drained and chopped (about 1 tablespoon)

10 kalamata olives, pitted and chopped

½ teaspoon coarsely ground black pepper

1½ cups jarred marinara sauce

2 (16-ounce) tubes fat-free polenta, cut into 24 (½-inch) slices

12 whole basil leaves

¾ cup shredded part-skim mozzarella cheese

1. Preheat the oven to 375°F. Spray a 9 x 13-inch baking dish with nonstick spray.

2. Combine the ricotta, Parmesan cheese, parsley, sun-dried tomato, olives, and pepper in a medium bowl; set aside.

3. Spoon about ½ cup of the marinara sauce into the bottom of the baking dish. Place 12 of the polenta rounds over the sauce, then top each with a scant 2 tablespoons of the ricotta mixture and a basil leaf. Arrange the remaining polenta on top. Spoon the remaining 1 cup sauce evenly over all, then sprinkle with the mozzarella cheese.

4. Cover the dish loosely with foil and bake until heated through and the sauce is bubbly, about 30 minutes. Remove the foil and let stand 10 minutes before serving.

PER SERVING (¼ of lasagna): 322 Cal, 10 g Fat, 4 g Sat Fat, 14 mg Chol, 1004 mg Sod, 38 g Carb, 4 g Fib, 19 g Prot, 344 mg Calc. POINTS: 6.

tip For a lightly browned top, uncover the lasagna during the last 10 to 12 minutes of baking.

**Polenta Lasagna
with Olives and
Sun-Dried Tomatoes,
page 231**

Quinoa and Mango Salad with Arugula

Quinoa was one of the most sacred foods of the ancient Incas. It was so nourishing and delicious that it was named their "mother grain." It is the only grain that is a complete protein. Before cooking, be sure to rinse quinoa in a fine mesh sieve under cold water for a minute to remove the natural outer coating, which is bitter.

1 cup quinoa, rinsed well under running water and drained

2 cups water

¼ cup fresh lime juice

2 tablespoons honey

1 tablespoon extra-virgin olive oil

¾ teaspoon salt

1 ripe mango, peeled and cut into ½-inch cubes

1 red bell pepper, seeded and diced

1 yellow bell pepper, seeded and diced

4 scallions, chopped

2 jalapeño peppers, seeded and minced (wear gloves to prevent irritation)

3 cups arugula, coarsely chopped

¼ cup sliced almonds

MAKES 4 SERVINGS

1. Combine the quinoa and water in a medium saucepan; bring to a boil. Reduce the heat and simmer, covered, until most of the water has been absorbed, about 10 minutes. Transfer to a large bowl and cool slightly.

2. Meanwhile, whisk together the lime juice, honey, oil, and salt in a small bowl.

3. Add the lime mixture to the quinoa; toss to coat. Add the mango, red and yellow bell peppers, scallions, and jalapeño peppers; toss to coat. Gently stir in the arugula. Serve at once sprinkled with the almonds.

PER SERVING (2 cups salad and 1 tablespoon almonds): 320 Cal, 9 g Fat, 1 g Sat Fat, 0 mg Chol, 460 mg Sod, 55 g Carb, 6 g Fib, 9 g Prot, 94 mg Calc. *POINTS: 6.*

tip You can make this salad ahead (omitting the arugula and almonds) and refrigerate it for up to 24 hours. Stir in the arugula and sprinkle with the almonds just before serving.

Pork and Vegetable Fried Rice

Fried rice is best made from cold cooked rice, so it's best to purchase the rice from your favorite Chinese takeout the day before you need it and keep it in the refrigerator. Or order extra rice when you have a Chinese takeout meal and save the extra for up to four days for making this dish. If you prefer to cook the rice yourself, simply spread the cooked rice out onto a large baking sheet to cool thoroughly before using it. If you like, you can substitute fresh chopped spinach for the peas.

MAKES 4 SERVINGS

½ pound pork tenderloin, cut into ¼-inch dice
2 tablespoons bottled oyster sauce
2 teaspoons minced peeled fresh ginger
1 garlic clove, minced
2 teaspoons Asian (dark) sesame oil
2 teaspoons canola oil
6 scallions, thinly sliced diagonally
1 carrot, cut into ¼-inch dice
1 large egg, lightly beaten
2 cups cold cooked white rice
1 tablespoon reduced-sodium soy sauce
1 cup frozen peas

1. Combine the pork, 1 tablespoon of the oyster sauce, the ginger, garlic, and 1 teaspoon of the sesame oil in a small bowl; set aside.
2. Heat the canola oil in a large nonstick skillet over medium-high heat. Add the pork mixture and cook, stirring constantly, until the pork begins to brown, about 3 minutes.
3. Reserve 2 tablespoons of the chopped scallions for garnish. Add the remaining scallions and the carrot to the pork in the skillet. Cook, stirring constantly, until the vegetables are tender, about 3 minutes. Add the egg, stirring quickly and constantly with a wooden spoon until the egg begins to set, about 2 minutes.
4. Stir the rice, soy sauce, the remaining 1 tablespoon oyster sauce, and the remaining 1 teaspoon sesame oil into the skillet. Cook, stirring frequently, until the rice is heated through, about 5 minutes. Stir in the peas and cook, stirring, until heated through, about 2 minutes. Serve sprinkled with the reserved 2 tablespoons scallions.

PER SERVING (1 cup): 283 Cal, 8 g Fat, 2 g Sat Fat, 89 mg Chol, 566 mg Sod, 31 g Carb, 3 g Fib, 19 g Prot, 34 mg Calc. POINTS: 6.

Jasmine Rice with Shrimp and Peas

Jasmine rice is a fragrant long-grain rice, popular in Thai cuisine. The grains become slightly sticky when cooked and the flavor is subtly sweet. Pickled ginger (fresh ginger preserved in sweet vinegar) is used in many Asian dishes and is sometimes served as a condiment. You can find jasmine rice and jars of aromatic pickled ginger in Asian markets and most supermarkets.

1½ cups low-sodium chicken broth
3 tablespoons bottled oyster sauce
2 tablespoons juice from the pickled ginger jar
1 tablespoon reduced-sodium soy sauce
1 teaspoon Asian (dark) sesame oil
¼ teaspoon crushed red pepper
2 teaspoons canola oil
½ pound large shrimp, peeled and deveined
1 carrot, cut into matchstick-thin strips (about 1 cup)
6 scallions, thinly sliced
1 tablespoon pickled ginger, drained and chopped
2 garlic cloves, minced
½ cup jasmine rice
1 cup frozen peas

MAKES 3 SERVINGS

1. Whisk the broth, oyster sauce, ginger juice, soy sauce, sesame oil, and crushed red pepper in a small bowl; set aside.
2. Heat 1 teaspoon of the canola oil in a medium nonstick skillet over medium-high heat. Add the shrimp and cook, turning often, until opaque in the center, about 3 minutes. Transfer the shrimp to a bowl.
3. Add the remaining 1 teaspoon canola oil to the same skillet, then add the carrot, scallions, ginger, and garlic. Cook, stirring constantly, until fragrant, about 2 minutes. Add the rice, tossing to coat. Stir in the broth mixture; bring to a boil. Reduce the heat and simmer, covered, until the liquid is absorbed and the rice is tender, about 20 minutes.
4. Add the shrimp and peas to the skillet and cook, stirring frequently, until heated through, about 3 minutes.

PER SERVING (1⅓ cups): 291 Cal, 6 g Fat, 1 g Sat Fat, 71 mg Chol, 1064 mg Sod, 42 g Carb, 4 g Fib, 17 g Prot, 78 mg Calc. *POINTS: 6.*

tip To save time, purchase precut matchstick carrots from the produce section of the supermarket. They're available in a 10-ounce bag.

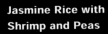

**Jasmine Rice with
Shrimp and Peas**

Chicken with Rice and Mushrooms

An important part of this recipe is cooking the vegetables in the oil long enough to turn them golden and slightly caramelized. The mushrooms give off liquid, which needs to be cooked off before the mushrooms can brown. After the liquid evaporates, you'll find that the vegetables' natural sugars are released; the vegetables will turn golden and begin to caramelize, making all the difference to the flavor of the dish.

MAKES 4 SERVINGS

2 teaspoons olive oil

1 pound skinless boneless chicken thighs, trimmed of all visible fat and cut into 1½-inch chunks

½ pound fresh white mushrooms, sliced

2 celery stalks, thinly sliced

2 carrots, chopped

1 small leek, cleaned and thinly sliced (about 2 cups)

1 tomato, chopped

¼ cup dry white wine

1 (6-ounce) box long-grain and wild rice mix

2 cups low-sodium chicken broth

2 tablespoons chopped fresh parsley

1. Heat 1 teaspoon of the oil in a large nonstick skillet over medium-high heat. Add chicken and cook, turning occasionally, until browned, about 6 minutes; transfer to a plate.

2. Heat the remaining 1 teaspoon oil in the same skillet. Add the mushrooms, celery, carrots, and leek. Cook over medium heat, stirring occasionally, until the vegetables are very tender and golden, about 12 minutes. Add the tomato and cook until soft, about 5 minutes. Stir in the wine and cook until the liquid evaporates, about 2 minutes.

3. Add the rice mix, stirring to coat the grains. Return the chicken to the skillet. Add the broth and bring to a boil. Reduce the heat and simmer, covered, until the liquid is absorbed, the rice is tender, and the chicken is cooked through, about 25 minutes. Remove the skillet from the heat and serve sprinkled with the parsley.

PER SERVING (1¼ cups): 420 Cal, 11 g Fat, 3 g Sat Fat, 77 mg Chol, 146 mg Sod, 47 g Carb, 5 g Fib, 33 g Prot, 74 mg Calc. *POINTS: 9.*

Barley Risotto with Sausage and Mushrooms

Cremini mushrooms are woodsy-flavored, earthy brown mushrooms that when allowed to grow fully, become portobello mushrooms. Substitute brown button or white mushrooms if cremini aren't available. If you're pressed for time, use quick-cooking barley instead of the pearl barley—it cooks in 10 to 12 minutes.

MAKES 6 SERVINGS

2 cups water
1 (¾-ounce) package dried shiitake mushrooms
2 teaspoons olive oil
1 (8-ounce) package fresh cremini mushrooms, thinly sliced
1 onion, finely chopped
¼ cup dry white wine
1 pound Italian turkey sausage, casings removed
3 cups low sodium chicken broth
1 cup pearl barley
¼ cup grated Parmesan cheese
2 tablespoons chopped fresh sage, or 2 teaspoons dried
1 teaspoon butter
½ teaspoon freshly ground pepper

1. Bring the water to a boil in a small saucepan. Remove from the heat and add the mushrooms; let stand 20 minutes. Drain, reserving the liquid, and coarsely chop the mushrooms.

2. Heat the oil in a large nonstick saucepan over medium-high heat. Add the soaked mushrooms, cremini mushrooms, and onion. Cook, stirring occasionally, until the mushrooms and onion are very tender, about 15 minutes.

3. Stir in the wine; bring to a boil. Cook until the wine evaporates, about 3 minutes. Add the sausage and cook, breaking the sausage up with a spoon, until it begins to brown, about 10 minutes.

4. Add the reserved mushroom soaking liquid, the broth, and barley; bring to a boil. Reduce the heat and simmer, covered, until the barley is tender, about 40 minutes. Remove the saucepan from the heat. Stir in the Parmesan cheese, sage, butter, and pepper and serve at once.

PER SERVING (generous 1 cup): 307 Cal, 11 g Fat, 4 g Sat Fat, 49 mg Chol, 707 mg Sod, 31 g Carb, 6 g Fib, 21 g Prot, 96 mg Calc. *POINTS: 6.*

**Three-Grain Salad
with Spicy Peanut Dressing**

Three-Grain Salad
with Spicy Peanut Dressing

Brown rice, barley, and wild rice give a subtle variety of colors and textures, while crisp, colorful vegetables add crunch and vibrant color to this healthy salad. The salad can be prepared several hours ahead of time, making it a perfect dish for entertaining, potluck suppers, and picnics.

MAKES 4 SERVINGS

½ cup brown rice
½ cup pearl barley
½ cup wild rice
2 tablespoons reduced-fat peanut butter
2 tablespoons seasoned rice vinegar
2 tablespoons reduced-sodium soy sauce
2 tablespoons low-sodium vegetable broth
1 tablespoon honey
1 tablespoon Asian (dark) sesame oil
2 garlic cloves, minced
2 teaspoons minced peeled fresh ginger
½ teaspoon crushed red pepper
1 yellow bell pepper, seeded and diced
1 red bell pepper, seeded and diced
6 scallions, thinly sliced
2 carrots, cut into ¼-inch dice
½ cup chopped fresh cilantro
¼ cup unsalted dry-roasted peanuts

1. Place the brown rice, barley, and wild rice in a large saucepan. Add enough water to cover by 2 inches; bring to a boil. Reduce the heat and simmer, covered, until the rice mixture is tender, 30–40 minutes. Drain the rice mixture and place in a shallow baking pan, separating the grains with a fork. Let stand, uncovered, at room temperature to cool, about 20 minutes.
2. Whisk together the peanut butter, vinegar, soy sauce, broth, honey, sesame oil, garlic, ginger, and crushed red pepper in a large bowl.
3. Add the rice mixture, the yellow and red bell peppers, the scallions, carrots, and cilantro to the peanut butter mixture; toss to coat. Serve sprinkled with the peanuts.

PER SERVING (1½ cups salad and 1 tablespoon peanuts): 445 Cal, 12 g Fat, 2 g Sat Fat, 0 mg Chol, 381 mg Sod, 74 g Carb, 10 g Fib, 14 g Prot, 69 mg Calc. *POINTS*: 9.

CUT *POINTS* Sprinkle each salad with just a teaspoon of peanuts instead of a tablespoon and save about a *POINT*.

Slow-Cooker Solutions

Dinners to greet you at the door

Beef Burgundy

Traditionally, the French use Burgundy wine when cooking their famous *boeuf bourguignon*, but any dry red wine would be fine. Avoid "cooking wines," as their taste is inferior and they can be high in sodium—cook only with wine that you would serve at the dinner table.

MAKES 4 SERVINGS

2	teaspoons canola oil
1	pound boneless lean beef round, trimmed of all visible fat and cut into 2-inch chunks
½	teaspoon salt
¼	teaspoon freshly ground pepper
1½	cups low-sodium beef broth
½	cup dry red wine
2	all-purpose potatoes (about ¾ pound), peeled and cut into 1-inch cubes
½	pound fresh white mushrooms, quartered
1	cup frozen small whole onions
2	garlic cloves, minced
1	tablespoon chopped fresh thyme, or 1 teaspoon dried
1	bay leaf
2	tablespoons all-purpose flour
3	tablespoons cold water
2	teaspoons browning and seasoning sauce
2	tablespoons chopped fresh parsley

1. Heat the oil in a large nonstick skillet over medium heat. Add the beef, then sprinkle with the salt and pepper. Cook, turning occasionally, until browned, about 6 minutes.
2. Transfer the beef to a slow cooker. Add broth, wine, potatoes, mushrooms, onions, garlic, thyme, and bay leaf. Cover and cook until the meat and vegetables are fork-tender, 4–5 hours on high or 8–10 hours on low.
3. About 20 minutes before the cooking time is up, combine the flour, water, and seasoning sauce in a small bowl until smooth; stir in about ¼ cup of the hot liquid from slow cooker until blended. Stir flour mixture into the slow cooker. Cover and cook on high, until mixture simmers and thickens, about 15 minutes. Discard the bay leaf. Stir in the parsley just before serving.

PER SERVING (1½ cups): 278 Cal, 7 g Fat, 2 g Sat Fat, 60 mg Chol, 375 mg Sod, 26 g Carb, 3 g Fib, 27 g Prot, 36 mg Calc. *POINTS: 6.*

tip Browning meats in a skillet before cooking in the slow cooker adds flavor and rich color to the finished dish. If you want a truly one-pot experience, however, you can omit this step and place the meat directly in the slow cooker with the remaining ingredients.

Corned Beef and Cabbage

Mustard is the condiment of choice to serve with this Irish favorite, and the Irish know just the kind of mustard to use—a biting hot, nose-tingling, eye-watering mixture of equal parts warm water and powdered mustard. A tablespoon, or two, of each should be enough to accompany this amount of food. For the tamer palate, serve a prepared mustard such as Dijon.

2 large onions, sliced

2 garlic cloves, chopped

1 (1¾-pound) lean corned beef brisket, trimmed of all visible fat

3 medium carrots, cut into 2-inch chunks

3 all-purpose potatoes (about 1 pound), peeled and cut into 2-inch chunks

½ head green cabbage (about 1 pound), cored and cut into 8 wedges

1¼ cups low-sodium chicken broth

MAKES 8 SERVINGS

1. Place the onions and garlic in a slow cooker. Place the corned beef on top of the onions. Arrange the carrots and potatoes around the meat. Place cabbage wedges on top of vegetables. Pour the broth over and around the vegetables. Cover and cook until the meat and vegetables are fork-tender, 4–5 hours on high or 8–10 hours on low.

2. Transfer the corned beef to a platter and cut into slices. With a slotted spoon, lift the vegetables from the broth and place around the meat.

PER SERVING (⅛ of dinner): 261 Cal, 14 g Fat, 4 g Sat Fat, 68 mg Chol, 821 mg Sod, 19 g Carb, 3 g Fib, 15 g Prot, 49 mg Calc. *POINTS*: 6.

tip To save precious time in the morning, assemble all the ingredients in the insert of the slow cooker the night before and refrigerate. In the morning, you'll only need pop the insert into the slow cooker and plug it in.

Country-Style Beef Short Ribs with Horseradish Cream

Boneless beef short ribs (sometimes called country-style ribs) require long, slow cooking to tenderize them, making them a perfect candidate for the slow cooker. Boneless short ribs contain less fat than bone-in short ribs, but they still need to be trimmed of all visible fat once you get them home.

6 tablespoons fat-free sour cream

2 tablespoons prepared horseradish

1 tablespoon Dijon mustard

¾ teaspoon salt

1¼ pounds boneless beef short ribs, trimmed of all visible fat and cut into 1½-inch chunks

½ teaspoon freshly ground pepper

2 onions, sliced

1 pound small whole white potatoes, scrubbed

1½ cups whole baby carrots

2 garlic cloves, chopped

1 bay leaf

1 cup low-sodium beef broth

2 tablespoons Worcestershire sauce

3 tablespoons all-purpose flour

3 tablespoons cold water

1 tablespoon chopped flat-leaf parsley

MAKES 4 SERVINGS

1. To prepare the horseradish cream, combine the sour cream, horseradish, mustard, and ¼ teaspoon of the salt in a small bowl. Cover and refrigerate until ready to use, at least 4 hours or up to overnight.

2. Sprinkle the ribs with the remaining ½ teaspoon salt and the pepper. Spray a large nonstick skillet with nonstick spray and set over medium-high heat. Add the ribs and cook, turning once, until browned, about 8 minutes.

3. Transfer the ribs to a slow cooker. Add the onions, potatoes, carrots, garlic, and bay leaf. Pour the broth and Worcestershire sauce over the meat and vegetables. Cover and cook until the meat and vegetables are fork-tender, 4–5 hours on high or 8–10 hours on low.

4. About 20 minutes before the cooking time is up, combine the flour and water in a small bowl until smooth; stir in about ¼ cup of the hot liquid from the slow cooker until blended. Stir the flour mixture into the slow cooker. Cover and cook on high, until the mixture simmers and thickens, about 15 minutes. Discard the bay leaf. Stir in the parsley just before serving. Serve with the horseradish cream.

PER SERVING (2 cups stew and 2 tablespoons horseradish cream): 311 Cal, 9 g Fat, 3 g Sat Fat, 33 mg Chol, 653 mg Sod, 42 g Carb, 5 g Fib, 17 g Prot, 110 mg Calc. *POINTS*: 6.

tip Making the horseradish cream a few hours ahead or the night before allows the flavors to meld and develop. If it's more convenient for you, however, make the sauce just before you're ready to serve the ribs, and add extra horseradish if necessary.

Country-Style Beef Short Ribs
with Horseradish Cream

Pork Loin with Sauerkraut and Apples

Slow cooking is a good way to cook lean cuts of pork, because steam from the long simmering helps to tenderize the meat. This comforting combination of tender pork, sauerkraut, apples, and beer is delicious with bakery-fresh rye or pumpernickel bread. Add *2 POINTS* for a 1-ounce slice.

MAKES 6 SERVINGS

1 (1½-pound) boneless pork loin roast, trimmed of all visible fat
⅛ teaspoon salt
½ teaspoon freshly ground pepper
1 teaspoon canola oil
1 (2-pound) package sauerkraut, rinsed and drained
1 onion, sliced
1 Granny Smith apple, cored and chopped
2 teaspoons caraway seeds
½ cup light beer

1. Sprinkle the pork with the salt and pepper. Heat the oil in a large nonstick skillet over medium-high heat. Add the pork and cook, turning frequently, until browned, about 6 minutes.
2. Place the sauerkraut, onion, apple, and caraway seeds in a slow cooker; stir to mix. Place the pork on top of the vegetables, then pour the beer over all. Cover and cook until the pork and vegetables are fork-tender, 4–5 hours on high or 8–10 hours on low.
3. Transfer the pork to a platter and cut into 6 slices. Spoon the sauerkraut mixture around the pork.

PER SERVING (1 slice pork and ¾ cup sauerkraut mixture): 193 Cal, 5 g Fat, 2 g Sat Fat, 67 mg Chol, 845 mg Sod, 11 g Carb, 4 g Fib, 25 g Prot, 51 mg Calc. *POINTS: 3.*

Irish Stew with Lemon-Parsley Dumplings

Use boneless lamb shoulder meat that you or your butcher cut into cubes—it will be leaner than packaged precut lamb stew meat. To save time, brown the lamb and cut the vegetables the night before. Keep the lamb in one covered container and the vegetables in a separate container in the refrigerator.

1 pound boneless lamb shoulder, trimmed of all visible fat and cut into 1-inch cubes
½ teaspoon salt
¼ teaspoon freshly ground pepper
1 teaspoon canola oil
1 onion, chopped
2 all-purpose potatoes (about ¾ pound), peeled and cut into 1-inch cubes
1 cup whole baby carrots
1 purple-top turnip, peeled and cut into 1-inch cubes
3½ cups low-sodium chicken broth
1 tablespoon browning and seasoning sauce
1 cup frozen peas
1⅔ cups reduced-fat all-purpose baking mix
⅔ cup fat-free milk
1 tablespoon chopped fresh parsley
1 tablespoon grated lemon zest

MAKES 6 SERVINGS

1. Sprinkle the lamb with the salt and pepper. Heat the oil in a large nonstick skillet over medium-high heat. Add the lamb and cook, turning occasionally, until browned, about 6 minutes.

2. Transfer the lamb to a slow cooker. Add the onion, potatoes, carrots, turnip, broth, and seasoning sauce. Cover and cook until the lamb and vegetables are fork-tender, 4–5 hours on high or 8–10 hours on low.

3. About 40 minutes before the cooking time is up, stir the peas into the stew, then prepare the dumplings. Combine the baking mix, milk, parsley, and lemon zest in a bowl until a soft dough forms. Drop the dough by rounded tablespoonfuls onto the simmering stew, making 6 dumplings. Cover and simmer until the dumplings have doubled in size and have cooked through, about 30 minutes.

PER SERVING (1⅓ cups stew and 1 dumpling): 397 Cal, 15 g Fat, 6 g Sat Fat, 53 mg Chol, 691 mg Sod, 43 g Carb, 4 g Fib, 20 g Prot, 104 mg Calc. *POINTS: 8.*

**Lamb Shanks
and White Beans**

Lamb Shanks and White Beans

One of the benefits of slow one-pot cooking, aside from convenience, is that as the meat cooks, delicious juices develop and make a wonderfully rich sauce. Although you trim all fat from the lamb before cooking, some fat may accumulate on top of the stew after simmering. Be sure to skim it away from the top before adding the beans. If it is hard to skim the fat with a spoon, blot the top of the stew with a paper towel.

MAKES 4 SERVINGS

1   tablespoon dried
    oregano
2   garlic cloves, minced
½   teaspoon salt
1   teaspoon extra-virgin
    olive oil
4   (7-ounce) lamb shanks,
    trimmed of all
    visible fat
1   large onion, chopped
1   carrot, chopped
1   celery stalk, chopped
1   (14½-ounce) can
    stewed tomatoes
1   cup low-sodium
    chicken broth
⅔   cup dry white wine
2   (15-ounce) cans
    cannellini (white
    kidney) beans, rinsed
    and drained
2   tablespoons chopped
    fresh parsley

1. Combine the oregano, garlic, salt, and ½ teaspoon of the oil in a small bowl. Rub the oregano mixture onto the lamb shanks.

2. Heat the remaining ½ teaspoon oil in a large nonstick skillet over medium-high heat. Add the lamb and cook, turning once or twice, until browned, about 8 minutes.

3. Place the onion, carrot, and celery in a slow cooker. Place the lamb shanks on top of the vegetables. Pour the tomatoes, broth, and wine around the shanks. Cover and cook until the lamb and vegetables are fork-tender, 4–5 hours on high or 8–10 hours on low.

4. About 35 minutes before the cooking time is up, skim away any fat that is on top of the stew, then stir in the beans. Cover and cook until heated through, about 30 minutes. Stir in the parsley just before serving.

PER SERVING (1 lamb shank and 1½ cups vegetables and beans): 430 Cal, 12 g Fat, 4 g Sat Fat, 98 mg Chol, 1190 mg Sod, 38 g Carb, 9 g Fib, 42 g Prot, 97 mg Calc. *POINTS: 9.*

tip Since in slow-cooked dishes, foods tend to lose their vibrant colors and flavors tend to become mellow, we use fresh chopped herbs to perk things up at the last minute. Double the parsley and sprinkle with a little chopped fresh oregano too, if you like.

Blanquette de Veau

Blanquette, from the French word *blanc*, is a creamy "white" stew. In the classic tradition, veal is used along with small whole white onions and white button mushrooms—none of which is browned. If you prefer, you can substitute cubed skinless boneless chicken thighs or lean pork for the veal. The stew is delicious over noodles (add *2 POINTS* for every ½ cup cooked egg noodles).

1   pound boneless veal shoulder, cut into 1½-inch chunks
½   pound fresh white mushrooms, quartered
1   cup frozen whole small onions
¾   cup low-sodium chicken broth
½   cup dry white wine
3   tablespoons fresh lemon juice
½   teaspoon dried thyme
½   teaspoon salt
1   bay leaf
3   tablespoons all-purpose flour
3   tablespoons cold water
1   cup frozen peas
1   tablespoon chopped fresh parsley

MAKES 4 SERVINGS

1. Place the veal, mushrooms, and onions in a slow cooker. Stir in the broth, wine, lemon juice, thyme, salt, and bay leaf. Cover and cook until the veal and vegetables are fork-tender, 4–5 hours on high or 8–10 hours on low.

2. About 30 minutes before the cooking time is up, combine the flour and water in a small bowl until smooth; stir in about ¼ cup of the hot liquid from the slow cooker until blended. Stir the flour mixture and peas into the slow cooker. Cover and cook on high, until mixture simmers and thickens, about 25 minutes. Discard the bay leaf. Stir in the chopped parsley just before serving.

PER SERVING (1¼ cups): 233 Cal, 6 g Fat, 2 g Sat Fat, 99 mg Chol, 420 mg Sod, 16 g Carb, 3 g Fib, 28 g Prot, 50 mg Calc. *POINTS: 5.*

tip There's no need to thaw any frozen vegetables before using them in a recipe for a slow cooker.

Chicken and Turkey-Sausage Gumbo

This Creole specialty is a favorite in New Orleans and is traditionally simmered for a long time, making it a natural for the slow cooker. The name "gumbo" is derived from the African word for okra. Okra, along with the flour, helps to thicken the stew. For an extra *2 POINTS*, serve this with ½ cup cooked rice.

MAKES 6 SERVINGS

1 onion, chopped

1 green bell pepper, seeded and chopped

1 celery stalk, chopped

¾ pound skinless boneless chicken thighs, trimmed of all visible fat and cut into 1½-inch chunks

¾ pound Italian turkey sausage, cut into 2-inch chunks

1 tablespoon Cajun seasoning

2 cups low-sodium chicken broth

1 (14½-ounce) can stewed tomatoes

2 teaspoons Worcestershire sauce

3 tablespoons all-purpose flour

3 tablespoons cold water

1 (10-ounce) package frozen sliced okra

1 cup frozen whole-kernel corn

1. Place the onion, bell pepper, and celery in a slow cooker. Place the chicken and sausage on top of vegetables; sprinkle with the Cajun seasoning. Add the broth, tomatoes, and Worcestershire sauce. Cover and cook until the chicken, sausage, and vegetables are fork-tender, 4–5 hours on high or 8–10 hours on low.

2. About 50 minutes before the cooking time is up, combine the flour and water in a small bowl until smooth; stir in about ¼ cup of the hot liquid from the slow cooker until blended. Stir the flour mixture, okra, and corn into the slow cooker. Cover and cook on high until the mixture simmers and thickens slightly, about 45 minutes.

PER SERVING (generous 1½ cups): 258 Cal, 9 g Fat, 3 g Sat Fat, 69 mg Chol, 955 mg Sod, 20 g Carb, 3 g Fib, 25 g Prot, 87 mg Calc. *POINTS: 5.*

Barbecue Chicken Chili

Ground-meat chili dishes with plenty of seasonings are terrific cooked in a slow cooker. Dark-colored seasonings, such as molasses, brown sugar, and chili powder, compensate for the lack of browning of the meat before simmering. Cornbread makes a great accompaniment to this zesty chili—a 2-inch square will add *3 POINTS*.

1   pound ground skinless
    chicken breasts
1   large onion, chopped
1   green bell pepper,
    seeded and chopped
3   garlic cloves, chopped
2   (15½-ounce) cans red
    kidney beans, rinsed
    and drained
1   (15½-ounce) can pinto
    beans, rinsed and
    drained
1   (14½-ounce) can diced
    tomatoes
1   (12-ounce) bottle chili
    sauce
1   (4½-ounce) can
    chopped green chiles
¼   cup chili powder
2   tablespoons
    Worcestershire sauce
1   tablespoon molasses
1   tablespoon packed
    brown sugar
1   tablespoon ground
    cumin

MAKES 8 SERVINGS

Place the chicken, onion, bell pepper, and garlic in a slow cooker; stir with a fork to blend. Add the kidney and pinto beans, tomatoes, chili sauce, green chiles, chili powder, Worcestershire sauce, molasses, brown sugar, and cumin; mix well. Cover and cook until the flavors are blended and the chili thickens slightly, 4–5 hours on high or 8–10 hours on low.

PER SERVING (1¼ cups): 280 Cal, 3 g Fat, 1 g Sat Fat, 31 mg Chol, 1172 mg Sod, 44 g Carb, 10 g Fib, 22 g Prot, 97 mg Calc. *POINTS: 5.*

tip You can mix all the ingredients for this chili in the insert of the slow cooker the night before and pop it in the refrigerator. The next morning, simply place the insert into the slow cooker and set it on low before going to work.

Sunday Meatloaf and Vegetables

Finely chopped vegetables mixed in with the ground turkey give moistness and flavor to this turkey meatloaf, while large chunks of vegetables surrounding the meatloaf add texture and color to the meal.

MAKES 6 SERVINGS

3 slices firm white bread, cut into 1-inch squares

⅓ cup fat-free milk

3 carrots

2 small onions

1 celery stalk, coarsely chopped

1 pound ground skinless turkey breast

1 large egg

¼ teaspoon salt

6 small red potatoes, scrubbed and halved

½ pound fresh white mushrooms, sliced

1. Place the bread in a large bowl. Pour the milk over the bread and let stand 10 minutes.

2. Coarsely chop 1 of the carrots and cut the remaining 2 carrots into 2-inch chunks. Coarsely chop half of 1 onion and slice the remaining onions. Set aside the carrot chunks and sliced onions.

3. Place the chopped carrot, chopped onion, and celery in a food processor; pulse until finely chopped. Transfer to the bowl with the bread mixture. Add the turkey, egg, and salt; mix with hands until combined. Shape the mixture into an oval loaf and place in a slow cooker.

4. Arrange the potatoes, mushrooms, and reserved carrot chunks and onion slices around the meatloaf. Cover and cook until the meat and vegetables are fork-tender, 4–5 hours on high or 8–10 hours on low.

5. Transfer the meatloaf to a platter and cut into 6 slices. Spoon the vegetables around the meatloaf.

PER SERVING (1 slice meatloaf and ⅙ of vegetables): 275 Cal, 4 g Fat, 1 g Sat Fat, 81 mg Chol, 250 mg Sod, 36 g Carb, 4 g Fib, 24 g Prot, 72 mg Calc. **POINTS: 5.**

tip If you have any leftover meatloaf, it makes a great sandwich the next day.

Desserts

We all need a little something sweet

Rice Pudding with Dried Cherries

Dried tart cherries give this pudding a distinctive tang that offsets the sweet creaminess of the rice. Dried sweet cherries could be substituted for the tart cherries if you prefer their flavor. For crunch and an extra *POINT*, sprinkle the top of each serving with a tablespoon of toasted sliced almonds just before serving.

2 cups whole milk
1¼ cups water
½ cup long-grain white rice
½ teaspoon salt
½ cup sugar
½ cup dried tart cherries
½ teaspoon almond extract

MAKES 6 SERVINGS

1. Bring 1 cup of the milk, the water, rice, and salt to a boil in a medium saucepan, stirring occasionally. Reduce the heat and simmer, covered, until the rice is tender, about 30 minutes.

2. Stir the remaining 1 cup milk, the sugar, cherries, and almond extract into the saucepan; return to a simmer. Cover and simmer, stirring occasionally, until the mixture is creamy, 20–25 minutes. Remove from the heat and let stand 5 minutes. Serve at once while still warm or let cool to room temperature before serving.

PER SERVING (½ cup): 213 Cal, 3 g Fat, 2 g Sat Fat, 11 mg Chol, 234 mg Sod, 42 g Carb, 1 g Fib, 4 g Prot, 107 mg Calc. *POINTS: 4.*

tip If you prefer to serve the rice pudding cold, cover and refrigerate until chilled, at least three hours or up to three days. Leftovers make a wonderfully tasty snack another day.

Apricot Tapioca Pudding

This is a refreshing nondairy dessert, but you can substitute 1 cup of low-fat milk for 1 cup of the apricot nectar for a creamy version. Tapioca is a starch made from the root of the cassava plant and is used mainly in the form of quick-cooking tapioca to make puddings or to thicken pie fillings. Look for it in the baking section or pudding section of your supermarket.

2 cups apricot nectar or orange juice
⅓ cup dried apricots, chopped
⅓ cup sugar
3 tablespoons quick-cooking tapioca
½ teaspoon vanilla extract

MAKES 4 SERVINGS

1. Bring the apricot nectar and apricots to a boil in a medium saucepan. Remove from the heat and let stand 20 minutes.
2. Strain the liquid from the apricots and add enough water to equal 2 cups. Return liquid to the saucepan with the apricots, sugar, and tapioca. Let stand 5 minutes.
3. Cook over medium heat, stirring constantly, until the mixture comes to a boil. Remove from the heat and let cool about 20 minutes. Stir the vanilla into the pudding. Serve warm or cover and refrigerate until chilled, at least 3 hours or up to 3 days.

PER SERVING (½ cup): 131 Cal, 0 g Fat, 0 g Sat Fat, 0 mg Chol, 2 mg Sod, 33 g Carb, 2 g Fib, 1 g Prot, 13 mg Calc. *POINTS: 2.*

tip Don't be concerned if the tapioca mixture still seems runny just after cooking—it will thicken as it cools.

Butterscotch Pudding and
Apricot Tapioca Pudding

Butterscotch Pudding

This nostalgic, silky-smooth sensation is a breeze to make and has a natural butterscotch flavor that you won't find in a boxed version. It goes well with bananas, but it's also good with sliced just-ripe pears. For those of us who equate satisfaction with something to bite on, serve this with a graham cracker or two—2 crackers are a *POINT*.

2 egg yolks
⅔ cup packed dark brown sugar
¼ cup cornstarch
1 tablespoon vanilla extract
2½ cups low-fat (1%) milk
2 tablespoons cold unsalted butter
2 medium bananas, sliced

MAKES 8 SERVINGS

1. Combine the egg yolks, sugar, cornstarch, and vanilla in a large bowl; mix well.

2. Heat the milk to a simmer in a large saucepan over medium heat. Slowly pour the hot milk into the egg mixture, beating constantly with a wire whisk. Return the mixture to the pan and bring to a simmer over medium-low heat, whisking constantly. Let the mixture simmer, whisking constantly, until thickened, about 2 minutes. Remove from the heat, then stir in the butter until it melts.

3. Pour the hot pudding into 8 custard cups. Immediately place a piece of wax paper directly onto the surface of each pudding to prevent a skin from forming. Cover and refrigerate until chilled, at least 3 hours or up to 3 days. Top with the sliced bananas just before serving.

PER SERVING (scant ½ cup pudding and ¼ of a banana): 188 Cal, 5 g Fat, 3 g Sat Fat, 64 mg Chol, 49 mg Sod, 32 g Carb, 1 g Fib, 4 g Prot, 118 mg Calc. *POINTS: 4.*

tip For ginger lovers, sprinkle each pudding with a few pieces of chopped crystallized ginger.

Southern Bread Pudding

Bread pudding is an old and simple comfort-food classic, enjoyed in many parts of this country. Southerners make it their own by adding a few rich, crunchy pecans. We add apples for flavor, fiber, and nutrients. Try serving this with a teaspoon of warmed apricot preserves or raspberry jam drizzled on top.

MAKES 8 SERVINGS

1¼ cups low-fat (1%) milk
4 large eggs
⅓ cup sugar
2 teaspoons vanilla extract
½ teaspoon cinnamon
⅛ teaspoon ground nutmeg
12 slices cinnamon-raisin bread, crusts discarded, bread cut into 1-inch squares
1 Granny Smith apple, peeled, cored, and cut into ½-inch cubes
3 tablespoons chopped pecans

1. Preheat the oven to 350°F. Spray a 1½-quart shallow baking dish with nonstick spray.

2. Combine the milk, eggs, sugar, vanilla, cinnamon, and nutmeg in a large bowl; whisk until blended. Add the bread, apple, and pecans. Let the mixture stand, stirring occasionally, until the bread absorbs some of the liquid, about 10 minutes. Pour the mixture into the baking dish.

3. Bake until the pudding is puffed and a knife inserted in the center comes out clean, 25–30 minutes. Remove the pudding from the oven and let cool 15 minutes. Serve warm.

PER SERVING (⅛ of pudding): 199 Cal, 6 g Fat, 2 g Sat Fat, 108 mg Chol, 168 mg Sod, 29 g Carb, 2 g Fib, 7 g Prot, 90 mg Calc. *POINTS: 4.*

tip If you have time, cut up the bread, spread it on a baking sheet, and let it stand on a countertop, uncovered, overnight. The stale bread will be drier and better able to absorb the milk mixture, giving the baked pudding a firmer texture.

Southern
Bread Pudding

Chocolate Zucchini Cake

Zucchini cakes are a great way to use abundant summer squash from the garden or from the supermarket. It is also a great way to add moisture to a cake while cutting back on the amount of fat used. Try this chocolate version for a real treat.

2¾ cups all-purpose flour
1 cup granulated sugar
1 cup packed light brown sugar
½ cup cocoa
1 teaspoon baking soda
½ teaspoon salt
¾ cup fat-free milk
½ cup canola oil
4 large eggs
1½ teaspoons vanilla extract
1 pound zucchini, grated (about 2½ cups)
Confectioners' sugar (optional)

1. Preheat the oven to 350°F. Spray a 9 x 13-inch baking pan with nonstick spray, then sprinkle lightly with flour.
2. Combine the flour, granulated sugar, brown sugar, cocoa, baking soda, and salt in a large bowl.
3. Combine the milk, oil, eggs, and vanilla in a medium bowl; whisk until blended. Stir the milk mixture into the flour mixture until all of the flour is just moistened.
4. Stir in the zucchini just until blended. Pour the mixture into the baking pan. Bake until a toothpick inserted in the center comes out clean, 35–40 minutes. Let cool in the pan on a rack 15 minutes. Remove from pan and let cool on the rack 30 minutes. Sprinkle with confectioners' sugar, if using. Cut into 24 squares.

PER SERVING (1 square): 182 Cal, 6 g Fat, 1 g Sat Fat, 36 mg Chol, 120 mg Sod, 30 g Carb, 1 g Fib, 3 g Prot, 29 mg Calc. *POINTS: 4.*

tip To enjoy zucchini cake long after summer has passed, wrap individual squares in foil, place in a zip-close freezer bag (remember to label the bag), and freeze for up to six months.

Macerated Fruit with Pound Cake

Macerating a variety of fruits allows the juices to mingle and infuse each fruit with new flavor combinations. The greater the variety, the more intriguing the flavor becomes. A liqueur, such as Grand Marnier, is often added to macerating fruit for extra sparkle— 2 tablespoons would add **2 POINTS** (or ½ **POINT** per serving).

MAKES 4 SERVINGS

1 pint fresh strawberries, sliced

2 fresh peaches, pitted and sliced

1 orange, peeled and cut into segments

1 mango, peeled, pitted, and sliced

1 red pear, cored and sliced

2 tablespoons orange juice

2 tablespoons sugar

1½ teaspoons grated lemon zest

4 (1-ounce) slices fat-free pound cake, toasted

1. Combine the strawberries, peaches, orange, mango, pear, orange juice, sugar, and lemon zest in a large bowl; mix well. Cover the fruit with plastic wrap and refrigerate at least 1 hour or up to 24 hours.
2. Place 1 slice of pound cake on each of 4 plates. Top each slice with 1 cup of the fruit salad.

PER SERVING (1 plate): 231 Cal, 1 g Fat, 0 g Sat Fat, 0 mg Chol, 103 mg Sod, 56 g Carb, 5 g Fib, 3 g Prot, 44 mg Calc. *POINTS:* 4.

tip For a quick dessert, use 4 cups of your favorite cut-up fruit from the supermarket salad bar instead of cutting up your own fruits.

Lemon-Blueberry Bundt Cake

Lemon-Blueberry Bundt Cake

Bundt cakes—cakes baked in a fluted tube pan (Bundt pan)—are wonderful because they look so impressive. To prevent the cake from sticking, be sure to get into all the crevices of the pan with both the nonstick spray and the flour. You can use a plain 10-inch tube pan if you don't have a Bundt pan. If you are using frozen blueberries in this cake, there is no need to thaw them.

MAKES 24 SERVINGS

3 cups all-purpose flour

2 cups sugar

1 teaspoon baking powder

¾ teaspoon baking soda

½ teaspoon salt

½ teaspoon cinnamon

¼ teaspoon ground nutmeg

1 cup fat-free buttermilk

3 large eggs

½ cup canola oil

1 tablespoon grated lemon zest

½ teaspoon vanilla extract

2 cups fresh or frozen blueberries

1. Preheat the oven to 350°F. Spray a 10-inch Bundt pan with nonstick spray then dust with flour; set aside.

2. Combine the flour, sugar, baking powder, baking soda, salt, cinnamon, and nutmeg in a large bowl.

3. Combine the buttermilk, eggs, oil, lemon zest, and vanilla in another bowl. Add the buttermilk mixture to the flour mixture and stir just until the flour is moistened. Stir in the blueberries and pour into the Bundt pan.

4. Bake until a toothpick inserted in the center of the cake comes out clean, about 1 hour and 10 minutes. Let cool in the pan on a rack 15 minutes. Remove the cake from the pan and let cool completely on the rack. Cut into 24 slices.

PER SERVING (1 slice): 182 Cal, 5 g Fat, 1 g Sat Fat, 27 mg Chol, 128 mg Sod, 31 g Carb, 1 g Fib, 3 g Prot, 30 mg Calc. *POINTS: 4.*

tip This cake makes a delicious and decadent breakfast treat when toasted and topped with fruit preserves. Cut any leftover cake into single-serve slices, wrap in foil, place in a zip-close freezer bag, and freeze for up to three months. For best results, defrost the wrapped cake by leaving it out on the counter the night before.

Zabaglione Parfaits

Zabaglione is a wonderfully light dessert or sauce that is made airy and voluminous from beating egg yolks, sugar, and Marsala wine over simmering water. This rich delight is often served alone, but we prefer to stretch it by serving it as a sauce over fresh fruit. A gift from Italy, zabaglione is also served in France, where it is known as *sabayon*.

3 egg yolks

⅓ cup sugar

3 tablespoons dry
   Marsala wine

1 pint fresh
   strawberries, quartered

1 pint fresh blueberries

MAKES 6 SERVINGS

1. Place the egg yolks, sugar, and Marsala in the top part of a double boiler; beat with a wire whisk until well combined. Fill the bottom part of the double boiler half full of water; bring to a simmer. Set the top part of the double boiler over the bottom part and cook the egg-yolk mixture, whisking constantly, until the yolks thicken and cook and the volume triples, 8–10 minutes. Remove the top part of the double boiler from the bottom half of the double boiler and let the mixture cool slightly, about 1 minute.

2. Divide the strawberries and blueberries among 6 parfait or sundae glasses; top each with one-sixth (about ¼ cup) of the zabaglione. Serve at once.

PER SERVING (1 parfait): 124 Cal, 3 g Fat, 1 g Sat Fat, 106 mg Chol, 8 mg Sod, 22 g Carb, 2 g Fib, 2 g Prot, 22 mg Calc. *POINTS: 2.*

tip Zabaglione is wonderful cold as well as hot. To make ahead, simply cool the mixture quickly over a bowl of ice water. Transfer the zabaglione to an airtight container and refrigerate for up to 24 hours.

English Trifle

Trifle originated in England and traditionally is made with either ladyfingers or sponge cake. This version takes advantage of ready-made, fat-free angel food cake, which has a light, airy texture that soaks up plenty of juice from the fruit.

MAKES 16 SERVINGS

3 pints fresh strawberries, halved

½ pint fresh raspberries

1 cup seedless red grapes, halved

¼ cup sugar

1 (10-ounce) fat-free angel food cake, cut into ½-inch-thick slices

1 cup apricot preserves

1 (16-ounce) container fat-free nondairy whipped topping

¼ cup walnuts, coarsely chopped

1. Combine the strawberries, raspberries, grapes, and sugar in a bowl; let stand 15 minutes.

2. Line the bottom of a 12-cup trifle dish or glass bowl with one-third of the cake slices. Brush the cake with ⅓ cup of the apricot preserves. Top with one-third of the fruit mixture (about 2 cups), then one-third of the whipped topping (about 2 cups). Repeat the layering twice more with the remaining ingredients, ending with the whipped topping.

3. Cover the trifle with plastic wrap and refrigerate until the cake absorbs the juices, at least 2 hours or up to 8 hours. Sprinkle with the nuts just before serving.

PER SERVING (¹⁄₁₆ of trifle, about ⅔ cup): 197 Cal, 2 g Fat, 0 g Sat Fat, 0 mg Chol, 158 mg Sod, 44 g Carb, 2 g Fib, 2 g Prot, 18 mg Calc. *POINTS: 3.*

tip If you use a bowl that slopes outward rather than a straight-sided trifle bowl, you'll find the layers need to be spread thinner near the top.

Apple Turnovers

We spike these easy-to-make pastries with ginger, but if traditional cinnamon is your choice, use about 1½ teaspoons. You can also substitute pears for the apples, if you like.

4 Granny Smith apples, peeled, cored, and cut into ½-inch cubes

⅓ cup raisins

3 tablespoons plus 1½ teaspoons sugar

1 teaspoon ground ginger

¼ cup water

6 (12 x 17-inch) sheets phyllo dough, thawed according to package directions

MAKES 6 SERVINGS

1. Preheat the oven to 350°F. Spray a baking sheet with nonstick spray; set aside.

2. Spray a large nonstick skillet with nonstick spray and set over medium-high heat. Add the apples, raisins, and 3 tablespoons of the sugar. Cook, stirring, about 3 minutes. Stir in the ginger and water; cook until the apples are tender and the liquid evaporates, 3–4 minutes. Let the mixture cool slightly, about 15 minutes.

3. Place a scant ⅓ cup of the apple mixture in the center bottom of each strip. Place one sheet of the phyllo on a work surface with the long side nearest you. Spray lightly with nonstick spray and top with a second sheet. Spray lightly and top with a third sheet; spray lightly again. Cut the stacked phyllo sheets lengthwise into 3 strips. Fold each strip from the bottom right corner over the filling to the left side to form a triangle. Continue folding from corner to side, flag-style, to the top of each strip. Place the 3 triangles seam-side down on the baking sheet. Repeat with the remaining 3 sheets of phyllo and apple filling, making a total of 6 triangles.

4. Lightly spray the turnovers with nonstick spray, then sprinkle with the remaining 1½ teaspoons sugar. Bake until light golden, 20–25 minutes.

PER SERVING (1 turnover): 156 Cal, 1 g Fat, 0 g Sat Fat, 0 mg Chol, 56 mg Sod, 37 g Carb, 2 g Fib, 2 g Prot, 10 mg Calc. *POINTS: 3.*

tip These sweet treats are great to have on hand for dessert, a brunch treat, or a snack. Simply freeze the unbaked turnovers in a plastic storage container for up to three months. When you're ready, place the frozen turnovers on a baking sheet (as many or as few as you like) and bake as directed above, allowing an extra 7 to 10 minutes baking time.

Apple Turnovers

About Our Recipes

We make every effort to ensure that you will have success with our recipes. For best results and for nutritional accuracy, please keep the following guidelines in mind:

• All recipes feature approximate nutritional information; our recipes are analyzed for Calories (Cal), Total Fat (Fat), Saturated Fat (Sat Fat), Cholesterol (Chol), Sodium (Sod), Carbohydrates (Carb), Dietary Fiber (Fib), Protein (Prot), and Calcium (Calc).

• Nutritional information for recipes that include meat, fish, and poultry are based on cooked skinless boneless portions (unless otherwise stated), with the fat trimmed as specified in the recipe.

• All recipes include POINTS values based on the Weight Watchers FlexPoints Food System. POINTS values are calculated from a proprietary formula that takes into account calories, total fat, and dietary fiber.

• Before serving, divide foods—including any vegetables, sauce, or accompaniments—into portions of equal size according to the designated number of servings per recipe.

• Any substitutions made to the ingredients will alter the "Per serving" nutritional information and may affect the POINTS value.

• Additionally, substituting fat-free foods for any low-fat ingredients specified in a recipe may affect the consistency, texture, or flavor of the finished dish.

• If you prefer to avoid using alcohol in any recipe, you may substitute an equal amount of water, broth, or juice.

• It is implied that all greens in recipes should be washed or rinsed.

• All herbs called for are fresh, not dried, unless otherwise specified.

Dry and Liquid Measurement Equivalents

If you are converting the recipes in this book to metric measurements, use the following chart as a guide.

TEASPOONS	TABLESPOONS	CUPS	FLUID OUNCES
3 teaspoons	1 tablespoon		½ fluid ounce
6 teaspoons	2 tablespoons	⅛ cup	1 fluid ounce
8 teaspoons	2 tablespoons plus 2 teaspoons	⅙ cup	
12 teaspoons	4 tablespoons	¼ cup	2 fluid ounces
15 teaspoons	5 tablespoons	⅓ cup minus 1 teaspoon	
16 teaspoons	5 tablespoons plus 1 teaspoon	⅓ cup	
18 teaspoons	6 tablespoons	¼ cup plus 2 tablespoons	3 fluid ounces
24 teaspoons	8 tablespoons	½ cup	4 fluid ounces
30 teaspoons	10 tablespoons	½ cup plus 2 tablespoons	5 fluid ounces
32 teaspoons	10 tablespoons plus 2 teaspoons	⅔ cup	
36 teaspoons	12 tablespoons	¾ cup	6 fluid ounces
42 teaspoons	14 tablespoons	1 cup minus 2 tablespoons	7 fluid ounces
45 teaspoons	15 tablespoons	1 cup minus 1 tablespoon	
48 teaspoons	16 tablespoons	1 cup	8 fluid ounces

VOLUME	
¼ teaspoon	1 milliliter
½ teaspoon	2 milliliters
1 teaspoon	5 milliliters
1 tablespoon	15 milliliters
2 tablespoons	30 milliliters
3 tablespoons	45 milliliters
¼ cup	60 milliliters
⅓ cup	80 milliliters
½ cup	120 milliliters
⅔ cup	160 milliliters
¾ cup	175 milliliters
1 cup	240 milliliters
1 quart	950 milliliters

LENGTH	
1 inch	25 millimeters
1 inch	2.5 centimeters

WEIGHT	
1 ounce	30 grams
¼ pound	120 grams
½ pound	240 grams
1 pound	480 grams

OVEN TEMPERATURE			
250°F	120°C	400°F	200°C
275°F	140°C	425°F	220°C
300°F	150°C	450°F	230°C
325°F	160°C	475°F	250°C
350°F	180°C	500°F	260°C
375°F	190°C	525°F	270°C

NOTE: Measurement of less than ⅛ teaspoon is considered a dash or a pinch. Metric volume measurements are approximate.

Index

M

Notes